ENCYCLOPAEDIA OF WOMEN IN SOUTH ASIA
(BHUTAN)

ENCYCLOPAEDIA
OF
WOMEN IN SOUTH ASIA

(In 8 Volumes)

Bhutan

(Volume 7)

Editors

Sangh Mittra, Bachchan Kumar

KALPAZ PUBLICATIONS

Delhi-110052

Encyclopaedia of Women in South Asia *(Bhutan)*
(International Studies, Women)

Rs. 7000 (Set)

ISBN: 81-7835-187-0 (Set)
ISBN: 81-7835-194-3 (Vol. 7)

Published in 2004 in India by
Kalpaz Publications,
C-30, Satyawati Nagar, Delhi-110052
E-mail : Kalpaz@hotmail.com

Laser Typesetting at : Shree Vaishnavi Creations, Delhi
Printed at : Mehra Offset Press, Delhi

Contents

1

Historical Background, Geography and People

Located between India and China, its 47,000 square kilometres of territory form a stigmatic stair-case between the narrow lowland region of the south approx. 300 metres above sea-level and the lofty Himalayan peaks of the north over 7,000 metres high. The central valleys, the most densely populated region, are very difficult to reach from the south because of a 2,000 metre-high chain of mountains interspersed with unhealthy jungle-covered gorges. These previously made access both dangerous and difficult. Until the border with Tibet was closed in 1959, the high Himalayas gave easy access through certain mountain passes, and there was a considerable amount of trade between the two countries. These climatic variations, coupled with the dramatic changes in altitude, make Bhutan a country with an extremely rich flora. Over a mere 70 kilometres one passes from rice paddies, banana and orange groves at 1,300 metres in the Punakha region, through a deciduous forest and then an alpine forest (at Gasa), finally arriving in the Laya region where yaks are raised and only barley and winter wheat can be grown. Southern Bhutan consists of often impenetrable jungles full of tropical trees and fruits. In the central valleys apples, peaches, plums and apricots can be found, and rhododendrons grow side by side with fir trees, blue pines and oaks. An infinite variety of plants and flowers grow on the slopes and in the valleys, giving Bhutan its centuries-old name : "Southern Valleys of Medicinal Herbs".

The fauna also varies with the different types of vegetation. Elephants, tigers, buffaloes and snakes abund in the southern forests, while the central Himalayan region is full of pheasants, monkeys, wild boars and above all fearsome black bears. The desolate high valleys are the home of yaks, of the retiring blue sheep and the extremely rare snow leopard. Differing ethnic groups are also distributed according to the varying environments. Southern Bhutan is inhabited mainly by Nepalese farmers who arrived in the country at the end of the 19th century and are now fully integrated Bhutanese citizens. Small trading towns, such as Phuntsholing, Gaylegphug and Samdrup Jongkhar, prosper in this region on the Indian border. These towns boast small-scale industries, such as match factories, fruit juice and jam processing units and a cement plant.

The central Himalayan region is the home of the *Drukpa* people, who are of Mongoloid origin. Most breed cattle or cultivate the land and their dwellings are spread over a wide area, with small towns growing around the *dzongs,* or fortified monasteries, which used to defend each valley. The appearance of these towns is directly linked to the improvement in communications and to the formation of a middle class of civil servants and shopkeepers. The northern Himalayan zone, over 3,000 metres, is the haunt of semi-nomadic yak herdsmen. They spend most of the year in their black tents woven from yak hair, but also possess drystone-walled houses, where they spend the coldest months of the year and which are used to store their goods. Precious additives to a diet composed mainly of yak milk, butter, cheese and meat are barley and winter wheat, plus a few root vegetables which they grow in small fields.

This horizontal division of Bhutan into three ecological zones (northern, central and southern) would only give a very approximate idea of the country's ethnic and geographical diversity if we do not also consider its vertical divisions. In fact the mountain chains which divide the central valleys all run from north to south and form real barriers between different parts of the country barriers which are perceived as such by the people themselves. The central Himalayan region can thus be divided longitudinally into three parts which are each distinct but which are all inhabited by the *Drukpas,* who speak language of the Tibeto-Burmese group.

Western Bhutan is made up of the valleys of Haa (2,700 metres above sea-level), Paro (2,200 metres), Thimphu (2,300 metres) and Punakha and Wangdiphodrang (1,300 metres). With the exception of Haa valley, whose rigorous climate suits it more for animal breeding and which used to be very involved in trading with Tibet, western Bhutan is a region of rice-paddies and orchards. All types of vegetables and fruit flourish in the fertile valleys, and the relative wealth of the inhabitants can be inferred from their very large houses, in which several generations co-habit.

Traditionally wooden shingles were used for roofing but these have in some cases been replaced by corrugate iron. Fortunately, slate being mined from rich local deposits may again provide roofing material which enhances the traditional architecture. The mountain slopes are covered by rich coniferous and deciduous forests where forestry is strictly regulated, since Bhutan recognizes what a precious asset its woodlands are. All the valleys are strewn with reminders of the past, in particular with monasteries and fortresses. Since the fifties, the country's capital has been located in the Thimphu valley. The five valleys which make up western Bhutan are where *Dzongkha,* the "language of the Dzong (fortress)" is spoken. It has become the official language of Bhutan.

The boundary between eastern and western Bhutan is generally taken to be a 3,300 metre-high pass through the Black Mountains (5,000 metres) called Pele-la. Central Bhutan is made up of two valleys: Tongsa and Bumthang, plus the more southerly district of Khyeng, famous for its bamboo work. Khyeng is also the home of several isolated aboriginal tribes known as *Monpas* and considered by the Bhutanese as the first inhabitants of their country.

Tongsa (2,200 metres above sea-level) hardly deserves to be called a valley. It is in reality a gorge cut out by the Mangde river, with a few cultivated areas cut into its steep slopes. Tongsa is best known for its fortress, which is perhaps the most impressive in the country.

A 3,300 metre-high pass, the Yuto-la, leads to Bumthang which is a group of four valleys at altitudes from 2,700 to 4,000 metres: Chume and Choekhor which are mainly agricultural and Tang and Ura where yak and sheep herding are carried out. Bumthang is proud of its rich historical and artistic traditions and of its language which is close to that of Kurtoe in the north-east, and which still contains many archaic features. Religious traditions are very much alive here and each monastery, each holy place, is the focus of long tales in which reality and myth are closely interwoven. As in western Bhutan, the mountains are covered with dense forests but the cold climate precludes rice cultivation. Even though rice brought in from other valleys is eaten, buckwheat cakes are the staple food. The Thumshing-la pass, over 4,000 metres high, separates central from eastern Bhutan. The latter consists of the Kurtoe, Mongar and Tashigang regions, plus that part of southern Bhutan adjacent to the Indian border. The eastern region is the land of the *Sharchops* – the "people of the east" - who speak their own language known as *Sharchopkha.* The climate there is generally warmer and direr, and the slopes barer than in the west. It is a region of deep valleys which often consist of no more than the river itself, with fields and houses clinging to their steep slopes. Rice, wheat and barley are cultivated widely but corn (maize) is the staple crop and numerous cattle may be seen grazing by the sides of the roads. Most of the houses follow the traditional Bhutanese pattern, in stone and wood, but toward the south some are made of bamboo matting and are raised up on piles.

The *Sharchops* are well known for their piety, and the region is dotted with small temples where *gomchens,* laymen trained in religious particles, live with their families away from monastic communities. The women are un-equalled in their skill ar weaving beautiful fabrics of raw silk known as *bura* - and of cotton with infinitely varied designs. Two days on foot to the east of Tashigang fortress, one finds the astonishing valley of Sakteng, 3,000 metres above sea-level, and virtually unknown to the outside world. For the moment, we will simply mention that the inhabitants of the valley, sometimes known as *Brogpas* (shepherds), *Dakpas* or *Daps* are herdsmen and are related to the peoples known as *Monpas,* from the Tawang region of Arunachal Pradesh in N.E. India.

Bhutan is made up of a mosaic of varied populations which, right up to the present day, have lived in valleys isolated from one another by formidable mountain passes and cut off from the outside world by mountain barriers which are extremely difficult to cross. And yet this is a country which is a real nation of one million inhabitants united in the same desire for stability and peace and who share the same pride in being Bhutanese. This keen sense of belonging to the Bhutanese nation is rooted in a mutual respect for the cultural values of each of the peoples which the forces of history have formed into the Bhutanese nation.

Stone implements found in Bhutan seem to indicate that the country was inhabited fairly early, probably around 2000 B.C. Moreover, the relatively large number of megaliths to be seen today may have been used to mark out territories or for ritual practices. However, it is difficult to draw conclusions concerning the prehistory of Bhutan, since almost of archaeological research has yet been carried out. As for the history of Bhutan, this was for centuries so closely bound up with the religious history of the country that the religious school which became dominate from the 17th century, the Drukpa school, gave its name to the country and its inhabitants" in *Dzongkha*, Bhutan is called *Druk-yul* and the Bhutanese people *Drukpas*. A more poetic translation is often given: "Druk-yul" also means "Land of the Dragon", and this is explained by the following anecdote: when Tsangpa Gyare Yeshe Dorje (1161-1211) was consecrating a new monastery in Central Tibet at the end of the 12th century, he heard the thunder which popular belief holds to be the voice of the dragon ("druk"). He therefore decide to name this monastery "Druk", and so the religious school which he founded was called "Drukpa". Bhutan's other traditional names are *Lhomon Khashi* or "The Southern Mon (pa) Country of Four Approaches".

The origin of the present name of Bhutan is not clear. One interpretation is that it comes from the Indian term *Bhotanta* which refers to all those regions bordering on Tibet.

In order to provide a brief sketch of the history of Bhutan up to the end of the 19th century, we must consider the main religious figures who were not only important in their own time but who live on in the minds and memories of the people today.

After this first introduction of Buddhism and probably the first migration from Tibet, the 9th and 10th centuries form a period of great obscurity. Following the assassination of the anti-Buddhist King Langdarma of Tibet in A. D. 842, Tibet itself plunged into great political turmoil and Buddhism almost completely disappeared, surviving only in remote regions.

The 11th century saw the revival of Buddhism in Bhutan, this was the period of the activity of the *tertons* or "discoverers of treasures" in Paro and Bumthang. These treasures were usually texts hidden by Padmasambhava and other saints and discovered by the predestined *tertons* at a favourable moment. The end of the 11th century and the beginning of the 12th saw a period of religious expansion in Tibet and a number of different religious school came into being including the Kadampa, Kagyupa and Sakyapa schools. The missionary activity of these new schools was also directed at the "Southern Valleys", and at the end of the 12th century, Gyelwan Lhanangpa (1164-1224) arrived in western Bhutan. He was the founder of the Lhapa school, a branch of the Kagyupa school, and had special links with the valley of Paro, since he had inherited land in this fertile region from his great-grandfather. He accordingly established the Lhapa school in western Bhutan.

In the first half of the 13th century, a monk by the name of Phajo Drugom Shigpo (1208-1276) arrived in Bhutan. He belonged to another branch of the Kangyupa, the Drukpas, founded by Tsangpa Gyare Yeshe Dorje (1161-1211). He came to Bhutan following a prophecy of Tsangpa Gyare who ordered him to go to the South. As soon as he arrived, Phajo Drugom Shigpo came into conflict with the Lhapas, who were already firmly established in western Bhutan. However, Phajo Drugom Shigpo finally won his struggle with the Lhapas and, having married a women from the Thimphu valley, he founded the first Drukpa monasteries at Phajoding and Tango. The Lhapa school nevertheless continued until the 17th century when it was totally crushed by the Shabdrung Ngawang Namgyel. However, many monks, whether belonging to the Drukpa school or not, continued to come to Bhutan between the 12th and the 17th centuries. Barawa (1320-1391), for example, founded a sub-sect of the Drukpas and had monastery at Brangyekha in the Paro valley. In the same way, the distinctive Neyingpa school founded several monasteries in western Bhutan, amongst which was Dzongdrakha in the Paro valley.

Longchen Rabjampa (1308-1363), the great philosopher of the Nyingmapa school, went to Bumthang where he founded the monasteries of Tharpaling, Samtenling and Shinkar and in 1355 wrote an eulogy on the valley of Bumthang. In the 15th century a man arrived in western Bhutan who is unquestionably the most popular of the religious figures: Drukpa Kunley, "the divine madman" (1455-1529). All Bhutanese are familiar with his adventures. In fact, he belonged to the Drukpa school and to the princely family of Gya, from which came the successive abbots of Ralung, one of the main Drukpa monasteries. His wandering life style, the eccentric and shocking behaviour with which he taught the essence of religion and his songs give him a special place in the history tantric Buddhism. His descendants became equally famous in Bhutan, especially Tenzin Rabgye (1638-1696) who was the famous 4th Temporal Ruler (*Desi* or *Deb*) of Bhutan. Although only monks who came from Tibet to Bhutan have so far been mentioned, it should not be forgotten that from the 14th century onwards many eminent monks were born on Bhutanese soil.

The most famous among them is Pema Lingpa, a descendant of Gyalwa Lhanangpa, who was born in Bumthang in 1450 and died there in 1521. Pema Lingpa, however, did not belong to Lhapa school but to the Nyingmapa school, which was very powerful in central Bhutan. He was the reincarnation not only of Guru Rinpohce but also of the great Nyingmapa scholar Longchen Rabjampa. Pema Lingpa, in addition to his activities as a *terton* or discoverer of treasures, founded the temples of Petsheling, Tamshing and Kunzangbrag in Bumthang. He was the originator of a number of sacred dances, which came to him in visions, and he also left behind him important writings. He is intimately linked to the history of the Bumthang valley, where his memory has left traces everywhere. His descendants played an important role in the development of the Nyingmapa school and one of them set up Gangtey monastery, built on the borders of central and western Bhutan in the Black Mountains.

This brief outline indicates how Bhutan was an important area of missionary activity for the religious schools between the 12th and the beginning of the 17th centuries, but it also highlights the lack of political unity which characterized Bhutan during this period. It was in the 17th century that Bhutan became a unified states, thanks to the political and religious charisma of Ngawang Namgyel (1594-1651) of the Drukpa school. He took the honorary title of Shabdrung, "at whose feet one submits" but his history is too long to be told in detail and we shall limit ourselves to its broad outlines.

In 1616, Shabdrung Ngawang Namgyel, fleeing from Tibet, arrived in western Bhutan. He had been born into the princely Gya family and he was the 18th abbot of Ralung, a great Drukpa monastery. He had been recognized as the incarnation of the famous Drukpa scholar Pema Karpo (1527-1592) but this recognition had been challenged by the Tsang Desi, the head of the province of Tsang in Tibet, who had his own candidate. Under these circumstances, Ngawang Namgyel was obliged to flee from Ralung and to take refuge in western Bhutan, where, as we have seen, the Durkpa school was firmly established. Shabdrung Ngawang Namgyel accordingly went to the valleys of Thimbhu and Paro, where his great-great-grandfather Ngawang Choegyel (1465-1540) had founded the monasteries of Panri Zampa and Druk Choeding respectively. In the upper Thimphu valley, the Shabdrung himself founded the monastery of Cheri in 1619, and in 1629 he founded his first dzong, Simtokha, near Thimphu.

The system of dzongs built in each valley not only symbolized the might of the Drukpa school, since each dzong contained a monastery, but also constituted an unrivalled instrument of government and unification of the country. However, before he could bring about the unification of Bhutan, the Shabdrung had to fight against his enemies both at home and abroad. His foreign enemies were the Tibetans, whose army was first organized by the Tsang Desi in order to invade Bhutan. Their first attempt, which took place shortly after the arrival of the Shabdrung, was repelled, and their renewed attacks in 1634 and 1639 met with no greater success. In 1645 and 1648, the Tibetans, now aided by the Mongol army which supported the new Tibetan government of the 5th Dalai Lama, made further fruitless attempts at conquest.

The enemies of the Shabdrung at home were the "five groups of lamas", in other words the religious schools which had long been established in Bhutan and against which the Shabdrung had fought in order to consolidate his own power and that of the Drukpa school. The Shabdrung gave Bhutan a system of laws based on the unwritten laws then in common use, established a state monk-body under a religious leader, the *Je Khenpo* and a theocracy administrated by monks at whose head he put a temporal leader, the *Desi*. This dual system of government, known as *choesi,* was unified and transcended in the person of the Shabdrung Ngawang Namgyel. In 1651, the Shabdrung went into retreat in Punakha dzong and died while he was there. His death was kept a secret for over half a century. The reasons for this concealment no doubt lie in the concern to avoid turmoil—in a nation which had only just came into existence—which might have broken out before a worthy successor to the Shabdrung could be found.

It was in the first half of the 18th century that the theory of the triple incarnation of the Body, Speech and Mind of the Shabdrung was finally established. However, only the successive "mental" incarnation were recognized as successors of the Shabdrung as heads of state. Hierarchically inferior to the incarnation of the Shabdrung, to whom the British gave the name *Dharma Raja*, came the head of the monk-body, the *Je Khenpo* and the temporal ruler, the *Desi* (or *Deb Raja* as the British called him). They continued the dual system of government which was to last until the coming of the monarchy at the beginning of 20th century.

The heads of dzongs (*Dzongpons*) were put in charge of the provinces. Some of these at Daga, Tongsa and Paro) were more important than others and were given the title of *Penlop.* In the course of the 18th and the 19th centuries, these regional governors increased their powers to the detriment of the central government. Moreover, the dual system of government favoured political inertia and encouraged inter-factional struggles.

Beyond its frontiers, the government was faced with a new factor in the form of British hegemony in Assam and British colonial ambitions in the Himalayas. In the 18th century, British missions, seeking preferential trading relations with Tibet and Bhutan, were successful in establishing good relations between the Bhutanese and the British, without however the concrete results for which the latter had been hoping. The conflicting interests of the Bhutanese and the British over the question of the Duars rapidly tarnished these good relations and the expeditions in the 19th century bore signs of hostility. Continual skirmishes on the southern border from the 1830's onwards reached such proportions in 1864 that what is known as the Duar War took place. In November 1865, the treaty of Sinchula brought the war to an end and re-established normal relation. Bhutan gave up its rights over the Duars and in exchange received an annual allowance from the British.

The progressive weakening of the central government became more marked at the end of the 19th century and conceded with the emergence of the power of the two main governors in Paro and Tongsa, who had *de facto* control over western and central Bhutan. The struggle for power between these two governor came to a head in 1904 at the time of the British expedition to Tibet under Younghusband. Whilst the Penlop of Paro was determined to side with Tibet, which was already in the Chinese zone of influence, the Tongsa Penlop, Ugyen Wangchuck, advised by Kazi Ugyen Dorji, was in favour of increased cooperation with the British. Ugyen Wangchuck became the intermediary in negotiations between the Tibetans and the British and won the respect and confidence of the latter. He therefore came to be seen as the strong leader which Bhutan needed after so much instability.

On 17th December 1907, Ugyen Wangchuck was unanimously elected as the first King of Bhutan by a constituent assembly made up of representatives of the monastic community, civil servants and the people. This marked the end of the dual system of government and the beginning of the hereditary monarchy which was to guarantee stability to the country. Ugyen Wangchuck died in 1926 and was succeeded by his son Jigme Wangchuck who reigned until his death in 1952.

The twenty-year reign of the third King, Jigme Dorji Wangchuck (1952-1972), was marked by the gradual opening up of the country to the outside world and by economic and social development. He was the father of modern Bhutan and an enlightened monarch. Amongst his achievements was Bhutan's entry into the United Nations in 1971.

His son, His Majesty Jigme Singye Wangchuck, today pursues the late King's policy of socio-economic progress. Bhutan now has a seat in a number of international organizations and UN agencies which provided aid for its development. These include the Colombo Plan, the Movement of Non-aligned Countries, the Economic and Social Commission for Asia and the Pacific, the Universal Postal Union, the United Nations Development Programme, UNESCO, UNICEF and the World Bank.

The system of government is that of the monarchy. His Majesty the King is the Head of State and the Head of the Government. He is aided by the Cabinet, which is the main executive body and consists of the members of the Royal Advisory Council and the Ministers of Home Affairs, Foreign Affairs, Communications and Tourism, Development, Finance, Trade and Industry, plus other high-ranking officials.

The Royal Advisory Council (*Lodoe Tshogde*), set up in 1965, consists of the Chairman, appointed by the King, five representatives of the people, two representatives of the clergy, two representatives from southern Bhutan and a women's representative. They have a five-year mandate.

The National Assembly (*Tshongdu*) is the main legislative body. It was created in 1953 and consists of 150 members who fall into three categories:

- one hundred representatives of the people, elected for three years.
- ten representatives of the Clergy, elected by the State monastic community.
- forty representatives of the government, appointed by the King. These consist of the members of the Cabinet and various officials.

The National Assembly, presided over by the King, meets twice a year in Tashichho Dzong in Thimphu with sessions of variable length, depending on the importance of the subjects being dealt with. The Je Khenpo is the head of the monk-body, which includes the central and regional State monastic communities. It should be mentioned that Bhutan is the only independent country in which Mahayana Buddhism is practiced as the State religion.

Bhutan is divided up into seventeen administrative districts (*Dzongkhags*) under the control of the Ministry of Home Affairs and headed by a *Dzongda* and a *Dzongda wogma,* his deputy. Each district is in turn subdivided and the subdivisions are each headed by a *Dungpa,* aided by the village headmen (*Gups*) who are elected for three years. Each Gup controls several villages and provides the link between the State administration and the villagers.

Judicial power is held in the last resort by the King, to whom all the Bhutanese may appeal. A High Court has its seat in Thimphu, and all the districts have a local court presided over by a magistrate or *Thrimpon*. The Bhutanese are tenaciously litigious, but the major crimes which afflict other societies are virtually non-existent.

The Economic Development of Bhutan has, since 1961, taken place in stages corresponding to five-year plans, with the fifth such plan now under way. The last twenty years have been marked by the efforts which have been made to bring about structural transformations in the socio-economic system, in other words to change a bearter economy into a modern economy.

The Planning Commission centralizes all economic data and advises as the which options should be given priority.

The economy of Bhutan is still essentially based on agriculture and cattle-rearing. Ninety-five per cent of the population live from these activities. The main crops are maize, rice, wheat, barley, buckwheat, mustard and peppers. Cultivation of some recently-introduced cash crops has undergone remarkable expansion: asparagus, mushrooms, potatoes, oranges, apples, cardamom, ginger a d tropical fruits, as well as high-quality seeds. A huge programme for the development of irrigation is under way which will enable previously unused land to be cultivated. Because of its low population, Bhutan has always been self-sufficient as regards its food-consumption. Cattle products—butter, milk, cheese and meat—are a major part of the Bhutanese diet. The animals reared for food are bovines, pigs and poultry in southern Bhutan and the central valleys, and yaks in northern Bhutan, Bumthang and Mera Sakteng. Intense efforts are being made to increase productivity, veterinary farms have been set up and crossbreeding with imported animals has produced good results. Horses and mules are used exclusively as pack-animals and for riding, whilst sheep are raised for their wool, since traditionally their meat is eaten very little.

Two-thirds of Bhutan is covered by forests containing a wide variety of species (tropical trees, deciduous trees and conifers in the temperate zone), which constitute one of the country's most important potential sources of wealth. A policy of reforestation and of scientifically controlled utilization of the forests is strictly applied by the Department of Forests which also created a school for foresters in 1971. A match factory, saw-mills and small private joinery businesses have been set up in agreement with the Department of Forests and this Department has itself established a factory for plywood, most of which is exported. In order to preserve the ecological balance of its environment, Bhutan has also created nine natural parks in which the fauna and flora are protected.

Mining resources were the object of prospecting in the period 1960-70 and amongst the minerals to be found under the ground in Bhutan are dolomite, coal, graphite, gypsum, marble, zinc, copper, lead, limestone and slate. Slate is now beginning to be worked and a cement plant, seventy per cent of whose production is intended for export, was inaugurated in southern Bhutan in 1982. The other industries in Bhutan, apart from saw-mills and joinery, which are depended on the products of the forest, are industries for processing agricultural products, such as factories and distilleries.

Two closely related sectors of economic activity are at present in a phase of rapid expansion: tourism and arts and crafts. Bhutan opened its doors to tourism in 1974. This industry is State operated and provides an important source of foreign exchange for the country. Individual tourism is very limited and almost all visitors must belong to a group. Their visit is organized by the government travel agency. In 1982-1983, the number of tourists to visit the country reached two thousand. The development of tourism had led to a boom in arts and crafts. This activity had in the past been entirely geared to producing for the home market but now has to adapt to different requirements. Traditional materials such as bamboo and wood are used to make items of furniture previously unknown in Bhutan, such as beds and lamp-shades. All the hotels in the country show their fidelity to traditional Bhutanese decorations, with a harmonious combination of Bhutanese and Western elements. Bhutanese arts and crafts are renowned for cloth woven on traditional looms, for bamboo, wood and precious metal work and for painted banners (*thangkas*) of religious inspiration. A painting schools has been established so as to preserve traditional techniques of drawing and painting.

Economic development, however, involves improvements in the means of communication and in energy production. Bhutan has no railways and until February 1983 the only means of access to Bhutan was by road. This date marked the opening of a regular air link between Calcutta and Paro, which undoubtedly means the beginning of a new era for Bhutan.

Bhutan has a wide-ranging network of mule-tracks and bridges which remain the only means of access to many areas of the country. The road system has however expanded considerably since work started on the first road linking Phuntsholing to Thimphu and Paro in 1960. By 1983 there were some two thousand kilometres of roads, of which one thousand two hundred kilometres are metalled. Road-building has been hampered by a shortage of labour and workers have had to be recruited from abroad. Many bridges have also been built throughout the country to improve transport communications. The Government runs a public transport service, which has linked the different valleys since 1962, and a government-supervised service of privately-owned lorries provides for transport of goods.

A regular postal service began operating in 1962. Bhutanese stamps are highly prized by collectors all over the world and the Government attaches great importance to their design and to their distribution. A telephone, telegraph and radio network links Bhutan to the outside world, as well as connecting different regions within the country. A radio station broadcasting in Dzongkha, Sharchopkha, Nepalese and English and a weekly paper in Dzongkha, Nepalese and English provide national and international news.

The large number of rivers, mountain streams and water-falls gives Bhutan an enormous hydro-electric potential. However, it is extremely expensive to set up hydro-electric power stations and this has been done only for the major urban centres. Diesel generators have also been installed since, although domestic energy requirements can be readily met with wood from the countryside, a quite understandable desire to have electricity is now being felt and the demand in urban centres has grown. A major Indo-Bhutanese hydro-electric project is now under construction in Chukha and this is expected to supply about 330 mega watts from 1985 onwards. This amount of electricity will not only cover Bhutanese requirements but will make it possible to export electricity to India.

Economic development has also enabled Bhutan to transform its barter economy into a monetary economy. A currency has been established-the *Ngultrum* divided into a hundred *Chetrums*-and in 1968 the Bank of Bhutan was created. In 1982, the Royal Monetary Authority, whose role is that of a central bank, was inaugurated.

Education is one of the main concerns of the Government, since the future of the country depends on its younger generations if Bhutan is to achieve its goal of self-reliance. Till the early 60's, there were virtually no modern educational facilities inside Bhutan, apart form the traditional education given in the monasteries. However it should be noted that some Bhutanese received a formal education first in Haa valley and then abroad under the patronage of the previous Kings and of the late Prime Minister Jigme Dorje. Today, there are one hundred and fifty-two primary and secondary schools with thirty-six thousand pupils spread over the country. Most of the pupils are boarders with the schools providing their board and lodgings free of charge. A college equivalent to the first two years of university has also been set up and a fully-fledged university is being planned. Many students pursue advanced studies abroad, with scholarships from the Bhutanese Government, the UN or from the host-country. Great importance has been attached to the creation of technical colleges, which correspond to the most urgent needs of the country, and teacher-training establishments.

The teaching of Dzongkha, the official language, is being very actively promoted, but English is the medium of education so as to facilitate contact with the outside world. Students are given guidance in their choice of subjects by a government commission which subsequently provides them with jobs in the various branches of Government where their services are required.

For centuries, the Bhutanese considered the illnesses from which they suffered to be the results of bad behaviour or of the influence of evil spirits. Oracles were consulted, followed by religious ceremonies, and this went hand in hand with treatment by medicinal plants, the use of which constituted a highly elaborate science. Today, centres for traditional medicine are being set up with the help of the World Health Organization. Parallel to the preservation of traditional medicine, one of the major projects of the Government since 1962 had been to establish modern medical facilities, available to all the Bhutanese right across the country.

Average life expectancy in Bhutan is 43, but the reason for which is the rate of infant mortality which is as high as one hundred forty seven per thousand. The mountainous nature of the country, which makes communications difficult, prevents the speedy development of natal and postnatal care.

The most frequent illnesses are respiratory and gastrointestinal, with a high incidence of goitres as a result of the lack of iodine in the traditional diet. Measles continues to ravage the child population.

Bhutan now has twelve hospitals, forty dispensaries and more than forty Basic Health Units, as well as three leprosy centres. Major campaigns for the control and elimination of malaria (in southern Bhutan), of tuberculosis (using BCG vaccinations), of goitres (by distributing iodized salt) and of leprosy are being carried out with the help of the WHO and UNICEF. Conditions of hygiene are far from perfect and the Government is making efforts to inculcate basic notions of hygiene by organizing training sessions throughout the countryside.

Whilst the Bhutanese still perform ceremonies in the event of illness, they are reacting favourably to the introduction of new methods of treatment and the two "systems" are used together in many families to the advantage of all concerned.

Has this introduction, however schematically, achieved its goal? Has it managed to show all the different facets of Bhutan? Has it made it possible to understand how a rich past and centuries of tradition have combined with steady but restrained economic development and spectacular social progress over the last twenty years to make Bhutan one of the most astonishing and fascinating countries in the world? During these years, this country had experienced profound changes and undergone cultural shocks which might have created instability or destroyed Bhutan's awareness of its cultural heritage. None of this has in fact happened, since the Government had always endeavoured to take account of the aspirations of the people and takes care never to offend against ancestral values. The monarchy, which in many countries is a conservative institution hampering change and progress, is in Bhutan a dynamic force which is instrumental in bringing about economic innovation and social progress.

Bhutan is neither a Shangri La nor a poverty-stricken country. It does not fit into any of the stereotyped images of the "least-developed nations". With its small population, abundant material resources, and its fidelity to tradition, there is every reason to hope for a well-balanced future for these "Southern Valleys" hidden in the folds of the immense Himalayas.

The name Bhutan is derived from the Sanskrit 'Bhotant', meaning 'the end of Tibet', or from 'Bhu-uttan', meaning 'high land'. Historically the Bhutanese have refered to their country as Druk Yul, 'land of the thunder dragon'. Bhutanese refer to themselves as Drukpa people. In the 8th century CE, Guru Rinpoche (Padmasambhava or second Buddha) made his legendary trip from Tibet to Bhutan on the back of a flying tigress to subdue the evil spirits who hindered Buddhism. An after defeating them, he blessed them as guardians of the doctrine. Introducing Tantric Buddhism to Bhutan. Taktshang or Tigers Nest in the Paro Valley is where he landed and remains one of most sacred places in Bhutan. Guru Rinpoche (Precious Master) is the father of the Drukpa Kagyu school of Tantric Mahayana Buddhism practiced in Bhutan. Shabdrung Ngawang Namgyal, a tibetan lama of the Drukpa School, arrived in Bhutan in 1616 CE. He introduced the present dual system of religious and secular government, creating and building the system of Dzongs through out Bhutan.

Shabdrung unified the country, and established himself as the country's supreme leader and vested civil power in a high officer known as the Druk Desi. Religious affairs were charged to another leader, the Je Khenpo. For two centuries following Shabdrung's demise, civil wars intermittently broke out, and the regional Penlops (governors) became increasingly more powerful. This ended when an assembly of representatives of the monastic community, civil servants and the people, elected the Penlop of Trongsa, Ugyen Wangchuck, the First King of Bhutan in 1907-1926. The monarchy has thrived ever since, and the present Fourth King, His Majesty Jigme Singye Wangchuck (1972 to present), commands the overwhelming support for his people. Geographically, the Kingdom of Bhutan lies in the Central Himalayas, between Tibet to the north the Indian territories of Assam and West Bengal, to the south and east, and Sikkim to the west. The Kingdom has a total area of about 47,000 square kilometres. Located in the heart of the high Himalayan mountain range, Bhutan is a land-locked country surrounded by mountains.

The sparsely populated Greater Himalayas, bounded to the north by the Tibetan plateau, reach heights of over 7,300 metres (23,950ft.), and extend southward losing height, to form the fertile valleys of the Lesser Himalayas divided by the Wang, Sunkosh, Trongsa and Manas Rivers. Monsoon influences promote dense forestation in this region and alpine growth at higher altitudes. The cultivated central uplands and Himalayan foothills support the majority of the population. In the south, the Daurs (the gates) Plain drops sharply away from the Himalayas into the large tracts of semi-tropical forest, savannah grassland and bamboo jungles.

Bhutan's indigenous population is the Drukpa. Three main ethnic groups, the Sharchops, Ngalops and the Lhotsampas (of Nepalese origin), make up today's Drukpa population. Bhutan's earliest residents, the Sharchops (people of the east) reside predominantly in eastern Bhutan. Their origin can be traced to the tribes of northern Burma and northeast India. The Ngalops migrated from the Tibetan plains and are the importers of Buddhism to the kingdom.

Most of the Lhotsampas migrated to the southern plains in search of agricultural land and work in the early 20th century. Bhutan's official language is Dzongkha. The current population is approximately 750,000. Given the geographic isolation of many of Bhutan's highland villages, it is not suprising that a number of different dialects have survived. Bhutan has never had a rigid class system. Social and educational opportunities are not affected by rank or by birth.

Bhutanese women enjoy equal rights with men in every respect. To keep the traditional culture alive Bhutanese people wear the traditional clothing that has been worn for centurys. Bhutanese men wear a gho, a long robe tied around the waist by a small belt called kera. The women's ankle length dress is called a kira, made from beautifully colored and finely woven fabrics with traditional patterns. Necklaces are fashioned from corals, pearls, turqoise, and the precious agate eye stones which the Bhutanese call 'tears of the gods'.

Bhutan is the only country in the world to retain the Tantric form of Mahayana Buddhism (Drukpa Kagyu) as its official religion. The Buddhist faith has played and continues to play a fundamental role in the cultural, ethical and sociological development of Bhutan and its people. It permeates all strands of secular life, bringing with it a reverence for the land and its well being. Annual festivals (tshechus and dromchoes) are spiritual occasions in each district. They bring together the population and are dedicated to the Guru Rinpoche or protective deities.

Throughout Bhutan, chortens or stupas (receptacle for offerings) line the roadside commemorating places where Guru Rinpoche or another high Lama may have stopped to meditate. Prayer flags dot the hills, fluttering in the wind. They allow Bhutanese people to maintain constant communication with the heavens.

In Bhutan, the majority of Bhutanese people live in small rural villages. An agricultural based economy, small family farms are the predominante way of life and the farmer the most common occupation. As the altitude rises crops give way to cattle and yak breeding. Large herds grazing in the high pastures. The Bhutanese diet is rich in meat and poultry, dairy, grain (particularly rice-red and white) and vegetables. Emadatse (chili pepper and cheese stew) is considered the national dish with many interpretations to this recipe throughout the country.

Poultry and meat dishes, pork, beef and yak, are lavishly spiced with chilies, and it is common to see bright red peppers drying on rooftops in the sun. Salted butter tea, or suja, is served on all social occasions. Chang, a local beer, and arra, a spirit distilled from rice, maize, wheat or barley, are also common and widely favored. Doma or betel nut, is offered as a customary gesture of greeting.

The Bhutanese way of life is greatly influenced by religion. People circumambulating the chortens with prayer beads and twirling prayer wheels are a common sight. Every Bhutanese home has a special room used for prayers, a chosum.

The rectangular national flag of Bhutan is divided diagonally and depicts a white dragon (druk) across the middle. The upper part of the flag is yellow, representing the secular power of the king, while the lower part is orange, symbolizing the Buddhist religion. The national emblem, contained in a circle, is composed of a double diamond-thunderbolt (dorji) placed above a lotus, surmounted by a jewel and framed be two dragons. The thunderbolt represents the harmony between secular and religious power. The lotus symbolizes purity; the jewel expresses sovereign poer; and the two dragons, male and female, stand for the name of the country which they proclaim with their great voice, the thunder.

National Day is celebrated on December 17 and commemorates the ascension to the throne of Ugyen Wangchuck, the first king of Bhutan. The national flower is the blue poppy, found in the high altitudes. The national tree is the cypress, which is often associated with religious places. The national bird is the raven, which adorns the royal crown. It represents the deity Gonpo Jarodonchen, one of the most important guardian deities of Bhutan. The national animal is the takin, an extremely rare bovid of the ovine-caprine family. Found in heards in the very high altitudes (13,000 ft and over), living on a diet of bamboo. The form of government in Bhutan is as unique as the country. It is the only Democratic Monarchy in the world. His Majesty King Jigme Singye Wangchuck is Bhutan's fourth king. A very special man who has kept the culture and traditions of his county intact while listening to the voice of his people. One of the six development goals HM King Jigme Singye Wangchuck has expressed is: People's participation and decentralisation in the government. Inherited from Shabdrung Ngawang Namgyel's administrative system of the 17th century.Bhutan is divided into 20 Dzongkhags (dzong districts or states, see map above), each with its own elected 3 year representative, a Dzongdag (district chief).

In 1988, four Dzongde (zones) were set up as administrative units between the district level and the central government. A group of four districts make up one zone, which is headed by the Dzongde Chichab (Zonal Administrator) with authority over the district chiefs in the area.

All districts are divided into blocks, administrative units that include several villages. At the block level, government orders are transmitted through an elected representative the Gup (village headman). The Tshogdu, or National Assembly has 154 members who fall into 3 catagories. The largest group with 105 members are the Chimis. Representatives of Bhutan's 20 dzongkhags. The regional monk bodies elect 12 monastic representatives who also serve 3 year terms.

Another 37 representatives are civil servants nominated by

the king. They include 20 Dzongdags, (district administrators or mayors): The old term for Dzongdag is Penlop (Governor), the first king was the Penlop of Paro and Thimphu) ministers, secretaries of various government and other high ranking officials.

The Tshogdu meets in Thimphu twice each year and is presided over by an elected speaker. The speaker may also call special sessions during emergencies. The Tshogdu body passes all the kingdom's legislation by a simple majority vote.

Bhutan has three regions that are open to visitors. These three regions are distinctly different due to the prominent north, south mountain ranges that separate each area resulting in different topographical features.

Western Bhutan is comprised of the Haa Valley at 8860ft. (recently opened to limited travel), Paro Valley at 7200ft., Thimphu at 7500ft. the Punakha Valley and Wangdue Phodrang at 4200ft., separated by high passes or "La's": Cheli La (3988m, 13,084ft.), Dochu La (3050m, 10,007ft.), Pele La (3300m, 10,825ft., separates Western from Central). Western Bhutan is known for its stunning scenery with rice paddies and orchards cascading down magnificent mountains, the pristine rivers that flow through the main towns of Paro, Thimphu and Punakha, and unique two-story houses with brightly painted window designs. The Black Mountains separate Western Bhutan from Central Bhutan. This region includes Trongsa and the rich broad valleys of Bumthang including Chumey, Choekhor, Tang and Ura valleys. The passes crossed are Yotang La (3400m, 11,155ft.) Shertang La (3573m, 11,723ft) and Thrumshing La (3800m, 12,465ft.).

Central Bhutan is known for its buckwheat and apple production, its sturdy stone houses, and its plethora of monasteries. Its the ideal place for walking due to its broad valleys and sloping mountains. The beauty of the Bumthang valley is legendary.

Eastern Bhutan comprises Mongar, Lhuentse, Trashigang and Trashi Yangste. Sengor Valley separates Central from Eastern Bhutan. After Thrumshing La, passes crossed are Kori La (2400m), Yongphu La (2190m) and Narphung La (1698) at much lower altitudes than Western and Central. The forests dissipate and the altitude is lower. The warmer climate is suitable for growing corn, rice, wheat, potatoes and surprisingly lemon grass. Eastern Bhutan is known for its stunning hand-loomed textiles and the weavers are all masters of the supplementary weft-weave.

Women in Society

Women in Bhutan generally have a much higher status than in many countries, enjoying the same status and legal rights as men. The equal status of women in Bhutanese society has undoubtedly contributed to the rapid development of this society and the remarkable gains in health status over the last ten years.

Women are valued and respected members of families and society. There seems to be no preference for either sex amongst children and no discrimination with respect to the allocation of financial and emotional resources within the family. More girls are enrolling at all levels of education and in fact now outnumber boys in many schools, though the dropout rate from primary to secondary level is still higher for girls. Women have the right of inheritance and land ownership and keep their own names after marriage. Marriage does not require formal ceremonies: people often quite simply decide to live together and this is considered as a marriage. Husbands often go to live in the wife's community.

In some areas of Bhutan women may have several husbands, often brothers, just as men may have several wives. There is no dowry system or bride-price custom. In cases of divorce, which is frequent in Bhutanese society, young children normally go to the mother while older children may go to the father. Women have access to cash in the same way as men, and often sell or trade agricultural or textile products. There is no emphasis on virginity in Bhutanese society and women have the same sexual rights as men.

Women and men are both encouraged to use free contraception and to limit the size of their family to two children. Termination of pregnancy is permitted only on medical grounds. Illegal abortion is said to be virtually unknown, probably because of open and non-judgmental access to contraception, the lack of stigma attached to illegitimacy and the strong social and family networks. It is also said, however, that women do go to other countries to access legally-induced abortion.

According to the 1994 National Health Survey, 35% of births were attended by husbands (who should therefore be a target audience for IEC messages about danger signs in pregnancy and childbirth). Men also appear to take more responsibility for contraception: vasectomy is an increasingly popular method of permanent family planning. Maternal mortality is still high, but the

MOHE is putting added emphasis on improving reproductive health services. All peripheral health workers, both male and female, are trained in midwifery, but women generally seem to prefer a female health worker to assist at delivery, even though many women are attended by their husbands. In the past, many remote BHUs did not have a female health worker, but where a male health worker is married to a nurse they are both posted to the same BHU. There are a few areas where equality is not the norm. One is in southern Bhutan, where Hinduism influences the society. Women there live with their husbands' families and their status is somewhat less secure. It is also striking how few women are in senior positions in the civil service, including the MOHE. There are two reasons for this. Traditionally it has been considered dangerous and difficult for women to travel long distances because of wild animals and difficult river crossings.

Since primary schools were few and scattered and higher education was only available in India, women had less access to education than men. There are therefore fewer women in the present generation with a secondary or tertiary education, which accounts for the general under-representation of women in higher positions. The other reason is the practice of women leaving their jobs when they get married. Raising a family has been considered more important for a woman than making use of her professional qualifications. This will almost certainly change with the coming generation, and female representation in the civil service and in the political system is likely to increase substantially in the next ten years.

Women and Health

Within the health sector itself there have been other inequalities. Many remote Basic Health Units (BHUs) have been - and some still are - without female health workers, for the reasons explained above. Only males have been recruited for Health Assistant (HA) training and there are no female District Health Supervisors. The male HAs are automatically put in charge of a BHU, even if the (female) Auxiliary Nurse Midwife (ANM) is more experienced.

Male nurses are expected to do more field work than female nurses. Although the curricula for HAs and ANMs have recently been merged, males are still referred to as HAs and females as ANMs, an anomaly which should be resolved by the forthcoming review of the Royal Institute of Health Sciences. Both males and females are trained for the more senior post of General Nurse Midwife, but all ANMs are female. The MOHE is taking active steps to ensure that all communities have access to female health workers, who in turn have equal opportunities for promotion and career advancement.

It has recently introduced a policy to post Auxiliary Nurse Midwives directly to rural BHUs after graduation, rather than to district hospitals. Female health workers will also be expected to undertake more field work.

In the mid-1980s, high fertility rate, high maternal mortality rate, high infant and child mortality rates, and the gender gap in the adult literacy rate have improved enormously. The impact of these problems is particularly severe among the smaller, more remote communities, where isolation provides an extra dimension to the difficulty of resolving them. In parallel with an impressive performance in terms of economic growth and diversification, major strides have been made in human development indicators, although from depressingly poor initial levels and to levels that have to be improved further.

In the case of health indicators, life expectancy rose from 35 years in 1961 to 46 years in 1977, and to about 66 years in 1998. Similarly, between the mid-1980s and the mid-1990s, the infant mortality rate and the maternal mortality rate were reduced from 102 to 71 per 1,000 live births and from 7.7 to 3.8 per 1,000 live births, respectively, while the under-5 mortality rate fell from 162 to 97 per 1,000 live births.

In addition, while the crude birth rate remained high at close to 40 per 1,000 population over the same period, the crude death rate was reduced significantly by more than half to 9.0. Major advances in immunization to 90 percent of the children have virtually eliminated neonatal tetanus, polio, and diphtheria. Malaria and leprosy have been brought under control, although malaria remains a problem in the southern part of the country. The program to iodize salt has significantly reduced iodine deficiency.

By the mid-1990s, 90 percent of the population had access to free basic health care (up from 65 percent in 1987); 58 percent of the rural population and 70 percent of the urban population had access to safe water supplies (from 31 percent in 1987 and expected to reach 95-100 percent in the next five years); and 80 percent of the rural population had access to means for safe excreta disposal. Moreover, piped sanitation systems either have been completed or are under construction in Thimphu and Phuentsholing.

Although housing is generally considered adequate in Bhutan, urban slums and substandard housing have increasingly become a concern due to the rapid growth of the urban population. The main issues facing the country's health authorities are the scarcity of skilled personnel for service delivery and for undertaking promotional and preventive programs, and sustainable long-term finance to support a highly dispersed and expanding health care system that seeks to provide improved services to widely scattered communities.

Difficulties faced on both fronts, as indeed in many other areas of national development, will be made more acute if the population growth is not brought under control. The success achieved in reducing the mortality rate between the mid-1980s and mid-1990s was not matched by a similar decline in fertility, with the result that population growth rate by the mid-1990s had actually increased from 2 percent in 1984 to 3.1 percent in 1994.

The Eighth Plan accords high priority to population planning, aiming to reduce the growth rate to 2.1 percent by 2002, 1.6 percent by 2007, and 1.3 percent by 2012. Various aid agencies, such as United Nations Fund for Population Activities (UNFPA), World Health Organization (WHO), and United Nations International Children's Education Fund (UNICEF), are providing substantial assistance in this area, focusing on reproductive health care and family planning as well as on improving the population database and information system.

The Government aims to achieve a replacement rate of two surviving children per woman by 2012 by (i) increasing the contraceptive prevalence rate, currently 24 percent but rising; (ii) expanding education programs, targeting not only girls and women but also boys and men; and (iii) changing traditional attitudes with respect to the benefits of small families, particularly in an economy where population growth is often popularly seen as a solution to perennial domestic labour shortages.

As in health, considerable progress has also been made in education over the past 20 or more years. Considering that fewer than 450 children attended secular primary schools in the late 1950s and that the country had no secondary schools at that time, educational achievements in Bhutan have been impressive.

2

Education and Employment

The system of Non-formal education programme in Bhutan was conceived as an alternative educational channel to help people acquire literacy skills. Early school dropouts, young men and women are the main target groups of the programme. Because of the limited resources and experience, the programme was initiated on a very small scale in 1990. Also wherever possible, the NFE programme uses the formal schools as the NFE centres. Apart from the benefits of the physical infrastructure such as classrooms, this also enables the programme to draw on other resources from the school such as its teachers and library facilities. The curriculum tries to meet three broad objectives as defined below:

a) To provide literacy training in Dzongkha (national language) to both men and women who have not received such training through the formal education system.
b) to provide functional and basic life-skills related knowledge
c) to provide post literacy and continuing education programme to help establish a literate society.

The NFE programme in Bhutan has now a structured curriculum and reading and learning materials to support it. A total of 30 readers have been developed on a wide variety of subjects to help the learners. The programme at present is structured into 3 distinct levels beginning with very basic literacy skills in level 1 and continuing to much more complex skills.

The duration of the course ranges between 6 to 12 months. By the end of the course, learners are not only able to read and write but do simple, every day arithmetics. They also acquire basic knowledge on health, hygiene, family planning, agriculture, forestry, environment, culture and tradition. A full scale evaluation of the NFE programme was conducted by the Education Division in 1999. 1,556 persons from 18 Dzongkhags were interviewed and 600 tested on functional literacy/knowledge. The study compared scores on functional literacy/knowledge between old NFE learners and non-learners. The main findings showed that old NFE learners could fill out forms, read envelopes and sight words more easily while non-learners could not perform any of these functions. Old learners scored twice as high as non-learners in functional knowledge on health and hygiene and knowledge on STDs and in peforming simple math operations. Starting 1996, post literacy programmes have been introduced as an effort to help the neo-literates to retain and enhance their literacy skills.

Curriculum for Post Literacy Courses(PLC) has been designed in three different packages covering broad areas related to functional literacy, arithmetic, health care, agriculture, animal husbandry, environment, technical courses and value education. Each package takes 6 months to complete. The packages are not graded so as to facilitate the learners to choose any package they are most interested in. A total of 30 readers and work books have also been developed to help the learners at this level.

These materials were developed in workshop settings involving government staff from different line Ministries such as Agriculture, Health and National Environment Commission. So far, 333 learners have enrolled in this programme in the 11 centres established to date. To help promote this programme, two pilot Community Learning Centres (CLC) have been established and more CLCs are planned to be established within the next 5 years. Post literacy programmes are not confined to those who have passed from the Basic Literacy programme. They are extended also to those who have received literacy training through the monastic education system as well as the formal education system such as school dropouts.

Like the Basic Literacy classes, the post literacy programme also uses the formal schooling facilities including its teachers and library resources. An exception is in communities where they have community learning centres in which case such centres are utilized for both Basic and Post Literacy programmes. Training and creating a pool of competent NFE teachers is another important component towards making the NFE programme successful. As mentioned earlier, a majority of these teachers are primary teachers trained to deliver the formal education curriculum with little knowledge of adult learning.

Therefore, the Division of Education organizes short training programmes in the winter vacations to provide these teachers with special skills required to cope with the NFE curriculum and teaching adult learners. One of the strategies adopted by the Government to ensure that NFE programmes make significant impact in alleviating illiteracy has been to get the communities concerned to initiate the programme themselves.

The community concerned has to formally make a request through their local representative to the Dzongkhag Education Office, who can study the proposal and then recommend for its establishment. This ensures that literacy programmes are made available to communities who are already receptive of the programme and see the need for such skills thereby helping the implementors to get better cooperation and higher success rates. This has also been instrumental in ensuring that the small NFE sub-sector is not overloaded in terms of resources, both materials and teachers. A larger and much more significant achievement in this sub-sector is in the establishment of a programme which can now begin to address the needs of the wider population. The successful implementation of the programme in the various NFE centres have given invaluable experience and confidence amongst both educators and the administrators to take the challenge of mass implementation in the following decade.

While the concept of an all round and wholesome education has been an established philosophy of education in Bhutan, a number of initiatives were taken during the decade under review which has had far reaching impact on this objective. They are changes and enrichment within the formal education curriculum, introduction of basic skills development programme and youth programmes.

School Curriculum

Changes in the formal school curriculum

One of the most significant events in the domain of curriculum change is incidentally the articulation of a framework for learning which defines the purpose of education and describes its components to the barest details. This document helps not only curriculum workers but the implementors of the curriculum in the classroom, the teachers. This is a major achievement of the decade because it translates many of the abstract goals and aspirations to curriculum objectives easily comprehendible to ordinary teachers. The period 1990 to 1999 saw major efforts to enhance the students understanding about issues related to health and to enhance the personal health of the students.

While the school curriculum includes basic knowledge on health, nutrition and sanitation a major effort is also being expanded to improve the personal hygiene and health of the students. Since 1998, a comprehensive school health programme has been launched in schools. This is a collaborative effort between Health and Education Division which amongst others monitor the health of the children and help the schools to improve their sanitation and minimize health related hazards.

Population Education, environment and conservation have also received a lot of attention in the past decade. The Health Sector, National Environmental Commission, and the Royal Society for the Protection of Nature have been active partners in enhancing this component of education in the schools. Songs, dances and music form important part of the school's co-curricular activities. All efforts are made to encourage the students to explore their innate talents in different art forms. Within the confines of a limited resource, all efforts are made to provide musical instruments and art materials to the schools to help them in this effort. The government has been providing increasing attention to improving sports and recreation facilities in the schools. Organised physical activities such as games and sports are seen as being important to develop physical, social and mental skills in youths and improve their physical health. While extolling their benefits the programmes were until now left very much upto the schools without much monitoring and support from the centre.

However from 1999, the Division of Education has developed and is implementing a new physical education programme. The government is also making efforts to include Physical Education as an optional stream for teacher educators in its two teacher training institutions. Over 80% of the country's population live in rural areas and are dependent on agriculture.

Therefore, agriculture education has always been stressed as an important component of the education curriculum. In this regards, the schools are encouraged to maintain school vegetable and flower gardens, piggery and poultry farms. By involving students in such projects they gain experiences which encourage them to undertake similar projects in their homes. The programme was initiated with the Agriculture Ministry and for some time in the early 1980s, received funding from OXFAM.

Prompted by increasing rural-urban migration as well as the emerging problems related to educated unemployment, the Ministry of Agriculture and Education are joining hands to strengthen the school agriculture project. Furthermore, in higher classes, especially in IX and X, the students are encouraged to initiate and take up activities which are socially useful and productive.

Students carry out such activities in the form of individual or group projects with the help of teachers in the class. Such activities develop skills in youth which help them to be useful in the community where they live.

Basic Skills

This programme was initiated in 1997 by the Technical and Vocation Education Section (TVES) of the Education Division. BSDP is targeted at the students as well as out of school youth and adults to enhance dignity of labour, promote civic responsibilities, engage them in self supporting economic activities and encourage lifelong learning.

For the students, these are organized in the form of school clubs wherein a teacher takes the lead role in providing essential guidance. Tools and equipment are provided by the government. A total of 563 people constituting students, teachers, juveniles, villagers and support staff of schools have been trained in various occupational skills. Of the 563 trained from January 1997 to February 1999, 106 were trained in plumbing, 113 in house wiring, 86 in construction carpentry, 59 in furniture making, 29 in hair cutting, 145 in masonry and 25 in gardening.

Furthermore, starting1999, the TVES has instituted 9 vocational centres. In addition to providing basic vocational skills-training to school-leavers seeking employment, the vocational centres will be expected to promote vocational skills among their general students. These centres will be based in formal schools and institutions and provide training programmes as per local demands. So far ten vocational instructors have also been trained who will provide the lead role in running these centres. In addition, TVES expects to provide mobile technical staff to support these programmes.

Rigney Education

Another important programme that has been established recently by the government is the Rigney Education. This programme is mainly targeted at school leavers who wish to take up vocations in traditional arts and crafts. The Trashi Yangtse Rigney Institute in eastern Bhutan offers training in the 13 traditional arts and crafts known as Zorig Chusum.

The school which was established in 1997 has at present an enrolment of 30 students. In addition, the Painting school in Thimphu trains students in Bhutanese religious and traditional decorative arts.

A few of the emerging issues related to youth are the problems of educated unemployment, substance abuse, delinquencies, thefts, sexual offences etc. especially in the urban areas. While no specific targets were set for this issue, it was generally believed that this required to be tackled through the existing formal schooling programme as well as focused programmes targeted at the urban youth. In response to this, the government in 1996 established a new section within Education Division, called theYouth Guidance and Counselling Service (YGCS).

Since its inception, YGCS has established a comprehensive youth guidance and counselling programme to help youth cope with the multitude of issues that beset them. This includes providing information as well as working together with the youth to understand and guide them through their problems. YGCS also provides career education to all students to promote a realistic assessment of their own capability and interest relative to the world of work.

Programmes are also developed to impart physical and reproductive health education information to youth. Heads of tertiary institutes, secondary schools, primary schools, District Education Officers, and senior educationist have been trained to respond better to the issues of youth problems and provide counselling roles. Another programme which is gaining increasing popularity in the kingdom is the scouts programme. Established for a few students in early 1990s, this programme is increasingly being viewed as an important channel for imparting essential skills and values in our youth which will help them to cope with many of the issues facing them.

Educational Division

The Education Division also established a Youth Centre in Thimphu in May 1996 to cater to the needs of growing numbers of youths and adults. The centre aims at not only providing the recreational facilities but also providing skill based literacy programmes for self employment to youth such as computer literacy, tailoring, knitting, house wiring, painting etc.

The courses are being certified to help them get employment. The centre is also initiating club activities such as visual arts, youth environment education, sports, languages, yoga and so on. In future, the centre plans to open mini youth centres in all the districts to carry out similar activities. Besides the formal and the non-formal education programme, there are numerous government and non-government programmes which help provide skills, knowledge and values to the general population at large thus contributing to the EFA goals and objectives. One of the most important of these programmes is the monastic education system. Instituted in the 8th century a.d. this was the only form of education available in the country till early part of this century.

While the institution of modern education system has pushed this programme to the background, the programme nevertheless continues to play a major role in providing education to those who opt to take up monastic and ecclesiastic calling. In the Bhutanese context, such decisions are made quite early in life and a significant proportion of the Bhutanese population continue to be beneficiary of this form of education.

There are numerous types of programmes provided by different monastic institutions. The most organized of this is the programme which is directly administered by the Central Monastic Body. While the Headquarters remain Tashi-Chhodzong, this monastic order commands similar institutions in all the 20 Dzongs. These institutions also provide patronage to numerous Gomdeys (Lay monk's monasteries), Drubdeys (Meditation centres), Shedras (School for language and arts), Lobdras (Monastic schools) and Nunneries.

A less well organized institution but nevertheless covering a wider expanse of the country are the village temples (Goenpas) which also may house a respected Lama and his lay followers who study under him to become lay-practitioners of religion. The record of the Special Commission for Cultural Affairs indicate that there are 2002 monasteries and temples spread throughout the country.

Agriculture Extension Programme

Instituted early in the 1970s, the extension programme is seen as playing an important role in helping farmers improve farming practices and improving management of farming resources. The knowledge and skills are disseminated through exhibitions, demonstrations, farmer's training courses, study tours and distribution of information leaflets.

Farmer-Extension Communication Support Unit (FECSU) has been set up in the Ministry to produce leaflets, booklets, posters and charts for general distribution to extension agents and farmers. In the Seventh Five Year Plan (1992-1997) about 59,789 farmers were trained on improved farming and livestock rearing techniques, study tours were organized for 1210 farmers and 64 exhibitions were held throughout the country.

The programme is seen as being successful in enhancing the awareness and skills of the farmers on modern farming practices and management. It has been observed that farmers are growing improved seed varieties and cash crops and rearing more cross-bred cattle leading to higher income generation.

Educating the general public on basic health, hygiene, nutrition and family planning is one of the integral programmes of the Health Division. Information, Education, Communication for Health (IECH) Bureau has been created in 1992 primarily for educating the public on health related issues. The Bureau publishes pamphlets, leaflets, flip charts for distribution to the public. It also organizes health festivals, health exhibitions, skits and plays in public gatherings to enhance awareness. In addition, the basic health workers in the villages play a crucial role in transmitting health related information to the villagers. As a result there is an enhanced awareness amongst the rural population on the values of hygiene, nutrition and small family. Health records also show that an increasing proportion of the population are now availing modern health care facilities.

The National Environment Commission has trained so far 550 Block Development Committee members and farmers from forty seven blocks in six districts on environmental awareness and management. It has also carried out environmental awareness activities in schools throughout the country. These training and awareness activities have been very successful in raising awareness and understanding of the importance of environmental conservation.

To enhance the vocational skills and promote entrepreneurship amongst the population, the Ministry of Trade and Industries has set up Entrepreneurship Promotion Centre in 1991. Apart from providing training programmes on entrepreneurship, the centre also organizes basic skills training to the school drop- outs, the unemployed youth and villagers. Some of the courses offered by the centre are tailoring and design course, basic plumbing, basic hair cutting, electrical house wiring and cuisine preparation. It is evident from the below that a majority of the trainees in these programmes are women.

Technical and Vocational Education

Technical and Vocational Education Section (TVES) of Education Division also provides similar training to students, support staff of schools and villagers including women using a mobile training system approach. Furthermore, the National Women's Association of Bhutan has trained many women in income generating skills like weaving, knitting and tailoring.

In 1997 it started "Strengthening Capacities for Development Management and Decentralization" with assistance from the UNDP. Under this project, community leaders from ten blocks in six districts have been trained in local development of plans and programmes, effective communication and reporting system skills. They were also briefed on policies and guidelines like irrigation, water users association etc. that directly affect their lives. The traditional means of communication in Bhutan such as public gatherings during annual religious festivals and frequent block and village level meetings are still used as an important and effective tool for delivering most of the knowledge.

Besides, radio is also an important tool of communication particularly for the remote places. The national radio, Bhutan Broadcasting Service presents regular programmes on agriculture, health, education, environment, religion and culture, rural development and issues on women in Dzongkha, Sharchop and Nepali - three widely spoken languages in the country. The EFA plan was conceived within a highly charged environment of idealism and hope. Despite the emotive appeal to go all out, experience had persuaded Bhutan to moderate the targets to reflect what was conceived as being tenable.

While this has meant that some of the global EFA targets would not have been attained, the government still has a high success rate to report within the context of the national programmes. The strategies and plan outlined under the EFA action plan is seen as relevant and viewed as being largely effective for achieving the EFA targets. The strategies that were successful in addressing the EFA goals were those that were time tested.

For example the community schooling concept had already been proven as a cost-effective means to help increase primary enrolment coverage before launching the EFA programme. Similarly, NAPE approach had found wide acceptance amongst the administrators and educators as a medium to help improve the quality of education. The most successful programmes were also those that relied on community participation and involved little additional resources.

In particular, the community schooling concept now enables the establishment of primary schools anywhere in the country with significantly lower costs to the government. An important reason why the government has not achieved UPE is because of its inability at this stage to provide adequate trained teachers and learning resources to all such schools. However, it is realized now the EFA objectives could have been more successful if a high level body of EFA representatives were formed to facilitate better networking amongst the sectors concerned with issues related to EFA programmes. A case in example is the "rural-flavoured" education approach which is an important objective of EFA programme but still has not made much progress. Additional support from the Agriculture Ministry could have made this more successful. Similarly, while some of Divisions such as Health, Agriculture, Water and Sanitation are solicited for helping the Education Division develop its curriculum materials for both formal and NFE programme, not much of networking and support has been established at the field level for these sectors to support each others programmes.

While a major part of the programmes outlined under the EFA have been carried out, a few programmes could not be undertaken either due to other emerging priorities or because of unavailability of resources. One of the programmes planned was a radio programme on child care. This was not carried out as envisaged. Instead, a programme was launched titled "Education calling teachers" which covers a wide range of topics of professional interest to teachers.

This programme was considered a higher priority because of the need to keep teachers abreast of the changes as well as to keep up the morale of the teachers, especially those serving in the remoter parts of the country. Another important programme that could note properly implemented was the rehabilitation of primary schools. In order to provide quality education it was deemed necessary to provide at least basic minimum standards in the facilities accommodating academic and other student activities. In addition it has been noted that to get teachers to stay in the remote schools, they required better living quarters than were commonly available.

However, within the conditions of a perpetual resource constraint, the rehabilitation and improvements of existing school always feature last in a long list of priority programmes. This has been also the case during the period under review. Despite bewailing the terrible conditions under which some schools operate and teachers live, there has been very little that the government has been able to achieve in this area. Private sector involvement has been looked upon as a possible means of alleviating some of the admission pressures being felt by the education sector. However, there are only 7 private schools operating in the country, all located in the urban areas. Between them they enrol only 1,544 students constituting only about 2 percent of the total student enrolment.

The biggest disappointment in this programme has been questionable quality of the programme offered by some of these schools. Therefore, the government has taken a stance not to allow any more private primary schools to be established in the country, but to restrict it only to those that cater to the secondary and post-secondary levels. Major industries such as the Hydro Projects and the Cement Industries are assisting the government to provide schooling places for the children of their employees as envisaged in the EFA plan.

Another programme where the government has not been able to make much headway has been on education for children with disabilities. The proposed survey for disabilities did not take place as planned. However, the School for the Blind was renamed as the National Institute for the Disabled which demonstrates the intention of the government to use this institute as a focal point for developing programmes for a population with other forms of disability. Some vocational programmes for the blind students have been introduced so far. Some of the other strategies and activities that were not stressed very strongly in the EFA action plan but was nevertheless adopted in the course of the period were prompted by the emerging issues. This is particularly true of issues related to youth problems which have prompted both educators and the parents to review the education content and processes. This also has led to a renewed emphasis on these aspects of the education process.

Despite a number of strategies that have been implemented as mentioned in previous sections, these have been the biggest stumbling block in the achievement of the EFA goals. Inadequate resources even now heads the list of all other issues within the Education Division. A cursory analysis of the subject indicate that the government has increased the allocation to education from approximately 223.136 million in 1991 to Nu NU 841.188 million in 1999. Therefore, teacher shortage even now continues to head the list of problems faced by the schools and the education administration at all levels. The gap has been filled by a large number of expatriate teachers, 14% at primary and 39% at secondary levels or an overall dependence of 20%. Some of the progress being made in enhancing education coverage is being offset by the growth in population due to improved medical services. In addition, topography, climate, limited communication links and scattered pattern of settlement have also impeded access to education and contributed towards a very high unit recurrent costs.

While parental contribution for establishing new primary schools has increased over the past decade, the costs of teachers salaries, materials, stationery and books continue to be largely borne by the government. This has led the Government to look closely at the cost effectiveness of the system as well as review its free education policy. The "free" education policy originated during a time when few student numbers were involved and when most parents did not have the capacity to pay for their children's education.

With rapid expansion at the primary level, and the foreseen growth at the secondary levels and other levels of education, it is becoming quite difficult to sustain this system. In view of this, as well as considering the general improvement in the economy during the last 3 decades, the Government is convinced that some provisions of the free facilities could be withdrawn from certain sections of the population. This in fact would be the only way by which the education system could be made self sufficient and sustainable in the future.

Similarly boarding places of primary and junior high schools have been phased out and are available only for children qualified to continue to higher classes and where there are no such schooling facilities near their homes. However such moves are being implemented cautiously and closely monitored to ensure that it does not affect the enrolment of any groups of population. Compounding the above are the problems related to the mismatch between individual aspirations and national or social needs.

Bhutan still continues to employ a large number of expatriate in the field of education, construction industries and technical areas. And yet, while the existing schools combat with the problems of admission pressures and limited space, the two technical institutes continue to remain under-enrolled every year. While much of these have been determined by a wider societal milieu, education too is perceived as playing a role and therefore, there is an increasing call from the government circles as well as parents for the education system to tackle these issues.

Curriculum at all levels of education continue to be questioned on the aspect of its relevancy. Despite the large resources already expended on this, much more requires to be done. A major concern is that the existing curriculum does not address fully the objectives related to values, skills and knowledge required by the future generation and for the world of work. The emerging problems related to rural-urban migration and juvenile delinquency have also been blamed on the education system and its inability to address these issues adequately. The qualitative development of the system is impeded by resource constraints. While the concern for improving quality continues to be expressed in every plan document, the pace of expansion imposed by the demand from the communities have taken a disproportionate amount of resources thus impinging on the qualitative development of the system.

Because of the lack of maintenance funds, many school buildings have become dilapidated, sanitary facilities appalling, sports facilities non-existent and school library and other learning resources at best, rudimentary. The issue of resources, both internal and external aid, will continue to occupy a major part of the development agenda in the coming decade too.

Compared to the early years of the education system when

children were required to be conscripted into the schools, parents now not only demand schools for their communities but are willing to contribute much more for the construction and maintenance of these schools. As mentioned earlier, in many cases, it is the government which has to provide alternate strategies such as delaying the enrolment of the child, to restrain the pace of development because of the lack of resources such as teachers and materials. Many more parents are now themselves educated and can participate in the provision of education to their children meaningfully both at home and in schools.

A growing number of people are also able to pay for the cost of their children's education or at least some portion of it. The government's decision to withdraw the free supply of stationery from schools situated in the urban and Dzongkhag headquarters have not in any way diminished the demand for education in these schools.

Progressive Increase

Further, a progressive increase in the share of cost by parents could now become a possibility given the increase in the average earning of the Bhutanese as well as the prevailing high demand for education. Corresponding growth in the economy could also help enhance the budget being made available for education. Non-Formal Education which was initiated as a pilot programme just about 8 years ago is also gaining popularity as a viable means for adults and out of school youth to attain literacy skills.

The Education Division now faces an increasing challenge to keep at pace with the demand from the communities to establish NFE programmes and learning centres. Also important is the acceptance by the policy makers that such schemes can work and help not only enhance literacy rates but serve as important channels for disseminating essential knowledge on a variety of issues. On the political front, Bhutan has always believed in the concept of linking development to enhancing the quality of life of every individual in the country. This is aptly termed "Gross National Happiness". Within this broad development philosophy, education has always received a high priority with 10-18% of its planned expenditure being set for education sector during the last 40 years.

Over 80% of the Bhutanese population are engaged in subsistence farming. With a very low revenue base, high social service costs most of which is provided free, the government is concerned rightly about the sustainability of the programmes that are established. Other emerging issues are related to mismatch in expectations between the educated youth and the employment opportunities, youth related problems and issues of rural-urban migration.

Therefore, while the total resources for education may remain undiminished and even increase, less are available for expansion and qualitative development within the system because of the dispersion of the resources to tackle these other issues. With increasing level of community participation for all levels of the education programme, the provision of education through the formal and non-formal channels is now tenable in all parts of the country.

However, the government still suffers from a weak institutional base to support and help deliver the EFA programmes. The total staffing in the Education Headquarters is at present 150, comprising of 88 officers and 62 support staff. These officers are expected to provide general direction, policy analysis and support, develop curriculum, procure and deliver supplies to schools, recruit teachers and deploy them, provide professional support to all schools and institutions and so on, establish standards for buildings, conduct national level examinations and implement national projects. The country is divided into 20 districts (dzongkhags). Each Dzongkhag has a Dzongkhag Education Officer who is expected to plan and provide support to the educational programmes within the dzongkhag. Apart from two larger dzongkhags, the DEO is the sole officer representing the sector in the Dzongkhag administration. Under such circumstances the DEO is hard pressed to meet his/her professional responsibilities.

Therefore, with the growth of the education system both in terms of the number of schools and institutions as well as in the complexity of the programmes and issues, the administrative support and institutions are seen as increasingly being over-loaded and becoming inadequate. Unless this particular issue is addressed in a holistic manner, not only the EFA goals but all the other programmes of the education sector will be adversely affected.

The Bhutanese primary education system provides education to 31,000 more children than it did in 1991 or an increase of 68%. Despite the pressure of enrolment and the resulting increase in class sizes, the Bhutanese Education system has been able to maintain high standards in many of the core learning area especially in languages. Children nowadays also stay longer in the system and take less numbers of years to complete schooling. Many of the beneficiaries of expansion have been the children living in the peripheral and remote parts of the country and those engaged in transmigration practices.

In fact, one of the most disadvantaged groups of population in terms of education access as well as in many other respects has until recently been the yak herders who lead a semi-nomadic life moving with their yaks. Till 1991, there were only 3 schools catering to this group of population. Three more community schools have now been established to cater to these population groups and it is estimated that the coverage of education in these places is well above the national average now. Non formal education which began on a cautious pilot footing has proved its effectiveness and has won the trust from administrators and the general public. The programme has increased its annual coverage from 300 in 1992 to 1932 in 1999. Skills based learning programmes are beginning to increase in scope as well as quality. Even some private entrepreneurs are now beginning to show interest in this area. The resolve on the part of the government to improve the general quality of the lives of its population through extension of social service amenities in general and education in particular, continues.

Efforts are being made to ensure that the education infrastructure that is in existence as well as the demand that it has created in the process of its development can be supported with available resources, namely, human and financial. This means working towards a system of cost-sharing, cost-reduction, self-reliance and a constraint driven development model without compromising the quality of education services.

The system of community participation has already been established. It is anticipated that this will evolve over time for communities to play a much more active role not only in the domain of school building but in the content, school time table and other issues of importance. This is seen to be crucial if one is to make the concept of "rural-flavoured education" a reality. While Primary Education will continue getting the lion's share of the resources and will be the main conduit for achieving EFA targets, the NFE programme shall be provided with much more resources and be allowed to expand at a faster pace than was the case till now.

Early Child-hood Development has so far not been accorded

much attention because of other competing demands as well as the comforting knowledge that these were addressed through the traditional family care system. However, with the increasing transformation of the society putting added pressure on the traditional family ties and relationships, it is seen that ECCD would need to play a greater role in our society. An increasing body of knowledge in this field supports such a move.

Therefore, more resources shall be accorded to this programme. In particular, the Non Formal Education will be developed to provide stronger links to early childhood development. As one nears the Universal Primary Education coverage, the system will need to devise programmes and create facilities for enrolling the population groups who are not so visible at present. They include those that have physical and mental disabilities as well as those who adopt nomadic life styles.

Fortunately for Bhutan, the size of this population is small. Even considering this, it is expected to involve sizable additional costs to the system. It has become imperative for education system to provide in addtion to the 3 Rs, the essential life-skills and value systems that will enable the youth to survive and contribute to the larger society.

The main vehicle and focus for achieving the EFA goals has been through the expansion and improvements in the primary education system. Nevertheless, other channels of education were not entirely ignored by the Government. On the contrary, significant progress has been made in the area of NFE and other educational programmes which has helped realize in large measure the targets set under the EFA plan. Bhutan faced a set back in its educational programme when some disturbances in the Southern part of the country forced a decline in enrolment in 1990.

At the beginning of the 1990s, this dimension of the EFA Declaration was not viewed as a serious area of concern. Firstly, the Bhutanese Primary Education system incorporates a 1 year of pre-primary education which provides an opportunity for all children to prepare for formal education programme. Secondly it is generally accepted that the Bhutanese culture at present provides a high level of interaction between children, parents and the other family members in their early formative years which ensures the development of emotional and social skills required by children.

In addition to this, the Health sector was already moving in a big way to promote mother and child care to achieve a reduction in infant and child mortality rates. Therefore, no specific targets or goals were set for this dimension under EFA programme. However, the government has addressed ECCD through sectoral inputs in the area of health, nutrition and education.

The Royal Government declared Universal Child Immunization in 1991. This reflects the commitment and the progress already made to enhance health services to the children. Mother and Child Health(MCH) clinics have been established in almost all parts of the country. Rigorous extension services are carried out in the remote areas to check the health of young children.

A national nutritional assessment conducted in 1988 indicated 38 percent of children under-five were malnourished and that 56% were stunted. The Health Division has undertaken various activities to improve the situation of nutrition in the country. The government has moved in a big way to promote breast-feeding. Simple manuals and pamphlets on local weaning foods have also been developed by the IECH Bureau of the Health Division. Mirco-nutrient supplements such as iron/folate are being provided for women and children.

The Health Division also maintains a good record of the growth of children (weight) who visit the immunization clinics. From such data, it may be seen that there has been a perceptible decrease in malnutrition during the last 7 years. Bhutan also continues to monitor the Iodine Deficiency Disorders through its IDD project which ensures the commercial distribution of iodized salt to the population.

A nationwide study on iodine deficiency disorders(IDD) conducted in 1996 found that the goitre prevalence in Bhutan was 14%. Within schools, the school feeding programme provides support to the school cooks to cook more nutritious food. In addition the School Agriculture programme is being strengthened to help schools produce fresh and varied vegetables.

Children of 6+ age are given admission in PP in primary schools established across the length and breadth of the country. Since 1990, PP enrolment has increased by 5%. Within a child-centred learning approach, PP children are provided with the most stimulated environment essential to their physical and intellectual development. Such formal services have been established by the private sector in urban areas specially in Thimphu, the capital city.

Since 1990, 7 of them have been initiated.

With the introduction of Non-formal education (NFE) in 1992, parents who are the most important teachers of their children, have had access to learning about various life skills. Although, no specific learning material on ECCD have been developed, many of its related themes under health and nutrition, hygiene, family health, education, etc., have been covered. Moreover, discussions have been underway to include ECCD in the NFE curriculum.

Primary school enrolment increased from 46,517 in 1991 to 78,007 in 1998 or by 7.7% annually which is more than the projected target of 6%. The gross primary enrolment ratio is estimated at 72% which is much lower than the target of 90%. This apparent anomaly may be explained by the high population growth during this period, estimated at 2.6% from 1991-93 and 3.1% from 1994-98. It is also estimated that during this period, the proportion of primary education aged children to the total population increased from 15% to 18%. This numbers to 18,000 which equals half the increase in enrolment registered during this period.

Furthermore, the net enrolment ratio is estimated at only 53%. The Bhutanese education system is characterized therefore by a high number of overaged children.

One of the main reason for this is the late entry into schools. When a new school is established, it is quite common for parents to enrol anyone from 6 years to 12 years into the Pre-Primary classes. The other reason for this is the high repetition rate prevalent within the system. In 1998, primary education is provided in 115 community schools, 128 primary schools and in 42 of the 44 junior high schools and 7 private schools. Please see structure of Education on page 5. An interesting point as indicated by the table at right is a gradual decline in the growth rate from 10.5% between 1991-1992 to 4.5% between 1997-1998. The main reason for this is a result of the attempt made by the Government to slow the pace of enrolment expansion to match the availability of teachers and materials. Furthermore, this has also been contributed to by the application of more stringent rules to restrict the entry of under-age children in the schools as a measure of controlling grade repetition.

From the trend of the falling entry rate at PP, it is possible that Bhutan may be closer to the UPE level than indicated by the present statistics. Interestingly, the growth rate of 7.7% in the formal education system has not been so much as a result of increased intake as it is with the increased retention within the system. It may be seen from the table below that between 1992-1998, the intake at the primary education has increased by an average of 3.3% annually only.

During 1991-98, 158 new community schools were established in the most disadvantaged and remote parts of the Kingdom. The enrolment in the community schools has been growing steadily from 5,576 number of students in 1991 to well over 12,695 in 1998. Some of these schools have been converted to boarding primary schools thus catering also to other communities. Therefore at present there are only 115 schools retaining the name of community schools. It constitutes almost 17% of the total student population at the primary education level.

The establishment of community schools has made it possible for the Royal Government to provide educational opportunities to many of the population groups living in the rural and remote parts of the country without taxing the already limited resources of the government.

It has helped ensure the sustainability of an expanding education service and is credited for having helped curb rural urban migration and reduced overcrowding in the urban schools. These schools have also become the centre of continuing educational activity for many communities.

The school facilities are used for conducting non formal education classes for the community using the existing teachers after school hours. Other vocational skills training are also conducted for the benefit of the community using the school facilities. While 17% of the PP-VI enrolment expansion is attributable to the new community schools, the rest of the expansion was absorbed by the existing schools through additional developments in these schools such as creation of additional classrooms as well as increases in the class sizes.

The result of these efforts is that there is now a generally higher level of enrolment in almost all the schools than existing in 1991 with the result that the average size of a community school is now 110 as compared to 66 in 1991. Similarly the average size of a primary and junior high school is now 326 and 671 as compared to 252 and 505 respectively in 1991.

Feeding/Boarding Programme

Another programme which has helped enhance enrolment

and retain students in schools is the school feeding programme. The mid-day meal scheme as well as the boarding provision has been instrumental in attracting and helping retain a large number of children in schools. Despite the proliferation of Community schools across the country, there remains many households which are located away from walking distances of these schools. Therefore mid-day meals and boarding schemes play a critical role in the enrolment of children from such households. Two types of feeding schemes are provided to the schools a) boarding and b) mid day meals. Day students receive one meal a day while the boarders receive two meals a day. The third meal for primary schools is contributed by the parents.

Parental contribution can vary from school to school, while some collect food grain, vegetables and fire wood, some collect money to buy these items. 27% of the students studying in community, primary and junior high receive food. The proportion of girls receiving food is much lower at 24%. This is because food aid is targeted to those children who have to walk long distances to schools and need to board. The proportion of girls who board or walk long distances are understandably low compared to the boys.

The government was also able to continue providing free textbooks and stationery to children in the rural primary schools. However as a result of the increasing resource crunch, free supply of stationery to children in urban schools was withdrawn in 1993. Because of the relative economic advantage in these areas, this has not affected the enrolment.

A significant effort has also been made to improve the management of the education system at all levels to ensure better learning environment and effective utilization of both material and human resources. A study done by CAPSS recently indicates that while there is generally a good working atmosphere in the schools, learning materials are still far too short of the requirements.

Girls Enrolment

While the absence of social bias against girls has contributed to a steady growth of girls enrolment over the years, there have been certain factors which affect girls enrolment. In particular, the harsh terrain and the long distances children have to travel to reach schools have discouraged many girls from attending schools. Secondly, while many schools provide boarding facilities, these are of the barest kind and hardly suitable for the girls.

Therefore, measures such as locating the schools closer to their homes (community schools), and improvement in boarding facilities where required have been instrumental too in contributing to the growth of girls enrolment. The institution of the School Management Board which facilitates the school managers to interact and get the influential community leaders to participate in helping the school has also influenced to a large degree in mobilizing community support to enrol girls where there have been specific problems.

One of the inferences drawn from the study of gender balance in enrolment in different schools is that in many of the places which exhibit less girls ratio also have lower enrolment ratio, although at present there is limited population information to help us support this statistically. This follows from the premise that the harder the conditions for enrolment, the more it affects girls.

Education for the Disabled

The School for the Blind was upgraded to the National Institute for the Disabled and its management taken over by the Technical and Vocational Education Section of the Education Division. Consequently, the programme for the blind children was enhanced by including vocational skills into the curriculum. However, enrolment in the school remained constant at 1990 level of 30 students. A survey of the other disabilities which was planned is yet to be carried out.

Quality of Primary Education

Quality of education is determined to a large extent by the quality of teachers, the curriculum and learning organization as well as the availability of learning materials. Much effort and resources have been expended in improving these during the last 8 years.

The Bhutanese education system has historically relied heavily on the expatriate teachers. Compared to 683 (35%) expatriate teachers teaching in these schools in 1991, the expatriate staff has reduced to 305 (14%) in 1998. This has been as a result of the efforts made by the Government to increase the training capacities of the country's two teacher training institutions as well as to make the teaching profession much more attractive. Compared to a capacity of about 300 teacher trainees a decade ago, the two institutes can now accommodate over 600 teacher trainees. Teacher graduates for primary level have increased from 89 to 141 in 1998. The Royal Government recently also instituted a teaching allowance which provides an enhanced renumeration amounting to 15% of the basic pay for all primary school teachers to help attract better candidates to the teaching profession.

A comparison of the teacher profile in the primary schools between 1991-98 indicate a marked improvement in the quality of teachers. For example in 1991, 28% of the teachers in schools providing primary education were untrained. In 1998 only 10 % of the teachers remained untrained. The proportion of female teachers improved marginally during the same period. Compared to 560 female teachers (28.9%) in 1991, there were in 1998, 692 (31.7%) female teachers. Apart from these, a significant effort has also been made to enhance the knowledge and skills of serving teachers through in-service training programmes.

A comprehensive system of updating and keeping teachers abreast about the changes in curriculum and development issues have been instituted at the national level as well as the school level. A system for the Dzongkhag level was also tried out for two years but this was dropped due to difficulties for Dzongkhags to mobilize resource persons as well as financial support. Over 1000 teachers (over half of the total teaching force) are engaged in national workshops annually. These workshops are followed through at the school level in the form of School-Based In-Service Programmes (SBIP) where new methods and information are disseminated to the other teachers. The SBIP is also an important forum where teachers can share experiences and skills with their colleagues.

Distance Education

A distance education programme has also been instituted for serving teachers to upgrade their professional and academic knowledge through distance learning. Instituted in 1995, the programme at present has an enrolment of 60 candidates. A recent survey conducted by the Curriculum and Support Section of the Education Division show that generally teachers are now more prepared to provide better quality teaching than they did erstwhile. While there is no baseline survey for 1990/91 to provide a comparative development scenario, the survey result of 1998 provides a very positive response of the teachers on their preparedness for schools.

The period 1990-98 saw major activities related to improving the curriculum content in each of the subject areas to make it relevant and meaningful to the Bhutanese children. This has been carried out within the context of achieving defined basic learning competencies at every grade of primary education. Not only was the content restructured and revised but a significant effort and resources were expended on improving the learning materials for children.

A whole series of new and attractive supplementary readers were produced during this time. This was linked to teacher preparation through in-service programmes both at the national and school levels.

Teaching Learning Methods

The New Approach to Primary Education (NAPE) is widely credited for helping break the traditional chalk-talk method to activity related and a more effective learning system. Apart from helping enhance the learning process, NAPE is also credited for making the schooling process much more meaningful and enjoyable to the students. The NAPE system is now adopted throughout the whole primary education cycle. Another significant step in helping to improve the teaching learning process is the adoption of a class-teacher system for the lower primary classes as a distinct improvement over the traditional subject-teacher system.

In this new system, a single teacher teaches all the subjects in his/her class. Apart from facilitating the teacher to know the students better, the system also allows for flexibility in switching from one topic of interest to another and to show the interconnectedness of the education programme. Related to this is also the adoption of a system of multigrade teaching to deal with situations when a teacher has to teach more than a class at the same time. This is an extension of the NAPE system which amongst others encourages ability groupings and peer interaction while learning. Amongst others, this method facilitates maximum students participation thereby motivating and improving the learning environment for the individual.

Improvement of Student Assessment System

The education programme in Bhutan traditionally provided for heavy reliance on end of year examinations. One of the main drawbacks of such a system was that this did not make adequate provision for the wider aspects of education such as those related to values and attitudes which are not easily amenable for testing and examinations. Moreover much of the technique applied served a summative purpose and did not really help in improving the performance of the teachers or the students.

Therefore, since 1995, a lot of attention and emphasis is being provided to the development of a continuous assessment system throughout the year that caters to social and other important skills of students as well as serving an important feedback for both students and teachers who would use this process to improve themselves.

The Primary School Certificate Examinations which was once a 100% pen and paper test has throughout the past decade been changed to a combination of continuous assessment by the school and external examination with 50% weightage being provided to each component. Assessing the impact made by these programmes in improving the learning competence of students can be a rather complex exercise.

However, it is generally believed that one of the proxy measures that can be used for this is through the improvements made in pass rate of students in different grades of the primary cycle. The Bhutanese education system presently adopts a rigorous testing and examination system at every class. This is complemented by a national level examinations at the end of primary education.

The general belief within the Education system is that boarding facilities enable children to receive extra tuition and supervised coaching which help enhance their academic performance. The results for 1998 show boarding schools faring less well than day schools. This however must relate to the other factors associated with the boarding schools. In particular, it is important to remind here that boarding schools are mostly confined to rural and remote parts of the country. A comparison of schools by availability of electricity, playfield and Science laboratories again indicate no appreciable difference between haves and have nots. In addition to end of primary examinations, there is a general improvement in the pass rates at every class as reflected by the steady reduction in the rate of repetition rates in every class.

The professional support to the schools and teachers is also another important component which is crucial for improving the teaching learning processes in the schools. The Dzongkhag Education Officers (DEO) and the School Inspectors have always been responsible for providing such crucial support. However, because of the lack of adequate staff, this has been one of the most difficult and perhaps neglected aspects of the education programme in Bhutan. For example a DEO does not even have an assistant to help him in his tasks which also includes planning, administration as well as looking after new school construction programmes.

Similarly, there are only 10 officers manning the Inspectorate. A far reaching decision made recently in this regard has been to change the image and the role of the Inspectors to Education Monitoring Officers. The EMOs also receive help from qualified teachers and professionals who are appointed as focal persons to assist in their work. By the year, 2000, there will be 53. These teachers will be able to help the DEOs and the EMOs to help guide and support the other teachers in their respective localities.

Human Rights Developments

Since 1990, over 100,000 thousand southern Bhutanese of Nepalese ethnicity have been made refugees after being forcibly evicted, forced to flee persecution and repression, or expelled after being coerced into signing "voluntary" emigration forms.

Ten years later, the refugees remain in camps in Nepal administered by the United Nations High Commissioner for Refugees (UNHCR). The 1990s could have made it as the decade of human rights because the Second World Conference on Human Rights in Vienna in 1993 helped put this issue in the spotlight. But for all the lip-service of defenders of human rights, selective intervention by powerful nations to resolve international crises - jumping in only when and where it mattered to them - only underscored the international community's hypocrisy.

Powerful nations policed the world with a vengeance: they waged a full-scale war in the Gulf, sent UN forces to Bosnia-Herzegovina, and mounted military attacks on Serbia. The world imposed sanctions on countries and declared no-fly zones over sovereign territory. The international community even demanded the head of an elected head of government as a wanted criminal. Yet, when a hundred thousand people forcibly evicted from their homeland languished in refugee camps, these same leaders and governments would not make the effort to demand that the leadership of a tiny kingdom abide by internationally accepted rules of civilised behaviour.

During the last decade of the second millennium, the international community was active in resolving crisis after crisis across the globe. The full military might of the United States was on display in the Gulf, international forces policed the Balkans, went after the Serbs in Kosovo and Serbia, and Australia did its bit for international law and order in East Timor.

But just as the rapid intervention in some areas of conflict have been impressive, the deliberate unwillingness of the international community to be involved in resolving other crises has been shameful. The global apathy toward the issue of Bhutanese refugees in Nepal is one such example. If the international community wished to leave a mark before the end of the millennium by doing one good that did not appear to be swayed by economic and political interests, the opportunity was there in resolving the Bhutanese crisis.

Unfortunately, that this did not happen is an indicator of how human behaviour and political actions continue to be guided by vested self-interests. Bhutan is a country ruled by a hereditary monarch, His Majesty King Jigme Singye Wangchuck. The King is both the Head of State and Head of Government although since 1998 much of the powers have been transferred to a Council of Ministers nominated by the King and vetted by the 150-member National Assembly. By rotation one member of the council takes on the duties of Head of Government.

The population of Bhutan is a subject of much speculation since the exact figures have never been divulged by the government. In the mid-1960s the government instructed officials to state that the country's population was 900,000. When the kingdom became a member of the United Nations in 1971, the population was stated to be 1 million. This figure was routinely increased to reflect the growth rate and had crossed 1.4 million by 1990 when the King announced in an interview to an Indian journalist that the actual figure was closer to 600,000. Taking this figure as more likely, the total population at the end of 2000 AD is around 750,000.

The reason behind this secrecy regarding population statistics is political and stems from concerns over the break-up between the three main ethnic communities that live in Bhutan.

Western Bhutan, the centre of power, is inhabited by Ngalongs of Tibetan origin and make up between 15 and 20 per cent. Eastern Bhutanese, the Sharchops, are of Indo-Mongoloid or Tibeto-Burman origin and constitute around 40 to 45 per cent. Both these groups share a common religion (Buddhism) and Tibetan-derived culture. The third group, ethnic Nepalese who are mainly Hindus, comprise immigrants of more recent origin (late 19th century onwards) who were granted citizenship in 1958. This southern group makes up between 40 and 50 per cent.

Since 1990 some 110,000 southern Bhutanese have been forced to abandon their homes and flee to India and Nepal. The roots of the political crisis in southern Bhutan obviously lie in the leadership's concern over the growing southern Bhutanese population, both as a percentage and in terms of real numbers.

The perceived threat of being swamped by ethnic Nepalese was heightened during the 1980s by the wave of democratic movements across the globe and nearer home in Nepal and the Nepali-led Gorkhaland movement for a separate state in India. Recognising this threat, a policy with an eventual goal of balancing the demographic pattern was initiated in the mid-1980s; the idea was to set right a historical error of judgement - the grant of nationality in 1958 to ethnic Nepalese settled in the south. One might sympathise with the Bhutanese, but the methods employed were foul and in total disregard of international nationality laws.

The grant of citizenship in 1958 was by royal decree. The new citizens were not granted papers nor was there any major changes in the lives of the people then.

3

Status of Women

The social attitudes, traditional practices and outlook against women have contributed to the exploitation of women. This has made Bhutanese women lacking in confidence in handling the issues generally affecting themselves even in their day-to-day life. The situation in Bhutan is such that majority of women are not even aware of their basic rights. The practice of discrimination, gender-inequality and exploitation of women are not sudden emergence in the Asian societies. These are the legacy of the past feudal societies. Bhutan is still a feudal and autocratic society. Therefore, the presence of discrimination, gender inequality and exploitation of women in one or other form is the main characteristics of feudal society of Bhutan.

Bhutanese patriarchal system reflects male supremacy making women subservient to men. Government has made no efforts to protect and promote women's rights even though it has ratified the International Convention on the Elimination of All Forms of Discrimination Against Women. Participation by women in national life is almost nil. Women have least access to higher post in the government. They have never been appointed as Ministers, Judges, Chief District Officers, Ambassadors or to other senior important posts. Women comprising around 49 per cent of the population have least access to gainful employment. They do not have economic autonomy.

More than 95 per cent women are illiterate and are engaged in traditional agricultural farming. The government has done nothing to improve their lot. Less than 0.5 per cent women are employed in the civil service (bureaucracy). They are mostly employed in lower level jobs like, telephone operators, typists, clerks etc. Less than 0.5 per cent women are engaged in business. Around 0.2 per cent are engaged in other occupation and 3.5 per cent of women have no identifiable occupation. The plight of rural women is worse. They are most neglected lot. Sexual exploitation, illiteracy, superstition, disease, child mortality and ignorance are rampant in the rural villages. Although women's participation in higher levels of government and decision-making is quite limited, their participation in community meetings within their direct environment is as high as 70 per cent. Industrial development is as yet limited and does not provide significant employment. Unlike many other developing countries, unemployment is not yet a major problem. The Human Development Index (HDI) rank of Bhutan is 159th of 174 countries. However, if based on recent data available, the country would occupy the 125th position among 174 countries, well ahead of neighbouring countries like India and Bangladesh. Although Bhutan remains an LDC, poverty does not take the shape of abject poverty seen in many other South Asian countries. The Gender-Related Development Index (GDI) rank has not yet been calculated for Bhutan.

Although agricultural development is slowly changing the face of rural Bhutan, it is still overwhelmingly characterised by subsistence agriculture with high demand for labour and low levels of productivity. Crop production, livestock and forestry activities are closely interrelated and interdependent. Crops account for a 20 per cent share of GDP, livestock for 8 per cent and forestry for 9 per cent of GDP. More than 80 per cent of the population depend upon agriculture and animal husbandry for their livelihood. The gender division of tasks in agriculture is not very clear in Bhutan. While some tasks are generally allocated by gender, others may be performed by both men and women, and men and women can to a large extent take over from each other.

Bhutanese women are usually engaged in firewood collection, crop cultivation, vegetable gardening, yak herding, traditional weaving using vegetal dyes and other handicraft making. Men, by tradition, are engaged in ploughing, construction, trading and other business or manual activity. The division of labour by gender also differs between ethnic groups, so that it is most pronounced among Lotshampas, and least among Sharchopas.

Women in Bhutan have traditionally been involved in activities related to housekeeping, agriculture, animal husbandry and cottage industry, and would appear to play an important role equal to men in rural economics. But in all ethnic groups it is men's task to plough the fields with oxen. Unlike most other South Asian countries, Bhutanese society is mainly matriarchal and women have equal status to men not only in the eye of the law but also in the home.

Women own 70 per cent of the land. This pattern holds true in the ownership of the livestock as well. Most decisions are made jointly by women and men and in many areas such as spending of money earned from kitchen gardening and farm labour, women are free to decide independently. Around 70 per cent of the country is covered by forests. A total of 26 per cent of the country is now protected area, and 13 per cent of the forest are under management. Wood and wood products accounted for 11.9 per cent of total exports in 1994 and forestry for 9.2 per cent of GDP in 1995. Bhutan's forests are among the most important remains of natural Eastern Himalayan forests. They are characterised by exceptional biological diversity and Bhutan is considered one of the world's ten most important "hot spots". Forest in Bhutan is state owned, but rural people have traditional user rights for grazing, collection of fuelwood and non-wood forest products, and thus the forest is an important resource base for the rural communities. Forests provide over 90 per cent of the domestic fuel in the rural areas as well as timber for rural housing and farm buildings.Forests also play an important role in food security in Bhutan. Food from the forests becomes critical to the rural areas when transporting food to these areas is difficult, when people do not have money to buy food and when there is crop failure. Farmers collect 164 different plants from forests, including 22 types of mushrooms, 16 medicinal plants, 11 cash-generating non-timber forest products, 14 species for home use, 6 wild fruit species, 15 food and 8 beverage species.

Fuelwood and water collection is often undertaken by women. However, men sometimes take on fuelwood and water collection, and even child care. House-husbands are common in many communities in Bhutan. Heavy work like felling trees for house construction is done by men. Mushroom collection provides a sizeable income to many women and their families. About 45 per cent of the medicinal plants collectors are women. Some have even traditionally been involved in cultivating and harvesting medicinal plants. Livestock is an integral part of farming systems in Bhutan. 86 per cent of farmers own livestock. Almost every household maintains at least a few cattle for draft power, animal products and for manure. Horses are kept as pack animals, pigs and poultry for meat and eggs. Sheep and goats are also raised. In the alpine zone yaks replace the cattle and horses. The primary gender division of labour in livestock management is somewhat blurred. However, usually women tend small stock, especially poultry. Though men contribute their labour in caring for the livestock, it is women who share more responsibility for caring for livestock by collecting fodder and water, cleaning stalls and milking. Women also feed the cattle, while men usually take cattle for grazing. The environment in Bhutan is still relatively intact. This is partly due to the recent start of the development process, and partly to the high priority given to environmental sustainability and conservation by the Royal Government of Bhutan. The Government has declared its firm intention to maintain a 60 per cent forest cover and 26 per cent in the form of protected areas, even at the cost of economic opportunities foregone. Moreover, the Buddhist philosophy of love and respect to nature has greatly influenced people's attitude to the environment.

As women play a leading role in the fields as well as in communities they are in position to gather new varieties through farmer-to-farmer exchanges. Even so, emerging environmental problems like degradation of forests close to settlements cause longer working hours for the rural people, as they have to walk longer distances to collect fuelwood. These emerging problems may not be gender-biased, though. Off-farm activities are undertaken by both men and women. Women are traditionally engaged in weaving and petty trade. Cloth weaving is an important economic activity in the central and eastern regions. Basket- and shoe-making, portering and carpentry work are some of the non-farm income earning activities that men undertake. Producing fine bamboo baskets and other containers is a speciality of the people in the eastern districts, which are now becoming very popular among tourists. Bhutan has numerous family-operated traditional paper-making units. In the Bhutanese farming community the system of exchange labour is widely practiced. Both men and women work on another's farm as part of the labour-for-labour exchange. In this system men's and women's work are accounted as equal. Both men and women also take up jobs in road construction, but for unskilled labour men are paid higher daily wages than women. The National Women's Association of Bhutan (NWAB) was established in 1981 with the objective of "encouraging women to take an active part in the implementation of socioeconomic development programmes and in all other nation-building activities" and "improving the socioeconomic status of women, especially rural women".

NWAB is an NGO and receives government financial support. It had about 400 members nationwide in 1993. It carries out social work in a number of areas and provides handicraft training for women and credit to assist women in setting up their own businesses. Even though Bhutan is classified as a Low Income Food Deficit Country, poverty does not take the shape of abject poverty seen in many other South Asian countries. Subsistence agriculture at low productivity is still sufficient to provide for household food security in most regions of the country. This appears to be related to the small size of the population and relatively equitable distribution of landholdings. Coupled with this, a traditional extended family system provides security for the most vulnerable groups, and a system of lending/ borrowing food among rural households during the lean season helps the poorer families. The forest also provides a buffer for food security during the lean season. The profile of gender roles in Bhutanese farming systems bears evidence that women are key contributors to household food security.

The real condition of Bhutanes women do not come to the light of the foreigners yet. Bhutan does not have newspaper, its only weekly bulletin is owned by the government. The external media is not allowed to Bhutan. Whereas, the government churns out glossy picture of the economic indicators in the international forums. They are only meant for the consumption of international community without reality.

But hardly any information reaches the world outside. Especially the ruling Drukpa or Ngalong community treats women as an object of consumer goods. They have no dignity and continuously humiliated by the males. Behind the government rhetoric of good governance, wide spread incidents of female abuses and their sexual exploitation are hidden.

Bhutanese refugee women and children constitute around 49 per cent and 40 per cent of the total refugee population in exile. Hundreds of women were raped during the army crackdown after peaceful protests in 1990. While male members were jailed for joining the peaceful rallies, women folk were abused, tortured and terrorised to flee the country. A number of reports prepared by the International human rights organisations, like, Amnesty International, IMADAR, Japan depicted cases of torture, dishonour and rape of Bhutanese women by the security forces.

The government of Bhutan simultaneously introduced the new Marriage Act which had an even larger content of discrimination against Lhotshampa women and their children. The Act declared all foreign wives of the Bhutanese citizens as non-citizens, even though most of them were granted citizenship under previous citizenship laws.

In contravention of all international norms and civilised behaviour, the Government denied several thousand children (born out of marriages between Lhotshampa husbands and Nepali speaking wives from Nepal or India) of their right to nationality. They were evicted along with their parents. This Act was only enforced against the Lhotshampas.

The Marriage Act was enacted in 1980 and was forcefully implemented in 1988 to especially target the wives of Lhotshampas. This discriminatory law imposes a number of denial of benefits to those who married non-Bhutanese wives. The Lhotshampas who married non-Bhutanese wife did not have the right to vote in (became ineligible for election to) the National Assembly (Parliament) elections, they were denied promotion in civil services, denied training and fellowships and medical treatment abroad, they were also denied business and agricultural grants and loans given by the government and could not avail of government supplied fertilisers, seeds and farm machineries on subsidies. They could not get jobs in the Foreign Service and Armed Forces. This posed enormous problems for the Lhotshampas.There are many reasons as to why the Lhotshampa chose foreign wives of their own ethnic groups from Nepal and India. Some reasons are enumerated as follows:

Bhutan stepped out of its isolation in the mid-sixties. The government did not encourage cultural socialisation of various ethnic groups. Some ethnic groups were not allowed to own properties in the ruling Ngalung dominated areas. Even in-country migration was restricted. In country travel was also restricted for some ethnic groups. The transport and communications were also not developed. This led to the cultural isolation of various ethnic groups. Thus, each ethnic group developed their own intra-ethnic group matrimonial alliances. Lhotshampas had a wide ethnic area in Darjeeling, Sikkim and Nepal to choose their spouse from. As a result many Lhotshampas got their spouses from their own ethnic groups from these places.

The most important factor that prevented the encouragement of inter-ethnic group matrimonial alliances is culture. The Lhotshampas are by and large Hindus. Culturally and traditionally, the Lhotshampas are entirely different from ruling Ngalung ethnic group. Their language is a dialect of or is derived from Sanskrit, the oldest language. They prefer to live in the hot climate of the southern foot hills.

The Ngalungs are nurtured in Drukpa Kargyupa Buddhist culture. They speak Tibetan stock Dzonkha language which is entirely different from Nepali. They wear robe like dresses and prefer to live in cool climate of the north. While strict cultural values of the Lhotshampas triggered the search for wives from outside Bhutan, limited domestic society and geography also facilitated such marriages. The lack of communication and infrastructure within Bhutan were also factors which made Lhotshampas get their wives from neighbouring Indian states and Nepal as it is easier to travel to neighbouring countries than to visit other districts of Bhutan. Because of the lack of roads, Bhutanese are required to travel through India to reach from east to west in the south and south to north. Darjeeling district had excelled as a centre of education during the British rule in India. It is still regarded as the best place for education in the entire region of Bhutan, Nepal and Northeast India.

Both the Citizenship Act and the Marriage Act are racist, biased and discriminatory against Lhotshampa women of southern Bhutan. Moreover, the law is also implemented in a discriminatory manner; very rigidly against the Lhotshampas and not at all against Ngalung/Drukpas, who for example have a Chinese, English, Italian or American wives. For example, Mr. Ugen Tshering, a Drukpa married to an Italian wife in the early eighties has today been promoted as Foreign Secretary. Similarly, the then Chief Justice of the High Court was promoted even though he had an English wife. Today, of course, aside from bringing about a denial of benefits, marriage to non-Bhutanese wife has resulted in the very denial of citizenship rights to the Lhotshampa husbands.

Both the Citizenship Law, 1985 and the Marriage Acts have stripped several thousand Lhotshampas of their nationality. As a consequences of not granting citizenship to the foreign wives of Lhotshampa husbands, more than 60,000 children were deprived of their rightful claim to Bhutanese citizenship. This is more than 20 per cent of the total children population of Bhutan. Refugee children constitute about 10 per cent of the country's total population of around 767,000 of Bhutan. More than 10,000 Lhotshampa wives are deprived of their right to nationality. The government must repeal the discriminatory Citizenship Act, 1985 and the Marriage Act. It must enact new citizenship and marriage laws conforming to the international standards, and protect the right to nationality of all its citizens.

Bhutan became a party to the UN convention on the Elimination of All Forms of Discrimination Against Women on 31 August 1981. But the situation of Bhutanese refugee women is appalling. Among the 100,000 Bhutanese refugees, around 50 per cent of the population in the refugee camps are women, most of these women are illiterate and they participate less in social activities. In the cultural sphere the southern Bhutanese women had to bear the brunt of the government's cultural policy.

The Bhutanese government forgetting its responsibility

towards improving the status of women has deliberately attacked them in this campaign of ethnic cleansing. Some of the discriminatory policies of the government are, inter-ethnic marriage policy, the 1985 Citizenship Act and the Census of 1988 and the one nation one people policy.

Under one nation one people policy the culture of ruling elite was imposed on others thus banning the cultural pluralism in Bhutan. Southern Bhutanese women were deprived of their right to wear their dress; their ceremonial marriage necklaces were stripped off; they were made to cut short their hair. Instead, they were forced to adopt the dress and culture of the northern Bhutanese.

The women have always been the worst hit by government repression. In most cases, their husbands were imprisoned or had to flee the country for fear of persecution. The security forces plundered their homes, tortured, intimidated and raped these helpless women. There are 156 rape victims in Bhutanese refugee camps as per the records of CVICT Nepal.

According to Shangri-La Without Human Rights eight women were raped to death. The Bhutanese refugees under the ageis of Appeal Movement Coordinating Council demanded their right to return. The Bhutanes refugee women played a very active role in the Peace March both as peace marchers and organisers. There were female representation from all the camps in the Appeal Movement. Exercising the right to return and the right to peaceful assembly and association as enshrined in articles 13 and 20 respectively of the UN Universal Declaration of Human Rights, altogether around 1333 refugee women, in sixteen batches undertook the peace march to Bhutan from the vicinity of the refugee camps and from different places in India. There were tens of thousands of other refugee women who were involved in the demonstration, mass meetings and other activities.

But the peace marchers were intercepted, arrested and imprisoned by the Indian authorities as they entered the Indian soil after crossing over the Indo-Nepal border. The Indian authorities promulgated prohibitory orders although the refugees were peacefully traversing the land route through which they were driven to Nepal following forcible eviction from Bhutan. After a prolonged detention in Indian jails of Siliguri, Jalpaiguri and Baharampur in West Bengal, Bhutanese refugees entered Bhutan. But the Bhutanese security forces deported them back to India and from there they were sent back to Nepal by the Indian police.With the schools and the health services remaining closed for the last ten years in south Bhutan, women and children have no access to these facilities. The harassment in south and eastern Bhutan continues.

Amnesty International's report on Bhutan in 1998, states that, "Ms. Kinzang Chozam, who was pregnant, was among those arrested and was not allowed to see her children. Other women were arrested, apparently in an attempt to force their husband to give themselves up to the authorities." The most serious problems that the women in Bhutan are facing is the risk of rape, sexual humiliation, imprisonment and eviction from the country. Women of all ages have been the target of the police, army and even the civilian repressions.Women in the camps continue to be subjected to various forms of torture and suppression. Many women have become the victims of local toughs and the authorities working in the camps. The harassment of women within the family is no less inside the camps. But the women have become active in the awareness programmes within and outside the camps.

Camp Life

Role of women in running camp-life is often greater than men, their activities start from early morning until late night. Now many women in the camps with the help of OXFAM (UK) know how to read and write. They write poems and short stories, and many of them who did not earlier know how to read and write are teachers and social activists. They now say that if they had known reading and writing before, they would have never left the country, and would have rather fought back to remain within their country Bhutan.

Bhutan Women and Children Organisation (BWCO) is a non-profit, nonpartisan, politically un-aligned and grassroots non-governmental organisation. It was established on November 23, 1990 in exile by the Bhutanese refugee women to organise themselves for protection, promotion and defence of women's and child rights, and advancement and empowerment of women in Bhutan against the violation of their human rights by the Government of Bhutan. BWCO is the first women's and children's organisation of Bhutan and consists of women activists as its members. It is headed by a President. Its Board of Directors consists of women members, which formulates the plans and policies of BWCO. It is assisted by refugee volunteers

BWCO is compelled to function in exile as there is a ban on the formation of unions, associations, human rights organisations and political parties in Bhutan by the regime of an absolute monarch. It believes that practical application of international instruments, the Convention on the Elimination of All Forms of Discrimination Against Women, gender justice and gender equality are indispensable for achievement of women's real empowerment, gender equality, gender justice and social justice. Following are the aims and objectives of the organisation:

i) To work for establishment, protection and promotion of women's rights as set out in the Convention on the Elimination of All Forms of Discrimination Against Women (CEDAW), the Platform for Action and the Beijing Declaration, 1995 in Bhutan and to work for elimination of all forms of exploitation, discrimination, violence against women and trafficking.

ii) To raise awareness and consciousness of Bhutanese women about the principles of nondiscrimination, gender equality, gender justice and freedom as contained in the International Human Rights Instruments: the CEDAW, Declaration on the Elimination of Violence against Women and Platform for Action, Beijing Declaration among the Bhutanese people at grassroots level for achieving gender equality, gender justice and social justice. To educate Bhutanese women about women's human rights, about the phenomenon of cruelty, violence, trafficking and discrimination against them and work for their elimination.

iii) To raise women's consciousness about the social, cultural, economic, religious and legal injustices, gender issues and discrimination against them and develop their consciousness, self-confidence and esteem through training, discussions, workshops, publications, awareness raising and leadership development programmes.

iv) To organise seminars, workshops, training and public meetings with the objectives of educating and training Bhutanese women about women's human rights, their civil, political, social, economic and legal rights and about the phenomenon of cruelty, violence, sexual exploitation, trafficking and discrimination against them and mobilise all Bhutanese women to fight against all forms of discrimination, exploitation and violence against them.

v) To combat all forms of discrimination, exploitation and oppression of women and fight against all forms of sexual exploitation of women and children and trafficking in women and children

vi) To intensify the grassroots movement for effective promotion, propagation, and dissemination of the principles and provisions of CEDAW, Declaration on the Elimination of Violence against Women and Platform for Action, Beijing Declaration among the Bhutanese people at grassroots level for achieving gender equality, gender justice and social justice.

vii) To campaign and advocate for the enactment of national legislation on elimination of all forms of discrimination and exploitation against women based on CEDAW, Declaration on the Elimination of Violence against Women and Platform for Action, Beijing Declaration.

viii) To promote observance of practical application of CEDAW.

ix) To develop Bhutanese women's consciousness, capabilities and leadership roles for women's empowerment and advancement through better opportunities of better education, gainful employment, economic empowerment and a share in decision making in all spheres and work for their full participation in society. Work for removing the obstacles to women's full participation in decision making at all levels of family, social, economic, political and national life in compliance with the Platform of Action, Beijing Declaration.

x) To create awareness about AIDS among the Bhutanese refugee community as a part of prevention education.

xi) To advocate and monitor gender representation and

balance in national programmes, policies and processes. To contribute to the institutionalisation of gender perspectives in major national development programmes.

xii) To initiate safe motherhood and child health programmes for Bhutanese refugees in the refugee camps.

xii) To work for establishment of rule of law, civil, political, cultural rights and social justice for women.

xiii) To work for the establishment, protection and promotion of the rights of the child in Bhutan and work for elimination of all forms of exploitation and discrimination against children.

xiv) To raise awareness of Bhutanese people about the principles and provisions of the Convention on the Rights of the Child and other International Instruments on Child Rights through various demonstrative activities, publication, seminars, training and talk programmes. To intensify the grassroots movement for effective promotion, propagation, and dissemination of the principles and provisions of the Convention on the Rights of the Child among the Bhutanese people at grassroots level.

xv) To organise seminars, workshops, training and public meetings with the objectives of educating and training Bhutanese people in the defence of child rights.

xvi) To develop critical thinking on the rights of child through training, campaign, advocacy, education and publication and to advocate and campaign for the implementation of the provisions of Convention on the Rights of Child and its incorporation into the national law of Bhutan and promote observance of practical application of all international instruments on children.

xvii) To work for elimination of exploitation and oppression of Bhutanese children, child labour and all forms of discrimination and deprivation against them.

xviii) To combat child trafficking and sexual exploitation and abuses of children

xix) To intensify the grassroots movement for effective realisation of the rights of the child through promotion, propagation, and dissemination of the principles and provisions of the Convention on the Rights of Child among the Bhutanese people at grassroots level.

xx) To work for the protection and defence of the rights of the child and initiate local, regional and international alliances for the promotion and protection of the Rights of the Child in Bhutan.

xxi) Initiate programmes for rehabilitation of children at risk and under difficult circumstances. Develop and establish educational fund for helping the under privileged, deprived and poor Bhutanese children who have no access to formal education.

xxii) To take initiatives to establish child health care programmes for refugee children.

xxiii) To serve as a centre for dissemination of information, documentation and publication concerning the status of Bhutanese women and children.

Bhutan allows no overt gender discrimination-social, economic, political or legal. Yet, gender gaps do exist particularly in education/literacy, employment and decision-making. On its path of development, the country recognises the challenge of balancing modern and traditional values. Gender relations too are not static but respond to the socioeconomic changes in the society. The RGoB is committed to promoting decentralised governance and people's participation in development.

This calls for enhancing the existing understanding of the different needs, interests, and constraints on women and men; involvement of women and men in the development processes and the impact of the various programs in their lives. With the ninth plan process set in motion, it was the right time to undertake a Gender Study that could inform the next five year plan. The study was designed to support the Ninth Plan process, implementation of Convention on the Elimination of All Forms of Discrimination Against Women (CEDAW) and the UN Development Assistance Framework (UNDAF). The main objectives of the study were:

- To collect and analyse gender-disaggregated information on key sectors in select districts (urban and rural) to deepen understanding of gender relations in Bhutan
- To feed the key findings into the planning processes of the

Ninth five-year Plan, the Government CEDAW reports and the UN programmes

– Identifying existing strengths, best practices and coping mechanisms.

The study is a joint initiative of the Planning Commission and Central Statistical Office (CSO)—Royal Government of Bhutan; and UN Agencies—UNDP, UNICEF and WFP, Bhutan Country Office. The Technical support for the study was provided by UNIFEM, South Asia Regional Office, New Delhi.

Methodology—A consultative process was followed for the study with the key stakeholders—ministries at the central government, autonomous institutions, multilateral support organisations—involved at all the stages. The tools used for the study were questionnaires, guides for focus group discussion with adult and adolescent women and men and interviews with key informants that included district officers, teachers and gups. The six districts selected (two geogs in each district) were Thimphu, Ha; Bumthang, Trongsa; Mongar and Trashigang.

The two urban areas for the study were Thimphu City and Phuntsholing City. The study followed the method of stratified circular sampling for selection of the sample. 200 households in urban areas and 602 households in rural areas were covered by the study. 52 group discussions were held and 42 key informants interviewed. In all, 1135 respondents, 640 women and 495 male were covered.

Constraints—Though the study was conceived as a national baseline study, only six districts could be covered and hence does not present the national picture or even 'regional' picture. Equal number of women and men could not be covered by the study as men, especially in rural areas were not available at home. Time and resources were also a constraint. In the urban centres focus groups were conducted only with road workers.

Strengths—The strengths of the study can be seen in its scope and coverage of respondents across the six dzongkhags—reaching remote geogs—and the urban centres. The data generated from the study can be used to further investigate more specific aspects of gender relations. As discussions in the stakeholder workshop affirmed, the findings from the study validated the general notions of the positive gender situation in

Bhutan. Another aspect of the study was its approach, with a range of key stakeholders involved at every stage of the process.

The high commitment and interest among the stakeholders for the study affirmed that the findings and recommendations would be used for planning. The study complemented the Ninth Plan process and its results would feed into the forthcoming plans.

Demographic profile of the respondents—Almost 80% of both women and men in rural areas were engaged in agriculture/ farming. In urban areas 47% men were in government service compared to 18% women; while 31% men were in private business as compared to 9% women. Nearly 70% of the respondents were married. In urban areas men headed more than 80% Households. In Thimphu and Ha and Bumthang and Trongsa (70% women in both the clusters) twice as many women head their Households in comparison to one third in Trashigang and Mongar (30% women). While in rural areas, the head was the one in whose name the property was registered, in urban centres, a head was described as some one who takes all the decisions and is the main earner.

Agriculture was the primary economic activity in the rural areas with the other dominant activities being kitchen garden and livestock. For 13% of all the rural and urban Households financial contribution from the relatives settled outside was an important economic source. Rural women were not only engaged in main economic activities but were also main workers for the supplementary activities. In urban centres, it appeared that men are primary earners while women are supplementary earners.

Patterns of property ownership and inheritance—In rural areas, the ownership pattern showed a 60:40—female/male ratio. Most property in the rural areas was received through inheritance. In Trashigang and Mongar the study indicated a reverse ratio with less than 40% women owning/inheriting property. In the urban areas more men (55%) compared to women (36%) owned property. During discussions, most respondents said that usually daughters inherited property especially the one who took care of parents. Some stated that both sons and daughters had equal rights to the parents' property.

According to young boys and girls, property was given to the eldest daughter (normally the one who was not educated) in the family, while others said that it was divided equally among the children.

Household activities—In both rural and urban areas, more than two third women were engaged in primary reproductive tasks. In rural areas, there was seemingly more sharing of household work than urban. Women were involved in the productive as well as the household tasks - multiple responsibilities, multiple tasks.

Most of the household decisions were taken together by the husbands and wives. Though more males made decisions relating to external matters, while more females did so for internal/ in-house decisions.

Decision making patterns—Both men and women were involved in decision making about livelihood related activities, though the scale was tipped in favour of men. In decisions related to selling of crops as well as property, both male and female members were consulted in the households. However men were responsible for the decisions relating to purchase of equipment/farm machinery in over 60% households (nearly 70% in strata 2 and 3). Further investigation of this trend is needed to ensure that technology does not marginalise nor bypass women. For districts Thimphu and Ha, 'own business' was one of the significant activities. While women did comprise the work force for such activities, decisions were taken by men (100%).

The study suggests that as economic options widen and households move away from subsistence based activities, women may not be perceived as capable and equal partners in the new economic opportunities. A similar pattern also emerged during focus group discussions in districts that enjoyed a wider portfolio of livelihood options. This trend needs to be investigated further.

Intra-household decisions—In the households interviewed in both rural and urban areas, women and men, shared the decision making over use of income and most of the household decisions were taken together by the husbands and wives.

In rural areas almost half the households were saving in cash or kind, while almost two third households in urban centres were saving. Almost 80% of both women and men in the rural areas were aware of the credit programmes. Less than 30% of the total households in rural areas and 32% in urban areas had taken loans over the last five years. Fear of non-repayment was the major deterrent for not taking loans in rural areas, while in urban areas, respondents said that they did not need to take loans. In rural areas BDFC was a popular source (62%) while in the urban areas most of the loans (90%) loans were from commercial banks.

Only 15% of the households from districts Mongar and Trashigang had taken loans. The number was highest for districts Thimphu and Ha at close to 40%. The main reasons for taking loans shows interesting trends and highlights the economic strength of the various districts. While in Trashigang and Mongar, respondents had taken loans of smaller amounts for household purposes, in Thimphu and Ha, about 60% loans were investments in economic activities and the amount consequently was higher. Loans taken in urban areas were used for purchase of vehicles and construction. Overall more men were taking loans than women. Gender differentiation is seen in decision-making and tracking of repayment.

Migration—Generally both men and women migrate. However, where only men have migrated, women and children had to cope with a heavier workload and bear the onus of decision making. There was an indication that single women may feel unsafe.

For the purposes of the study, literacy was defined as the ability to read and write. Literacy rate of the respondents in the urban areas was almost three times that of the respondents in the rural areas (68% and 25% respectively). Literacy levels in Mongar and Trashigang were half that of the overall level. The female literacy rate among the respondents in the rural areas was 18%, half of that for men. A similar trend was seen in urban areas, though the literacy rate for women respondents was 52%.

The literacy rates at the household level showed an upward swing at nearly 50% for men and 30% women in rural areas. In the rural areas 75% of the women in the 'reproductive' age group 20-40 were illiterate, while in urban the figure was 46%. Only 4% of rural women respondents had joined the formal stream. Out of these, 85% dropped out after grade six. Key informants felt that though girls were at par with boys in all areas except for 'physical work', there seemed to be more tendency among girls to drop out after 6th standard for various reasons. They also said that "girls are sensitive and tend to give up easily".

Discussions with adults and the key informants affirmed the positive change in parents' perceptions for education, over the years. The youth had high aspirations in life but realised there may be limited employment opportunities. They considered farming a viable fall back option.

Non formal education—Only 6% respondents in rural areas and 3% in urban areas and comparatively more women/girls attended NFE classes. Most of them, though, did not complete the course. Key informant interviews affirm this pattern. For those who had an access to the NFE, lack of time was the main reason for not attending classes. Realising the importance of being literate, both male and female said that to be not literate is like having to "walk with eyes closed".

Access to information, training and skill building in enterprise development: Both male and female respondents showed a high level of access to information and use of services for agriculture and animal husbandry and health. The gups, maangap, chimi, tshogpa and chupen as well as relatives who frequently travel between the geog and the district were other important resources for information. Less than 50% of the respondents in rural areas, (40% women and 48% men) had participated in the training programmes of agriculture and animal husbandry department.

Participation was highest in Thimphu and Ha at 57%. In the same region, 70% male against 49% female respondents had attended any training programmes. Indicating that perhaps when services were available, women have lesser access to them. This seeming difference in access and participation needs to be studied further. Nearly half the respondents in rural areas did not receive adequate information for enterprise development. Women in all the three regions were less informed about the enterprise development programmes. Less than 10% of all the respondents had participated in training programmes. It appeared that more men had access to training opportunities then women—given their relatively higher mobility as well as interaction with outside market and resources. In the FGDs, women expressed their interest and keenness to learn new skills and felt that many skills training programmes were more apt for men.

Participation in governance—Both men and women equally voted for the gup and participate in the village level meetings. It appeared that women were active in the meetings at the village level, but their participation decreases as the level of governance rises. At present there were no female gups and very few female tshogpas and chimis. The gups felt that women adequately represented their concerns but were quick to change their minds; in a similar refrain the district Planning Officers felt that women did not voice their concerns well and were shy during the meetings. Women also perceived that important 'geog decisions' are better made by the men and feel that women are not taken so seriously'.

An interesting public-private difference in governance is evident, where men dominate the public domain, involved in the larger macro-level decisions while women are in the private real-making micro decisions.

Socio-cultural dimensions: Boys and girls were equally valued in society. Overall, girls and women relatively enjoyed freedom from sexual abuse and harassment. Though instances of eve teasing and mistreatment of wives were said to occur. Many women said that men were relatively 'more free' and almost all the women said that they would prefer to be born male.

From the study the following conclusions can be drawn. Women enjoy fair amount of independence in their personal, social, economic and political spheres. They are involved in the decision- making processes within the household. There is no discrimination between girls and boys. In many areas girls inherit property. Women and girls do not have many fears. Women enjoy equal access to services and information including legal information.

Present socio-cultural perceptions of both men and women see women as less capable and confident than men specially in matters of governance and interaction with external agencies.

The study indicated that as people moved away from

agrarian economy or upscale their economic activities, women seemed to be losing their decision-making role. Gender specialisation was seen to be emerging in both economic and household-based activities, with women taking on most of the core · livelihood activities as well as the multiple household tasks. Women's access to training and technology was limited as also their involvement in decisions relating to business opportunities. This may lead to a situation where women are bypassed by technological advances and economic growth.

Limited skills base—Lower levels of education and skill-enhancement result in women being 'less employable', specially in urban centres Women's lack of such skills will further accentuate the perceived differences in their capabilities.

Heavy demands on women's time and mobility constrain their participation in geog level/dzongkhag meetings. Their lack of active participation further promotes the perceptions of women as shy and inarticulate in public forums, rather than attributing it to their minimal experience in decision making at higher levels. Despite equal opportunities and entitlements for both women and men, differences are seen in equitable access specially in education enterprise development and governance and have led to significantly lower levels of achievement for girls/women. Differences were also seen in interests on key elements in areas such as enterprise development, where women did not find the ongoing training useful.

Differential needs—Each village/geog within district has its own social, economic and cultural context that influence gender relations. Gender relations in the households are mediated by different stages of development of the different districts as can be seen in the various strata.

Bhutan has an extremely enabling environment for gender mainstreaming. This section includes and builds on the feedback of the stakeholders. Following are some key recommendations for RGoB and the UN agencies.

National Level study—As a next step, a wider and more representative sample was recommended in order that a true national scenario could be captured.

Gain more insights with micro studies: Further investigation and analysis were needed to fully understand the implications of the trends identified by the study. Thematic areas included—

exploring the impact of economic changes on gender relations; understanding emerging gender equations in the context of fast-changing urban reality and the various socio-economic and cultural dynamics at play; identifying and priortising areas for adaptation of technology that leads to saving time and reduces drudgery would be needed.

Since the introduction of planned development in the country, Bhutan has focused on enriching the lives of its people, improving standards of living and in augmenting people's economic, spiritual and emotional well being.

The tenets of Gross National Happiness (GNH), articulated by His Majesty, the King define the development framework for the country and emphasise on sustainable development and self-reliance of its people. GNH places the individual at the centre of development and articulates five priority areas:

- human development;
- governance;
- balanced and equitable development;
- culture and heritage; and
- conservation of environment.

Bhutan has ratified two of the six main UN human rights treaties, the Convention on the Elimination of All Forms of Discrimination Against Women and the Convention on the Rights of the Child. While Bhutan allows no overt gender discrimination- social, economic, political or legal-gender gaps, although steadily decreasing, do exist, particularly in education/literacy, employment and decision-making. The country today recognises the challenge of balancing modern and traditional values and that socio economic changes influence gender relations. Changes such as increased mobility, rising educational requirements, new opportunities for employment, urbanisation, access to and use of technology, may have differential impact on women and men. Women may find that they are not in a position to access the new opportunities especially in the area of technology and education.

The RGoB is committed to promoting decentralised governance and people's participation in development. This assumes that the institutions/mechanisms and processes that enable women and men to participate in the important task of nation building are in place. Yet, appropriate mechanisms and processes can not be evolved unless there exists an understanding of the different needs, interests and constraints on women and men; how women and men are involved in the development processes and the impact of the various programs in their lives. Not enough gender-disaggregated data is available across various sectors, especially at the geog and household level, to enhance that understanding.

The single overarching goal of the United Nations System in Bhutan is to achieve growth with equity for GNH, Bhutan's holistic and people-centred vision of development. This is consistent with national priorities as detailed in the Ninth Five Year Plan (2002-2007), as well as with Bhutan's global commitments. "Growth with equity" is understood in the broader context of human development as expansion of choices to contribute meaningfully to the multifaceted concept of GNH.

Because the capacity of making choices for oneself is an important part of human happiness, so is the absence of choices because of lack of income, education, health or participation in decision-making contradictory to GNH. Within this, the overall, long-term objective for the UN System activities is the reduction of human poverty in Bhutan, incorporating a focus on good governance and social services delivery through sustainable livelihoods. Operating within the context of the Royal Government's vision for accomplishing its national poverty goals by the year 2020, the UN System is committed to halving poverty in Bhutan by 2015. In support of the Royal Government, three specific crosscutting objectives that provide a common orientation and framework and that the UN System can collectively address are:

1) Measurable progress toward decentralisation, participation and efficiency in Government;
2) universal access to quality social services; and
3) improved livelihoods for the disadvantaged.

These strategic objectives though not inclusive of all UN interventions, represent the UN System's explicit common response in pursuit of the overall goal of growth with equity for GNH and the objective of reducing human poverty in Bhutan. The objective of gender mainstreaming will be pursued in all relevant activities, and the UN System will support the Royal Government in implementing its commitments relating to the Convention on the Elimination of All Forms of Discrimination Against Women.

Objectives

The study was designed to support the Ninth Plan process, implementation of CEDAW and the UN Development Assistance Framework (UNDAF). The main objectives of the study were:

- To collect and analyse gender-disaggregated information on key sectors in select districts (urban and rural) to deepen understanding of gender relations in Bhutan
- To feed the key findings into the planning processes of the Ninth five-year Plan, the Government CEDAW reports and the UN programmes
- Identifying existing strengths, best practices and coping mechanisms.

The study was a joint initiative of the Planning Commission and Central Statistical Office (CSO)—Royal Government of Bhutan, and UN Agencies—UNDP, UNICEF, and WFP, Bhutan Country Office.

The study followed a consultative approach: The first step of the study, set in motion in December 2000, involved discussions with a broad range of stakeholders from the central government ministries and other institutions. Based on the first phase consultations and a review of the secondary literature, a research framework was developed. The framework, identifying the strategic areas for the study, was shared with the stakeholders for their comments in February 2001.

Some members of the study team went for a field-visit to two districts in February 2001. The team held discussions with the district level officers, village communities and students. The next stage was development of research tools, sample design, and identifying and training the enumerators. In order to triangulate information, the tools included questionnaires, and guides for focus groups and key informants' interviews.

Twenty-two enumerators were hired for the fieldwork that included both the quantitative and qualitative data collection. A five-day training that covered concept and meaning of gender, communication skills, principles of fieldwork and data collection was given to the enumerators.

The sampling framework and the sample districts and geogs were drawn by Central Statistical Office (CSO). Sampling of the dzongkhags (districts) was based on stratified multistage sampling method. Four strata were determined based on the easy accessibility of one dzongkhag from another.

In the first stage of sampling - dzongkhags were arranged in alphabetical order under each stratum. Following circular systematic sampling, 2 dzongkhags were selected from each stratum, giving a total of 8 dzongkhags. In the second stage of sampling, 2 geogs (blocks) from each short listed dzongkhag were selected giving a total of 16 geogs.

Since the design required a total of 800 households in the rural stratum and 200 in the urban stratum, a total of 50 households were randomly selected from each geog. Using the same method, household selection was done by the supervisors at the geog level prior to the field survey.

However, of the 8 dzongkhags only 6 could be surveyed, as the team could not get permits for the two dzongkhags of Dagana and Tsirang. This resulted in a total of 600 households from the rural stratum keeping the urban totals unchanged. The geographical coverage of the study is given in the following table.

Geographical Coverage of the Study

Urban	*Rural*		
	Strata I	*Strata II*	*Strata III*
Thimphu city	Thimphu Geogs -Chang, Mewang	Bumthang Geogs - Ura, Chumey	Mongar Geogs- Drepung, Silambi
Phuentsholing city	Ha Geogs- Uesu, Sama	Trongsa Geogs - Langthel, Tangsibi	Trashigang Geogs - Khaling, Shongphu

The research team comprised 22 enumerators including 2 supervisors, and 4 facilitators for Focus Group Discussions. The enumerators were divided into two groups of 11 each for the actual survey. For each group 8 persons were assigned for data collection, 2 for FGDs and 1 was the team supervisor. One team covered the dzongkhags of Bumthang, Mongar and Trashigang, while other team covered the dzongkhags of Trongsa, Thimphu and Ha, including the two urban areas of Thimphu and Phuntsholing.

The fieldwork was completed in 38 days March 27 - May 4. Due to logistics and field reality, the teams took at least a day or two more for each geog. (45% of the households in the rural areas were at a distance of more than 1-hour walk from the road. In one instance the team had to walk for four days to reach a village.) In the urban centres the time schedule went a little awry as the team had to start by listing the households. The following table gives the distribution of respondents in the different strata.

Questionnaires - distribution of Respondents

Strata	*Female*	*Male*	*Total*
Rural			
Strata 1 (Thimphu and Ha)	128	72	200
Strata 2 (Bumthang and Trongsa)	133	68	201
Strata 3 (Mongar and Trashigang)	117	84	201
Urban			
Thimphu City	60	40	100
Phuentsoling City	63	37	100
Total	501	301	802

In each geog - 4 focus groups (Adolescent male/ female and Adult female/male) were conducted, taking the total to 8 focus groups in each district. In Urban areas, 4 focus groups discussions (Adult male/female with Road workers) were held. In all 52 focus group discussions were held. The following table gives the spread of the respondents for the focus groups.

Interviews with key informants: In each district: Planning Officer, Education Officer and Agriculture Officer, Gups (2) and Teachers (2) constituted the key informants. In all 42 key informants—18 district level officers, 12 Gups and 12 teachers—were interviewed. The study covered 1135 respondents, 640 females and 495 males.

Constraints and limitations of the study: Equal numbers of male and female respondents could not be reached, as male members were not present at the time of the interview. This was more a constraint in the rural areas. The information collected represents the perceptions of the respondents and not necessarily of the households.

The zones that were developed for the Demographic Survey of Thimphu by Health Department were used. Of the 4 zones a random selection of 2 zones were made for each town. For each selected zone, a listing of the households was made. The circular systematic sampling method was used to randomly determine the sample households to be surveyed. Focus groups were conducted only with the road workers in the urban areas. The data collected from urban centres could not be validated through triangulation.

Strengths of the study : The strengths of the study lie in its scope and coverage of respondents across the six dzongkhags—reaching remote geogs—and the urban centres. The data generated from the study can be used to further investigate more specific aspects of gender relations. Another aspect of the study was its approach, with a range of key stakeholders involved at every stage of the process. The high commitment and interest among the stakeholders for the study affirmed that the findings and recommendations would be used for planning. The study complemented the Ninth Plan process and its results would feed into the forthcoming plans. As discussions in the stakeholder workshop concluded, the findings from the study validated the general notions of positive gender situation in Bhutan.

Demographic Profile of the Respondents

Occupation – Almost 80% of both women and men in rural areas were engaged in agriculture/farming. In urban areas 47% men were in government service compared to 18% women; while 31% men were in private business as compared to 9% women. 16% students were male as compared to 8% female.

Age: In the rural areas, the representative age profile indicated that while there were 25% men (ranging from 6% in Thimphu and Ha to 35% in Trashigang and Mongar) and 40% women in the age groups 21-40 years; 25% men and women were in the age group 41-50 years, about 29% men and women in the age group 51-80. In the urban areas 71% women and 58% men were in the age group 21 - 40 years.

Marriage: Nearly 70% of all the respondents were married. In strata 1 (Thimphu and Ha), the percentage of women currently not married was close to 50%. This included about 30% women who were divorced/separated and those who had never married.

Heads of households: The reasons for a person being the head of the household varied in the rural and urban areas. While in rural areas, the head was the one in whose name the property was registered (almost 70%), in urban centres, a head was described as some one who took all the decisions and was the main earner. In urban areas more than 80% Households were headed by men. In Thimphu and Ha and Bumthang and Trongsa (70% women in both the clusters) twice as many women head their Households in comparison to one third in Trashigang and Mongar (30% women).

Languages spoken—In the Strata 1 (Thimphu and Ha) people speak Dzongkha, in the districts falling under Strata 3 (Trashigang and Mongar), the language spoken was Sharchopkha, and in the Strata 2 (Bumthang and Trongsa) the languages were Bumthap and Mangdep. In the urban areas over 30% of both men and women speak Sharchopkha and Dzongkha respectively and 20% speak Lhotsamkha.

Religion: Most respondents in the rural areas were Buddhists with 1% Hindus and in the urban areas, 83% were Buddhists and 17% Hindus.

Literacy—For the purposes of the study, literacy was defined as the ability to read and write. Literacy rate of the respondents in the urban areas was almost three times that of the respondents in the rural areas (68% and 25% respectively). More than 60% men and 80% women respondents in rural areas could not read and write. Literacy levels in Mongar and Trashigang at 12% were half that of the overall level in rural areas. In the urban centres 94% men and 52% women were literate.

Looking at the findings for the Households (as reported by the respondents) the literacy rates showed an upward swing. The literacy rate for the members of the households in rural areas was 38%, (nearly 50% men and 30% women) with Thimphu and Ha at 50% and Mongar and Trashigang at 27%. Affirming that the educated members of the family would have not been in the house at the time of household interview (attending school, office, or other businesses).

The analysis is based on triangulation of data through Focus Group discussions, key informants' interviews and the survey.

Livelihood Activities

Rural areas

Agriculture was the primary economic activity in the rural areas with the other dominant activities being kitchen garden and livestock. For 13% of all the rural and urban Households financial contribution from the relatives settled outside was an important economic source. Additional important activities in Thimphu and Ha (Strata 1) included own business; for Bumthang and Trongsa (Strata 2) sale of handicrafts and in Mongar and Trashigang (Strata 3), the activities were agricultural labour, sale of Ara, and construction work.

Farming activities—Both men and women were engaged in agriculture, though Thimphu and Ha (Strata 1) showed that more women were the main agriculture workers (in 54% of the households where agriculture was a significant activity and in some households (23%) both men and women were involved.). In both the other strata more men were involved in agriculture than women.

Though men and women shared most of the work, the data suggested to a gender division of labour based on the 'physical strength. Therefore while digging, weeding and transplanting were done by women, land preparation, ploughing, collection of firewood and pruning of apple trees, were tasks done mainly by men. In these areas there seems to be no flexibility as when men migrated out on work, these tasks were either done by other males or hired labour. Children contributed little at the farm since they were at school. During holidays they helped with household chores such as carrying water, cooking and gathering firewood, looking after livestock, carrying manure. Older children assisted in the fields also in staving off wild animals.

In the Chang geog, FGD participants mentioned that girls took on more domestic chores than boys did. In Bumthang the boys ploughed the field, chopped firewood, and helped in harvesting. Girls carried water, did weaving, cooked as well as helped in harvesting. Both men and women road workers lived on their daily wages and had no other source of income. At times they collected firewood from the forest to sell by the roadside and women grew maize and vegetables for own consumption.

Livestock—Both men and women were involved in taking care of the livestock in the households interviewed, though the number of women was a little higher. In Thimphu and Ha (Strata 1) more than three fourths of the workers were women while in Mongar and Trashigang (Strata 3), more men (58%) were involved in rearing of livestock.

Additional livelihood activities—Returns from kitchen gardening - an activity promoted by the government agencies mainly among women—were high as it was listed amongst top five activities in all the districts. Brewing of Ara in Strata 3 and making handicrafts in Strata 2 were the other activities done almost entirely by women. Agricultural labour was a significant activity for the households in Mongar and Trashigang (Strata 3). In both Strata 2 and 3, women too worked as labourers.

Urban areas

As indicated in the demographic profile, most of the male respondents in the urban areas were in the government service and engaged in own business. 60% of the women described themselves as 'housewives'. 18% women were in government service and 9% in private business. 16% students were male as compared to 8% female. The women from rural areas were not only engaged in main economic activities but were also main workers for the supplementary activities. In urban centres, it appeared that men were primary earners while women were supplementary earners.

Patterns of property ownership and inheritance: In rural areas, the ownership pattern showed a 60:40—female/male ratio. Most property in the rural areas was received through inheritance. In Trashigang and Mongar the study indicated a reverse ratio with less than 40% women owning/inheriting property. In the urban areas more men (55%) compared to women (36%) owned property. More men than women were buying property in urban areas, while there was little opportunity to buy in rural areas. Most respondents said that usually daughters inherited property especially the one who took care of parents. (Whether this leads to limiting her opportunities is a moot question.) While others stated that both sons and daughters had equal rights to the parents' property. (However, cases of property disputes are reportedly on the rise.)

According to young boys and girls, property was given to the eldest daughter (normally the one who was not educated) in the family, while some said that it was divided equally among the children. In Silambi geog, house was given to either eldest/youngest daughter and land was divided equally among rest of the children. Bhutan is perhaps one of the few countries in the world that places a value on taking care of the family. The inheritance laws in the country also promote this practice.

Household Level Activities

In more than 80% of the rural households, women cooked, washed clothes, cleaned house, worked in the kitchen garden, preserved food and collected manure. Nearly 60% men were engaged in firewood collection. More than two thirds of the women in rural areas took care of children, fetched water, collected manure, took care of domestic animals and distilled alcohol. Both men and women were equally engaged in collection of fodder, buying food, clothes and other items. In the households covered in Thimphu and Ha mainly women were responsible for reproductive tasks including collection of fodder, taking care of domestic a well as livestock animals.

Women in rural areas were involved in the productive as well as the household tasks -multiple responsibilities, multiple tasks. In more than 90% households in urban areas women cooked, purchased food, washed clothes and cleaned the house. While between 60-80% of women in urban areas took care of sick and children, and preserved food. In both rural and urban areas, more than two third women were engaged in primary reproductive tasks. In rural areas there was seemingly more sharing of household work than in urban areas.

Both men and women equally participated in community level activities. During village Pujas, men were responsible for 'physically' taxing tasks such as cooking while women took care of the guests. Annual Puja is an important religious occasion for every family. More men than women were lead organisers of the Pujas in their houses. Shaptolemi or Voluntary labour for activities such as construction of school building, village road, VIP visits, was contributed more by men than women.

Both men and women were involved in decision making about agriculture related activities, though the scale was tipped in favour of men. While Bumthang and Trongsa (Strata 2) showed both men and women being equally involved, in Thimphu and Ha (Strata 1) more women and in Mongar and Trashigang (Strata 3) more men took the decisions related to livelihood activities such as crops to be cultivated inputs required, hiring of equipment, use of agriculture output. In decisions related to selling of crops as well as property, both male and female members were consulted in the households.

However men were responsible for the decisions relating to purchase of equipment/farm machinery in over 60% households (nearly 70% in strata 2 and 3). Further investigation of this trend is needed to ensure that:

- women understand and use technology
- technology does not marginalise nor bypass women
- women can work with the extension workers to evolve appropriate technologies that will ease their workload.

For districts Thimphu and Ha, 'own business' was one of the significant activities. While women did comprise the work force for such activities, decisions were taken by men (100%). The study suggests that as economic options widen and households move away from subsistence based activities, women may not be perceived as capable and equal partners in the new economic opportunities. A similar pattern also emerged during focus group discussions in districts that enjoyed a wider portfolio of livelihood options. This trend needs to be investigated further.

In the households interviewed in both rural and urban areas, women and men, shared the decision making over use of income. Most of the household decisions were taken together by the husbands and wives. Though more males made decisions relating to outside matters, while more females take in-house decisions such as food to be cooked.

In the rural areas almost half the households were saving in cash or kind, and almost two third households in urban centres were saving. The main reasons stated for saving were security and investment for better life. Households that were not saving said they did not generate enough surpluses. During discussions in the rural areas both male and female participants said that usually women saved, as they were more reliable with money, unlike men who could be a little irresponsible and waste resources on gambling and drinking. Besides women were running the households and required money for daily expenses and thus needed easier access to the 'saved money'. In the Ha geog, men were more likely to save as they 'can make better investments' in business opportunities. (Families here owned apple orchards and land and investments in business ventures were higher.) A review of the credit patterns corroborates the dominant role of men in taking investment decisions. Road workers indicated that they did not generate any surplus. The women said that any savings at all were used for their children's education.

Credit

Almost 80% of both women and men in the rural areas were aware of the credit programmes. However only 36% of the 'aware' households and less than 30% of the total households had taken loans over the last five years. In urban areas, 32% of the households had taken loans. Fear of non-repayment was the major deterrent for not taking loans in rural areas, while in urban areas, respondents said that they did not need to take loans. Only 15% of the households from districts Mongar and Trashigang had taken loans.

The number was highest for districts Thimphu and Ha at close to 40%. Amongst the road workers, the men did not have any savings nor did they take any loans. They feared not being able to repay the loans. The women too were afraid and/or ignorant about taking loans. They had little or no savings and borrowed from friends when in need.

In rural areas BDFC was a popular source accounting for 62% of the loans taken. 24% loans were taken from the other banks, while loans from neighbours constituted 7%. In the urban areas most of the loans (90%) loans were from commercial banks.

Reasons – The main reasons for taking loans showed interesting trends and highlighted the economic strength of the various districts. Reasons for taking loans While in Trashigang and Mongar, respondents had taken loans for household purposes, in Thimphu and Ha, about 60% loans were investments in economic activities. Loans taken in urban areas were for purchase of vehicles, investing in business and construction. A similar pattern was seen for the amount of loans taken.

- in the districts Mongar and Trashigang nearly 60% loans taken were less than Nu 10,000
- In the districts Bumthang and Trongsa, more than two third of the loans taken were below Nu. 20,000 and 9% loans were above 50,000.
- more than 50% of the loans in Thimphu and Ha were above Nu. 20,000 (17% above 50,000)
- in the urban areas more than half the loans were for amounts higher than Nu. 50,000.

Decision-making—Overall more men were taking loans than women. In Mongar and Trashigang—more men were taking loans (77%) while in Thimphu and Ha marginally more women (57%) did so. In urban centres 22% loans were taken by women. Usually the head of the household or the owner of the property was selected to take the loan. More men took decisions and kept track of repayment than women in both rural and urban areas.

Migration

While only 12% migration was in respondents in rural areas—(for reasons of marriage, work in urban areas and higher education), a significantly higher number had migrated to the urban areas (46% for work and 26% for marriage). 13% of the Households (urban and rural) received financial support from their relatives outside. Migration out of the geog and village during the winter months was common in Thimphu and Ha districts primarily to earn cash incomes from sale of agricultural and dairy products, settle on the kidu lands, as well as take on some business works.

In some geogs for e.g.: Silambi, Chang, and Mewang no migration was reported. In Bumthang and Trongsa seasonal migration of men to work on the large hydro projects and other construction sites was reported. Some of the participants of FGDs felt that migration was an efficient economic option especially for families that did not have sufficient land for farming. Often during peak agriculture season, family members came back to contribute labour and many also returned to look after their parents. When families migrated to urban areas, men usually became the primary earners (service based) and women supplemented the household income by weaving, running shops etc.

The road workers in the urban areas had migrated due to inadequate land and education of their children. Generally both men and women migrated. However, in families where only men migrated, women and children had to cope with a heavier workload and also bear the onus of decision making. There was an indication that single women may feel unsafe and/or may receive proposals/or decide to enter into relationships with other men which in turn creates some difficulties in marital relationships. In the FGDs it was also reported that there was some occurrence of wife beating and quarrels out of jealousy.

Education and Literacy

More than 60% men and 80% women respondents in rural areas could not read and write. Literacy levels in Mongar and Trashigang at 12% were half that of the overall level in rural areas. The household level literacy details show that nearly 50% men and 30% women in rural areas are literate. Female literacy rates were highest for the households in Thimphu and Ha at 39% and least for Trashigang and Mongar at 19%. The age wise analysis of household level data reveals that in the rural areas, 75% of the women in the 'reproductive' age group 20-40 were illiterate. This has implications on their ability to make informed choices about their own selves and their families and may restrict their opportunities. For the school going age group of 11-20, fewer girls (65%) were literate than boys (75%). Only 7% of male respondents in rural areas reached above class eight, while 6% men had received monastic education.

Only 4% of rural women respondents had joined the formal stream. Out of these, 85% dropped out after grade six. Nearly all the male respondents and over half of the female respondents in the urban centres were literate. The household data revealed that 46% of women in the reproductive age group of 21-40 years were illiterate. The gap between male and female respondents who did not receive formal education was more in urban areas. Six times more women than men did not receive formal education in urban areas, as against rural areas where the number of women who did not receive formal education was twice more than men. Out of those who had joined the formal stream, 42% had studied up to class XII and only 6% had gone for higher studies.

Reasons for dropouts: In the rural areas, drop out rate among children was 21% for reasons of 'help needed at home' (>50%). Other reasons included lack of interest, failures in exams, marriage and school expenses. For urban areas the study showed a drop out rate of 10%. While validating the above information, key informants said that girls were likely to drop out between class 6 and 8. Key informants felt that though girls were at par with boys in all areas except for 'physical work', there seemed to be more tendency for girls to drop out after the 6th standard for various reasons. They also felt that "girls are sensitive and tend to give up easily".

Value for education: Discussions with adults and the key informants affirmed the changes in parents' perceptions over the years. Both mothers and fathers in the rural areas valued education for both boys and girls despite odds such as limited finances, distances to school and shortage of labour at the farm. All parents seemed confident that an educated person would certainly get a good job. "A good education means a secure job with the government or the civil service, or in some profession, that would benefit both parents and children".

However, in the remote areas such as Silambi geog in Mongar, parents felt that girls needed less education than boys. Among the road workers, women valued education for children. Parents did not want their children to be road workers and felt that educated children could do blue collar jobs and face less hardship.

School management: In both rural and urban areas over 70% parents were aware of the school management board and parent teacher meetings. The awareness levels were higher in Thimphu + Ha than Mongar + Trashigang. More parents in rural areas as compared to urban areas were attending the Parent-Teacher meetings. (It is compulsory to attend the meetings.) About 4% of the rural respondents (including six women) were members of the school management board.

Assessment of school facilities: Most parents were satisfied with the facilities. In many instances they had contributed labour for the construction and maintenance of the school premises. However there were observations about insufficient sports facilities which included playgrounds and sports equipment. Parents seemed quite happy with the teachers and noted that there were better teachers than in the past.

Parent-Teacher Meetings

Parent-Teacher meetings were said to be taking place about 2-3 times a year or more if needed. However shortage of Bhutanese Language Teacher (BLT) teachers was mentioned. While most of the parents were satisfied, both teachers and students listed a number of shortcomings. Teachers felt that school facilities such as dormitories, furniture and toilets required maintenance.

Extra curricular activities such as music, games and sports were lacking. In some remote areas schools required more basic amenities like electricity, more classrooms and books. Students felt the lack of teachers. They also listed facilities such as shortage of classrooms, toilets and sports equipment, which were inadequate. In the districts of Mongar and Trashigang, students complained about lack of basic furniture, beds, water, and small classrooms. While the students from more economically developed Thimphu and Ha fretted about lack of computers and library in addition to water and toilet. Girls also said that they seldom got to play in the ground, as boys were always using it. In Bumthang and Trongsa students reported about improper toilets, lack of basketball court and shortage of classrooms. One complaint common to all the districts appeared to be lack of proper toilets. The school curricula have a class on reproductive health, which was taught by the health workers of the district/geog. Young girls also talked to their mothers.

Key informants felt that women teachers, especially in remote areas were role models for young girls and also motivated parents to educate their daughters. But there were fewer women teachers, more so, in the remote areas (e.g. none in Silambi geog).

Professional aspirations: Parents (both mother and father) in rural areas considered nursing, government service, teaching and agriculture as preferred activities for the girls. For boys, government service, medicine, army and then agriculture were the possible options. In the urban areas, most parents wanted their boys to be in the government service and for girls both civil service and medicine were equally preferred.

There was however a differential set of expectations in Trashigang and Mongar geogs where parents did not have high and specific aspirations for their children, but placed a high value on destiny of the child. This was also reflected in the attitude of the children. Road workers aspired for blue-collar jobs for their children. The youth was aware of a range of careers—government service, medicine, engineering, media, information technology, hotel industry, police and army. Though there was no career counselling available, the youth did discuss the various options with their teachers and also with their peers. Boys felt that their parents would be happy as long as they got a job. The youth had high aspirations in life but realised that there may be limited employment opportunities. They considered farming a viable fall back option.

Non formal eaucation: Only 6% respondents in rural areas and 3% in urban areas and comparatively more women/girls attended NFE classes. Most of them, though, did not complete the course as they found it difficult to make time for the classes given their heavy workload. Key informant interviews affirmed this pattern. 55% of the households covered by the study had access to non-formal education centres. Of these 50% of the households were from Bumthang and Trongsa and 34% from Mongar and Trashigang. (This probably reflects the coverage of the NFE programme.)

More women than men thought NFE to be useful. For more than 40% of the illiterate women and 30% men in the rural areas, non-availability of NFE centres was an obvious reason for not joining literacy classes. However, for those who had an access to the NFE (40% of the total respondents and 53% of the total illiterate), lack of time (44% women, and 36% men) was the main reason for not attending classes. Amongst the road workers, most men and women were unable to access NFE due to busy workloads and physical exhaustion.

Completing the course—Out of 140 rural respondents who could read and write, 25 (18%) had attended non-formal education classes, out of which 20 were women. Only 37 respondents had attended NFE, out of which 31 were women

(84%). The main reason for attending classes was to learn to read and write. However, only 8 respondents, 7 being women had completed the course. Both male and female respondents realised the importance of being literate, yet could not attend classes for various reasons. They stated that to be unable to read and write was like having to walk with eyes closed.

Access to information, training and skill building in enterprise development: Access to different kinds of information in rural areas was found to be high, more than 70% of both males and females accessed information through the radio, while 10% received information through TV. More than 25% women and men read Kuensel, however in Trashigang and Mongar dzongkhags only 10% of the women reported getting information from the news paper. In the urban areas there was use of all the three sources of information. Both male and female respondents showed a high level of access to information and use of services for agriculture, animal husbandry and health.

The respondents were receiving regular information about the government laws and policies. More than 70% of both female and male respondents were receiving marketing and business related information. The gups, maangap, chimi, tshogpa and chupen as well as relatives who frequently travelled between the geog and the district were other important resources for information. People also exchanged information with each other on farming practices and problems. Less than 50% of the respondents in rural areas, (40% women and 48% men) had participated in the training programmes of agriculture and animal husbandry department. In Mongar and Trashigang, less than one third (29% male/female) of the respondents had attended any training programme. Participation was highest in Thimphu and Ha at 57%.

Awareness was least in Mongar and Trashigang (40% for male and 22% for females) and highest in Thimphu and Ha (about 90% male and 75% female). Women in all the three strata were less informed about the enterprise development programmes than men. More than 40% of the women respondents said they were not interested in the enterprise/ vocational training programmes. Almost 50% of the men attributed their lack of information to their living in remote areas or the place of training being too far.

Less than 10% of all the respondents had participated in training programmes. The reasons for non-participation included-lack of interest (female - 35%, male - 26%); lack of time (female 21%, male - 42%); place of the training being too far and lack of interaction with the extension agents (> 10%). It appears that more men had better access to training opportunities then women -given their relatively higher mobility as well as increased knowledge of dealing with outside market and resources.

In Mongar and Trashighang dzongkhags, due to geographical remoteness of the geogs both men and women were reluctant to travel the long distances for training. In some of the more remote villages, the communities have not yet moved beyond subsistence economy into selling of products (made from bamboo and cane, or weaving) and gaining entrepreneurial skills. In many cases heavy workloads kept both men and women from participating in the rural areas.

Men aspired for practical skills such as—such as carpentry, plumbing, house wiring, electric works and business techniques—to enhance their income. The male road workers said that they were interested in learning new skills to increase their incomes, but they did not have access to any enterprise development training. Women road-workers said that they could not find any time. In the FGDs, women expressed their interest and keenness to learn new skills.

Women felt that many skills training programmes were mostly suited for men. The high percentage of women who said they were not interested may not be fully informed about the various programmes or the programmes may not be available/ relevant to them.

Participation in Governance

An important aspect of public participation at the geog level is the election for the Gup held once every three years. Given that attending the meetings are mandatory, participation was dictated more by the availability of any household member. However the ability to understand and communicate were also mentioned as attributes for participation in meetings. The study findings show that both men and women equally vote for the gup and participate in the village level meetings.

Though in Trashigang and Mongar, where men reportedly had little external transactions—business or otherwise, more men (70%) than women were attending the meetings.

While at present there were no female gups, there were very few female tshogpas and chimis. The key informants felt that Gup's job required experience in public affairs. It was also physically demanding, as the person had to walk often through long and difficult terrain to reach villages. Also the work required a lot of time away from the house. One gup welcomed the idea of female gups in the future. He felt that after a few years, when women who were today tshogpas and chimis had gained sufficient experience, they could become gups. There was evidence that women were active in the meetings at the village level, but their participation decreases as the level of governance rises. While she may be participating in activities at the village level and to an extent at the geog level, her interaction at the dzongkhag level seemed to be limited. Both men and women considered the geog meetings of great value as they are able to own the development process.

The gups felt that women adequately represented their concerns but were quick to change their minds; in a similar refrain the district planning officers felt that women did not voice their concerns well and were shy during the meetings. Women also perceive that important 'geog decisions' were better made by the men as they were more literate and more experienced in pubic dealings. Besides women said they are not taken so seriously'. Some women felt that, there are no women leaders in their community.

Women did recognize the value of meetings at the higher levels but found extensive travel and night halts as major constraints for attending Geog/District level meetings. In addition, the burden of household and farm work coupled with long and inflexible hours of both public and political work, prevented women from being more active.

An interesting public-private difference in governance was evident, where men dominated the public domain, involved in macro-level decisions while women were in the private realm-making micro decisions and perceiving men to be more capable of making decisions at higher levels. Despite positive indicators, women in Bhutan do believe in the superiority of men and feel that men are better equipped to understand and participate in matters of governance.

Socio-Cultural Dimensions

Boys and girls are equally valued in the society. However some parents felt that boys were easier to raise as they were less vulnerable. In Thimphu and Ha, a significant number said that they incurred less expenditure on boys. Girls were seen to be more responsible and responsive by some parents and thus easier to raise. While in urban areas, the ideal number of children was seen as one boy and one girl, in rural areas, respondents felt that two boys and two girls made a family complete.

Overall, girls seemed to enjoy relative freedom from sexual abuse and harassment. Girls felt that they could raise a child outside marriage without feeling discriminated. While no sexual abuse was reported in the schools, girls were aware of such incidents occurring, possibly more in urban areas. Girls and boys acknowledged that eve teasing occurred. Girls mentioned no specific fears. They travelled together in groups and were generally cautious. They felt safe in the school hostel. In Khaling, they were afraid of being raped. In Silambi geog, girls said they feared wild animals, ghosts and strangers. All respondents said there was no case of drug abuse, prostitution and any other such problems in their villages.

Some respondents felt that such problems existed especially in the urban areas of Thimphu and Phuntsholing. They were all very critical about such problems as it brought discredit to the community. Several groups attested that males did mistreat their wives at home. There were occurrences of wife beating, quarrels arising due to jealousy and under the influence of alcohol. If the families failed to settle their disputes, neighbours and friends often intervened and acted as counsellors, in the absence of an institutional mechanism for counselling. Gups and Mangap were approached if the matter was not resolved within family and friends. Any matter beyond the gup and the chimi of the geog was then handled by the district court. The community was aware of the legal implications for any misbehaviour or mistreatment.

Social relations: Many women believed that it took nine births for a woman to be reborn as a man. They also said that men were relatively more free and did not experience suffering and pain of childbirth. Almost all the women said that they preferred to be born male—the only exception being in Chang geog.

Role models—The role model for the youth showed an interesting mix of people who had contributed to the development of the country, teachers, family members, social workers and of course popular film and sports personalities. This reflects that the youth is sensitive to and interested in national development.

For girls: His Majesty The King, Her majesty the Queen Ashi Sangay Choden Wangchuck, parents, teachers; Hindi movie heroes, Bhutanese singers- Nedup Dorji and Dechen Pem, Princess Diana, Mother Teresa. (In Silambi geog the adolescents had no idea about a role model).

For boys: Lyonpo Sangay Ngedup for his hard work in education and improving the health facilities in the country; Maradona—the football star; family member who earns and supports the younger ones at school; Shabdrung Ngawang Namgyal the founder of Bhutan who had built most dzongs in Bhutan; Mahatma Gandhi; Michael Jordan, and Hindi film heroes. In the Eastern and Central region, parents and teachers were some other favourite role models.

In the group discussions girls and boys shared their dreams that revolved around a good job and a small family. Boys wanted three while girls were happier with two children.

By the age of 30, boys wished to have a secure job, marry and have 2-3 children preferably 1 boy and 2 girls. Most wished to settle in urban areas like Thimphu. Girls too wished for a decent job and wanted to get married by the age of 28 years (at a relatively later age than their parents) and have a son and a daughter. In Thimphu and Ha they wished to live in urban areas. However in Silambi geog, they all want to work as farmers and live in their own village after marriage.

Enabling environment—Women enjoy fair amount of independence in their personal, social, economic and political spheres. They are involved in the decision-making processes within the household. In rural areas specially, there is sharing of productive and some reproductive tasks as well between men and women.

There is no discrimination between girls and boys. In many areas girls inherit property. Women and girls do not have many fears. There are no sexual taboos against women. Women enjoy equal access to services and information including legal information.

- *Socio-cultural perceptions:* Present socio-cultural perceptions of both men and women see women as less capable and confident than men specially in matters of governance and interaction with external agencies. Women are considered physically weak and positions of gups etc. deemed unsuitable as the jobs are physically demanding. Socio-cultural perceptions validate male superiority while not adequately recognizing female capabilities.
- *Changing roles*—A trend indicating a change in women's participation and decision making consequent to the gradual shift from traditional subsistence based agrarian forms to more diversified 'surplus' based livelihood options, seems to be emerging. The study indicated that as people moved away from agrarian economy or upscale their economic activities, women seemed to be losing their decision-making role. Women's access to training and technology was limited as also their involvement in decisions relating to business opportunities. This may lead to a situation where women are bypassed by technological advances and economic growth.

  Gender specialisation was seen to be emerging in both economic and household-based activities, with women taking on most of the core livelihood activities as well as the multiple household tasks. As the study indicated, property ownership and inheritance patterns varied in the districts studied. However in urban centres clearly more men owned property than women.

  In rural areas, head of the household was usually the person who owned the property. Whereas in urban areas the person who was the main earner and who took all the decisions was considered the head, and was usually the man.
- *Limited skills base*—Lower levels of education and skill-enhancement result in women being less employable. Unlike rural areas, a different set of skills is required in

urban areas. Consequently women find themselves as supplementary earners in urban centres. Women's lack of such skills will further accentuate the perceived differences in their capabilities.

– *Limited participation*—Heavy demands on women's time and mobility constrain their participation in geog level/ dzongkhag meetings. Held outside the village, participation in the meetings often requires night stay. Their lack of participation further promotes the perceptions of women as shy and inarticulate in public forums rather than attributing it to their minimal experience in decision making at higher levels.

Despite equal opportunities and entitlements for both women and men, differences are seen in equitable access specially in education, enterprise development and governance and have led to significantly lower levels of achievement for girls/women. These differences are intrinsically linked to women's constraints of time and mobility. An indication of this is the fact that girls after Class VIII seem to lag behind boys. Women want to, but are unable to attend non-formal education course. Differences were also seen in interests on key elements in areas such as enterprise development, where women did not find the ongoing training useful. There seemed to be a clear gender divide in training where kitchen gardening, weaving were earmarked for women and carpentry, electrical works for men.

– *Differential needs*—While differential needs may get expressed at the village meetings, there is probably not much focus on strategic gender interests at the district level and higher. This is also linked to limited participation of women in governance at higher levels.

Each village/geog within district has its own social, economic and cultural context that influence gender relations. Gender relations in the households are mediated by different stages of development of the different districts as can be seen in the various strata.

The following are some key recommendations for RGoB and the UN agencies:

– *National level study:* As a next step a wider and more representative sample was recommended in order that a true national scenario could be captured. This would also enable national reporting processes on the various International Conventions. The next step should be a study in urban areas as well as in rural areas that builds upon the current pilot study and constitutes a baseline in a true sense.

– *Gain more insights with micro studies:* The gender pilot study had highlighted certain trends. Further investigation and analysis were needed to fully understand their implications on gender relations. Thematic areas included - exploring the impact of economic changes on gender relations; understanding emerging gender equations in the context of fast-changing urban reality and the various socio-economic and cultural dynamics at play; identifying and priortising areas for adaptation of technology that leads to saving time and reduces drudgery would be needed.
– *Capacity building*: The 'how to do it' was an important element of discussions. Following are some of the measures suggested.
– *Common conceptual framework*: Gender equality is often misconstrued as forwarding the interest of women at the cost of men and thus creating a divide between men and women, and tearing the social fabric of the society. This leads to a certain level of hesitation in identifying and addressing gender concerns. The first step should thus be building a common understanding within the system at all levels.
– *Skill building*: Technical inputs for areas such as leadership development, enterprise development, situational analysis, and micro planning need to be designed and delivered at decentralised levels of governance. A cadre of trainers could be strengthened at district levels.
– *Core group*: A core group cutting across sectors could be the most important mechanism for gender mainstreaming. The existing forum of gender focal points in the various ministries needs to be revitalised under the leadership of the planning commission. Such a group needs the necessary mandate to monitor programmes and provide technical inputs. Greater sharing, learning, and capacity

building of the focal points is thus important.

- *Programme strategies*: Programmes should be designed to take cognisance of the different constraints, interests and levels of readiness between women and men in different regions/ districts.
- *Develop tools:* Tools that enable gender disaggregated analysis and its use for various stages of planning, implementation, monitoring and evaluation should be prepared specific to the requirements of the sectors. The analysis should complement the ongoing processes, to ensure that mainstreaming is seen as a routine activity and not a separate process.
- *Clear measurable results and indicators:* The core group can identify a set of clear, measurable results and indicators for specific sectors and programs. The indicators should evolve through a participatory process in consultation with the district and block level officers as well as women and men from the community. The exercise could be first done at a pilot level in selected districts with a particular line ministry.
- *Building Linkages/Communication and networking:* Cross-sectorial linkages result in a rich cross-fertilisation of ideas and experiential learning. Such interactions also help in refining as also adapting concepts and strategies to the social, economic and cultural context of the country. Strengthening linkages and networking of the different Government agencies and departments with other Aid agencies, media, regional and international forums. To be able to do this, regular collation and dissemination of information is important.
- *Demonstrating good practices:* Organisations like UN should take the lead in demonstrating good practices such as flexible working hours and day care support, in recognition of the multiple responsibility of women, as a first step towards engendering the organisation. Another good practice is using simple language, specially necessary for demystifying concepts and practices of gender equality. Language also reflects the user's orientation.

Both the UN and the government agencies need to commit

resources. Resources that include people—key people in key positions identified as focal points; information—to share, to learn from; time-people assigned must be able allocate sufficient time to the activities; and finally finances without which many of the action points. UNIFEM, during the workshop, reaffirmed its commitment to provide technical support and also facilitate the country's participation in regional and global forums.

4

Discrimination Against Women

The National Assembly, established in 1953, has 150 members. Of these, 105 are elected by citizens, 10 are selected by a part of the Buddhist clergy, and the remaining 35 are appointed by the King to represent the Government. The procedures for the nomination and election of National Assembly members are set out in an amendment to the country's Basic Law proposed by the King and adopted by the 73rd session of the National Assembly in 1995. It provides that in order to be eligible for nomination as a candidate for election to the National Assembly, a person must be a citizen of Bhutan, be at least 25 years of age, not be married to a foreign national, not have been terminated or compulsorily retired for misconduct from government service, not have committed any act of treason against the King, the people, and country, have no criminal record or any criminal case pending against him, have respect for the nation's laws, and be able to read and write in Dzongkha (the language, having different dialects in the eastern and western areas of the country, spoken by Bhutanese Buddhists).

Each National Assembly constituency consists of a number of villages. Each village is permitted to nominate one candidate but must do so by consensus. There is no provision for self-nomination and the law states that "no person . . . may campaign for the candidacy or canvass through other means." If more than one village within a constituency puts forward a candidate, an election is conducted by the district development committee, and the candidate obtaining a simple majority of votes cast is declared the winner. Individuals do not have the right to vote. Every family in a village is entitled to one vote in elections. The law does not make clear how a candidate is selected if none achieves a simple majority. It does state, however, that in case of a tie among the candidates in the election, drawing of lots shall be resorted to. The candidate whose name is drawn shall be deemed to be elected. Human rights activists claim that the only time individual citizens have any involvement in choosing a National Assembly representative is when they are asked for their consensus approval of a village candidate by the village headman.

The Assembly enacts laws, approves senior Government appointments, and advises the King on matters of national importance. Voting is by secret ballot, with a simple majority needed to pass a measure. The King may not formally veto legislation, but may return bills for further consideration. The Assembly occasionally rejects the King's recommendations or delays implementing them, but in general, the King has enough influence to persuade the Assembly to approve legislation that he considers essential or to withdraw proposals he opposes.

The Assembly may question government officials and force them to resign by a two-thirds vote of no confidence. The National Assembly has never compelled any government official to resign. The Royal Civil Service Commission is responsible for disciplining sub-ministerial level government officials and has removed several following their convictions for crimes including embezzlement. In June 1998, the King issued a decree setting out several measures intended to increase the role of the National Assembly in the formation and dissolution of his Government. The decree, later adopted by the 76th session of the National Assembly, provided that all cabinet ministers are to be elected by the National Assembly and that the roles and responsibilities of the cabinet ministries were to be spelled out.

Each cabinet minister is to be elected by simple majority in a secret ballot in the National Assembly from among candidates nominated by the King. The King is to select nominees for Cabinet office from among senior government officials holding the rank of secretary or above. The King is to award the portfolios of his ministers, whose terms will be limited to 5 years, after which they must pass a vote of confidence in the National Assembly in order to remain in office. Finally, the decree provided that the National Assembly, by a two-thirds vote of no confidence, can require the King to abdicate and to be replaced by the next in the line of succession. After adopting the decree, the National Assembly elected a new Cabinet of Ministers consistent with the decree. Human rights groups maintain that since only the King may nominate candidates for cabinet office, their election by the National Assembly is not a significant democratic reform.

The King also removed himself as Chairman of the Cabinet of Ministers in 1998; Foreign Minister Jigme Thinley was elected to that position by the National Assembly for one year, and was replaced by Minister for Health and Education Sangay Ngedup in July. Women are underrepresented in government and politics, although they have made small but visible gains. Three women hold seats in the National Assembly. All major ethnic groups, including ethnic Nepalese, are represented in the National Assembly. There are 16 "southern Bhutanese" in the National Assembly. Section 4 Governmental Attitude Regarding International and Nongovernmental Investigation of Alleged Violations of Human Rights. There are no legal human rights nongovernmental organisations (NGO's) in the country.

The Government regards human rights groups established by ethnic Nepalese exiles—the Human Rights Organisation of Bhutan, the People's Forum for Human Rights in Bhutan, and the Association of Human Rights Activists—Bhutan—as political organisations and does not permit them to operate in the country. Amnesty International (AI) visited Bhutan in 1992 to investigate and to report on the alleged abuse of ethnic Nepalese.

ICRC representatives continue twice yearly prison visits, and the Government has allowed them access to detention facilities, including those in southern districts inhabited by ethnic Nepalese. The chairman and members of the United Nations Human Rights Commission Working Group on Arbitrary Detention made a second visit to the country in May 1996 as a follow-up to an October 1994 visit. In addition to meetings with government officials, members of the working group visited prisons and interviewed prisoners in Thimphu, Phuntsoling, and Samtse.

In the 1980's and early 1990's, concern over rapid population growth and political agitation by ethnic Nepalese resulted in policies and abusive practices that led to the departure of tens of thousands of ethnic Nepalese, many of whom were expelled forcibly. The Government claims that ethnic and gender discrimination in employment is not a problem. It claims that ethnic Nepalese fill 22 per cent of government jobs, which is slightly less than their proportion of the total population.

Bhutanese human rights groups active outside the country claim that ethnic Nepalese actually make up about 35 per cent of the country's population and that the Government underreports their number. Women are accorded respect in the traditions of most ethnic groups; however, persistence of traditional gender roles apparently accounts for the low proportion of women in government employment. Exile groups claim that ethnic and gender discrimination is a problem.

There are credible reports by refugees and human rights groups that security forces raped large numbers of ethnic Nepalese women in the southern area of the country in 1991 and 1992. According to Amnesty International, some women were said to have died as a result. In one independent survey of 1,779 refugee families, 26 per cent of the respondents cited rape, fear of rape, or threat of rape as a prime reason for their departure from the country. The Government has denied these reports.

Rape was made a criminal offence in 1953, but that law had weak penalties and was enforced poorly. In 1993 the National Assembly adopted a revised rape act with clear definitions of criminal sexual assault and stronger penalties. In cases of rape involving minors, sentences range from 5 to 17 years. In extreme cases, a rapist may be imprisoned for life.

Women constitute 48 per cent of the population and participate freely in the social and economic life of the country. Forty-three per cent of enrolment in school is female, and 16 per cent of civil service employees are women. Inheritance law provides for equal inheritance among all sons and daughters, but traditional inheritance practices, which vary among ethnic groups, may be observed if the heirs choose to forego legal challenges.

Dowry is not practiced, even among ethnic Nepalese Hindus. Among some groups, inheritance practices favouring daughters are said to account for the large numbers of women among owners of shops and businesses and for an accompanying tendency of women to drop out of higher education to go into business.

However, female school enrolment has been growing in response to government policies. Women are increasingly found among senior officials and private sector entrepreneurs, especially in the tourism industry. Women in unskilled jobs are generally paid slightly less than men.

Polygamy is sanctioned provided the first wife gives her permission. Marriages may be arranged by partners themselves as well as by their parents. Divorce is common. Recent legislation requires that all marriages must be registered and favours women in matters of alimony. The Government has demonstrated its commitment to child welfare by its rapid expansion of primary schools, health-care facilities, and immunisation programs.

The mortality rates for both infants and children under 5 years have dropped dramatically since 1989, and primary school enrolment has increased at 9 per cent per year since 1991, with enrolment of girls increasing at an even higher rate. In 1995 the participation rate for boys and girls in primary schools was estimated at 72 per cent, with the rate of completion of 7 years of schooling at 60 per cent for girls and at 59 per cent for boys.

Children enjoy a privileged position in society and benefit from international development programs focused on maternal and child welfare. Amnesty International reported that at least 23 students, between 7 and 21 years of age, whose relatives had been arrested for supporting the pro-democracy movement, were expelled from school in eastern Bhutan in 1998. A study by UNICEF found that boys and girls receive equal treatment regarding nutrition and health care and that there is little difference in child mortality rates between the sexes. Government policies aimed at increasing enrolment of girls have increased the proportion of girls in primary schools from 39 per cent in 1990 to 43 per cent in 1995. Ethnic Nepalese have lived in the southern part of the country for centuries, and the early phases of economic development at the turn of the century brought a large influx of additional ethnic Nepalese.

In the late 1980's, concern over the increase in the population of and political agitation among ethnic Nepalese prompted aggressive government efforts to assert a national culture, to tighten control over southern regions, to control illegal immigration, to expel ethnic Nepalese, and to promote national integration.

Beginning in 1989, more discriminatory measures were introduced, aimed at shaping a new national identity, known as Drukpa. Drukpa is based on the customs of the non-ethnic Nepali Ngalong ethnic group predominant in the western part of the country.

Measures included a requirement that national dress be worn for official occasions and as a school uniform, the teaching of Dzongkha as a second language in all schools, and an end to instruction in Nepali as a second language (English is the language of instruction in all schools). Also, beginning in 1988, the Government refused to renew the contracts of tens of thousands of Nepalese guest workers. Many of these workers had resided in the country for years, in some cases with their families. Citizenship became a highly contentious issue. Requirements for citizenship were first formalised in the Citizenship Law of 1958, which granted citizenship to all adults who owned land and had lived in the country for at least 10 years.

In 1985, however, a new citizenship law significantly tightened requirements for citizenship and resulted in the denaturalisation of many ethnic Nepalese. While previously citizenship was conferred upon children whose father was a citizen under the 1958 law, the 1985 law required that both parents be citizens in order to confer citizenship on a child, and that persons seeking to prove citizenship through their own or their parents' residency in 1958 be able to prove residency in the country at that time.

In many cases, persons were unable to produce the documentation necessary, such as land tax receipts from 1958, to show residency nearly 30 years before. The law permits residents who lost citizenship under the 1985 law to apply for naturalisation if they can prove residence during the previous 15 years. The Government declared all residents who could not meet the new requirements to be illegal immigrants. The 1985 Citizenship Act also provides for the revocation of the citizenship of any naturalised citizen who "has shown by act or speech to be disloyal in any manner whatsoever to the King, country, and people of Bhutan."

The Home Ministry, in a circular notification in 1990, advised that "any Bhutanese nationals leaving the country to assist and help the anti-nationals shall no longer be considered as Bhutanese citizens . . . such people's family members living in the same household will also be held fully responsible and forfeit their citizenship." Human rights groups allege that these provisions were widely used to revoke the citizenship of ethnic Nepalese who were subsequently expelled or otherwise departed from the country. Beginning in 1988, the Government expelled large numbers of ethnic Nepalese through enforcement of the new citizenship laws.

Outraged by what they saw as a campaign of repression, ethnic Nepalese mounted a series of demonstrations, sometimes violent, in September 1990. The protests were spearheaded by the newly formed Bhutan People's Party (BPP) which demanded full citizenship rights for ethnic Nepalese, the reintroduction of Nepali as a medium of education in the south, and democratic reforms. Characterising the BPP as a terrorist movement backed by Indian sympathisers, the authorities cracked down on its activities and ordered the closure of local Nepalese schools, clinics, and development programs after several were raided or bombed by dissidents. Many ethnic Nepalese schools were reportedly turned into Army barracks.

Local officials took advantage of the climate of repression to coerce ethnic Nepalese to sell their land below its fair value and to emigrate. Beginning in 1991, ethnic Nepalese began to leave southern areas of the country in large numbers and take refuge in Nepal. Many were forcibly expelled. According to Amnesty International, entire villages were sometimes evicted *en masse* in retaliation for an attack on a local government official. Many ethnic Nepalese were forced to sign "voluntary migration forms" wherein they agreed to leave the country, after local officials threatened to fine or imprison them for failing to comply. By August 1991, according to NGO reports, 2,500 refugees were already camped illegally in Nepal, with a steady stream still coming from Bhutan.

The UNHCR began providing food and shelter in September of that year, and by year's end, there were 6,000 refugees in Nepal. The number of registered refugees grew to approximately 62,000 by August 1992, and to approximately 80,000 by June 1993, when the UNHCR began individual screening of refugees. The flow slowed considerably thereafter; there were no new refugee arrivals from Bhutan to the camps during the year. As of late 1999, there were approximately 97,000 refugees registered in camps in Nepal, with much of the increase since 1993 the result of births to residents of the camps. An additional 15,000 refugees, according to UNHCR estimates, are living outside the camps in Nepal and India.

Ethnic Nepalese political groups in exile complain that the revision of the country's citizenship laws in 1985 denaturalised tens of thousands of former residents of Bhutan. They also complain that the new laws have been selectively applied and make unfair demands for documentation on a largely illiterate group in a country that has only recently adopted basic administrative procedures. They claim that many ethnic Nepalese whose families have been in the country for generations were expelled in the early 1990's because they were unable to document their claims to residence.

The Government denies this and asserts that a three-member village committee—typically ethnic Nepalese in southern districts—certifies in writing that a resident is a Bhutanese citizen in cases where documents cannot be produced.

The Government maintains that many of those who departed the country in 1991-92 were Nepalese or Indian citizens who came to the country after the enactment of the 1958 Citizenship law but were not detected until a census in 1988. The Government also claims that many persons registered in the camps as refugees may never have resided in the country. A royal decree in 1991 made forcible expulsion of a citizen a criminal offence.

In a January 1992 edict, the King noted reports that officials had been forcing Bhutanese nationals to leave the country but stressed that this was a serious and punishable violation of law. Nevertheless, only three officials were ever punished for abusing their authority during this period. According to the UNHCR, the overwhelming majority of refugees who have entered the camps since screening began in June 1993 have documentary proof of Bhutanese nationality. Random checks and surveys of camp residents—including both pre- and post-June 1993 arrivals—bear this out.

A Nepal-Bhutan ministerial committee met seven times between 1994 and 1996, and a secretarial-level committee met twice in 1997 in efforts to resolve the Bhutanese refugee problem. During 1998, Foreign Minister Jigme Thinley took office with a mandate to resolve the refugee issue, and several meetings were held with representatives of the Nepalese Government, the UNHCR, and NGO's. However, the dialogue lost momentum in 1998 and was suspended by the Bhutanese Government pending the formation of a new government in Nepal in 1999. After a 3-year hiatus, the foreign ministers of Nepal and Bhutan met in September in Kathmandu to resume discussions on the refugee issue.

In March 1996 refugees began a series of "peace marches" from Nepal to Bhutan to assert their right to return to Bhutan. The marchers who crossed into Bhutan in August, November, and December 1996 were immediately detained and deported by Bhutanese police. In the December 1996 incident, police reportedly used force against the marchers. Such marches were also held in 1998 and 1999; the marchers charge that the police assaulted them during each march, injuring several demonstrators, and then arrested and deported all marchers.

A resolution adopted by the National Assembly in July 1997 prohibits the still-resident family members of ethnic Nepalese refugees from holding jobs with the Government or in the armed forces. Under the resolution, those holding such jobs were to be involuntarily retired. The Government made clear that for the purposes of this resolution, family member would be defined as a parent, a child, a sibling, or a member of the same household. The Government states that 429 civil servants, many of them ethnic Nepalese, were retired compulsorily in accordance with the July 1997 National Assembly resolution, and that the program was terminated in November. The Government states that those forced to retire were accorded retirement benefits in proportion to their years of government service.

The Government also began a program of resettling Buddhist Bhutanese from other regions of the country on land in the southern part of the country vacated by the ethnic Nepalese now living in refugee camps in Nepal. Human rights groups maintain that this action prejudices any eventual outcome of negotiations over the return of the refugees to the country. The Government maintains that this is not its first resettlement program and that Bhutanese citizens who are ethnic Nepalese from the south are sometimes resettled on more fertile land in other parts of the country.

There is no collective bargaining in industry. Industry accounts for about 25 per cent of the gross domestic product, but employs only a minute fraction of the total work force. The Government affects wages in the manufacturing sector through its control over wages in state-owned industries.

The Government abolished its system of compulsory labour taxes in December 1995. Labourers in rural development schemes previously paid through this system are now paid regular wages. There is no evidence to suggest that domestic workers are subjected to coerced or bonded labour. The law does not specifically prohibit forced and bonded labour by children, but such practices are not known to occur.

The law sets the minimum age for employment at 18 years for citizens and 20 years for noncitizens. A UNICEF study suggested that children as young as 11 years are sometimes employed with road-building teams. The law does not specifically prohibit forced and bonded labour by children, but such practices are not known to occur.

The Government provides free and compulsory primary school education, and 72 per cent of the school-aged population is enrolled. Children often do agricultural work and chores on family farms. There is no law barring ethnic Nepalese children from attending school. However, most of the 75 primary schools in southern areas that were closed in 1990 remain closed today. The closure of the schools acts as an effective barrier to the ability of the ethnic Nepalese in southern areas to obtain a primary education.

A circular effective February 1, 1994, established wage rates, rules and regulations for labour recruiting agencies, and regulations for payment of workmen's compensation. Wage rates are periodically revised, and range upward from a minimum of roughly $1.50 per day for unskilled and skilled labourers, with various allowances paid in cash or kind in addition. This minimum wage does provide a decent standard of living for a worker and family in the local context.

The workday is defined as 8 hours with a 1-hour lunch break. Work in excess of this must be paid at one and one-half times normal rates. Workers paid on a monthly basis are entitled to 1 day's paid leave for 6 days of work and 15 days of leave annually. The largest salaried work force is the government service, which has an administered wage structure last revised in 1988 but supplemented by special allowances and increases since then, including a 25 per cent increase in July 1997. Only about 30 industrial plants employ more than 50 workers. Smaller industrial units include 69 plants of medium size, 197 small units, 692 "mini" units, and 651 cottage industry units.

The Government favours a family-owned farm policy; this, along with the country's rugged geography and land laws that prohibit a farmer from selling his last five acres and that require the sale of holdings in excess of 25 acres, result in a predominantly self-employed agricultural work force. Workers are entitled to free medical care within the country. They are eligible for compensation for partial or total disability, and in the event of death, their families are entitled to compensation.

Existing labour regulations do not grant workers the right to remove themselves from work situations that endanger health and safety without jeopardising their continued employment. With one sixth of the population in exile, the tiny kingdom of Bhutan has the dubious distinction of being one of the world's highest per capita generator of refugees. The roots of the problem lie in the government's attempts to alter the kingdom's demography in favour of the ruling ethnic group.

Since 1990, over 100,000 thousand southern Bhutanese of Nepalese ethnicity have been made refugees after being forcibly evicted, forced to flee persecution and repression, or expelled after being coerced into signing "voluntary" emigration forms.

The section of society most notably excluded from the process of all-round development of Bhutan in terms of both the beneficiaries and the contributors - is women. Women population, which comprises almost half of the total population in Bhutan, has been so far neglected, discriminated and exploited. They have been deprived of most of the opportunities including access to business and industry, gainful employment, skill development training, education, health etc. They do not have access to education, gainful employment, economic resources, political process and decision-making institutions. Their representation at the policy and decision making bodies is negligible. In total, the status of women is very low in Bhutan.

The social attitudes, traditional practices and outlook against women have contributed to the exploitation of women. This has made Bhutanese women lacking in confidence in handling the issues generally affecting themselves even in their day-to-day life. The situation in Bhutan is such that majority of women are not even aware of their basic rights.

The practice of discrimination, gender-inequality and exploitation of women are not sudden emergence in the Asian societies. These are the legacy of the past feudal societies. Bhutan is still a feudal and autocratic society. Therefore, the presence of discrimination, gender in-equality and exploitation of women in one or other form is the main characteristics of feudal society of Bhutan. Bhutanese patriarchal system reflects male supremacy making women subservient to men.

Government has made no efforts to protect and promote women's rights even though it has ratified the International Convention on the Elimination of All Forms of Discrimination Against Women. Participation by women in national life is almost nil. Women have least access to higher post in the government. They have never been appointed as Ministers, Judges, Chief District Officers, Ambassadors or to other senior important posts.

Women comprising around 49 per cent of the population have least access to gainful employment. They do not have economic autonomy. More than 95 per cent women are illiterate and are engaged in traditional agricultural farming. The government has done nothing to improve their lot. Less than 0.5 per cent women are employed in the civil service (bureaucracy). They are mostly employed in lower level jobs like, telephone operators, typists, clerks etc. Less than 0.5 per cent women are engaged in business, Around 0.2 per cent are engaged in other occupation and 3.5 per cent of women have no identifiable occupation. The plight of rural women is worse. They are most neglected lot. Sexual exploitation, illiteracy, superstition, disease, child mortality and ignorance are rampant in the rural villages.

The real condition of women do not come to the light of the foreigners. Bhutan does not have newspaper, its only weekly bulletin is owned by the government. The external media is not allowed to Bhutan. Whereas, the government churns out glossy picture of the economic indicators in the international forums. They are only meant for the consumption of international community without reality.

Bhutan tops the list on women's sexual exploitation among Asian countries. But hardly any information reaches the world outside. Especially the ruling Drukpa or Ngalong community treats women as an object of consumer goods. They have no dignity and continuously humiliated by the males. Behind the government rhetoric of good governance, wide spread incidents of female abuses and their sexual exploitation are hidden..

Women constitute 49 per cent of the total population of Bhutan. Bhutanese refugee women and children constitute around 49 per cent and 40 per cent of the total refugee population in exile. Hundreds of women were raped during the army crack-down after peaceful protests in 1990. While male members were jailed for joining the peaceful rallies, women folk were abused, tortured and terrorised to flee the country. A number of reports prepared by the International human rights organisations, like, Amnesty International, IMADAR, Japan depicted cases of torture, dishonour and rape of Bhutanese women by the security forces. Sorry saga of women and children in Bhutan

The Marriage Act

The government of Bhutan simultaneously introduced the new Marriage Act which had an even larger content of discrimination against *Lhotshampa* women and their children. The Act declared all foreign wives of the Bhutanese citizens as non-citizens, even though most of them were granted citizenship under previous citizenship laws. In contravention of all international norms and civilised behaviour, the Government denied several thousand children (born out of marriages between *Lhotshampa* husbands and Nepali speaking wives from Nepal or India) of their right to nationality. They were evicted along with their parents. This Act was only enforced against the *Lhotshampas.*

The Marriage Act was enacted in 1980 and was forcefully implemented in 1988 to especially target the wives of *Lhotshampas.* This discriminatory law imposes a number of denial of benefits to those who married non-Bhutanese wives. The *Lhotshampas* who married non-Bhutanese wife did not have the right to vote in (became ineligible for election to) the National Assembly (Parliament) elections, they were denied promotion in civil services, denied training and fellowships and medical treatment abroad, they were also denied business and agricultural grants and loans given by the government and could not avail of government supplied fertilisers, seeds and farm machineries on subsidies. They could not get jobs in the Foreign Service and Armed Forces. This posed enormous problems for the *Lhotshampas*. There are many reasons as to why the *Lhotshampa* chose foreign wives of their own ethnic groups from Nepal and India. Some reasons are enumerated as follows: Bhutan stepped out of its isolation in the mid-sixties. The government did not encourage cultural socialization of various ethnic groups. Some ethnic groups were not allowed to own properties in the ruling Ngalung dominated areas. Even in-country migration was restricted. In-country travel was also restricted for some ethnic groups. The transport and communications were also not developed. This led to the cultural isolation of various ethnic groups. Thus, each ethnic group developed their own intra-ethnic group matrimonial alliances. *Lhotshampas* had a wide ethnic area in Darjeeling, Sikkim and Nepal to choose their spouse from. As a result many *Lhotshampas* got their spouses from their own ethnic groups from these places.

The most important factor that prevented the encouragement of inter-ethnic group matrimonial alliances is culture. The *Lhotshampas* are by and large Hindus. Culturally and traditionally, the *Lhotshampas* are entirely different from ruling Ngalung ethnic group. Their language is a dialect of or is derived from Sanskrit, the oldest language. They prefer to live in the hot climate of the southern foot hills. The Ngalungs are nurtured in Drukpa Kargyupa Buddhist culture. They speak Tibetan stock Dzonkha language which is entirely different from Nepali. They were robe like dresses and prefer to live in cool climate of the north.

While strict cultural values of the *Lhotshampas* triggered the search for wives from outside Bhutan, limited domestic society and geography also facilitated such marriages. The lack of communication and infrastructure within Bhutan were also factors which made *Lhotshampas* get their wives from neighbouring Indian states and Nepal as it is easier to travel to neighbouring countries than to visit other districts of Bhutan. Because of the lack of roads, Bhutanese are required to travel through India to reach from east to west in the south and south to north. Darjeeling district had excelled as a centre of education during the British rule in India. It is still regarded as the best place for education in the entire region of Bhutan, Nepal and Northeast India.

Jesuit fathers and Christian missionaries established the best schools in Darjeeling. Due to the absence of good schools and colleges throughout the sixties, seventies and the eighties in Bhutan, the government used to send young Bhutanese for studies to Darjeeling on Indian government scholarships. Most *Lhotshampa* students married with their schoolmates of their own ethnic community from Darjeeling, Sikkim and Nepal.. Bhutan does not have enough colleges to cater to the need of students. Its only college is affiliated with Delhi University. Therefore, Bhutanese students have no alternatives but to go to Darjeeling as it is less expensive to study in neighbouring Darjeeling than in Delhi or Kalkata.

As a consequence of increasing developmental activities after 1960 more opportunities were being created for educated people in the government services and in the private sector. Bhutan has a very low literacy rate. The available manpower was not sufficient to meet the demand. As a result, educated *Lhotshampa* took educated and conscious wives of their own ethnicity from neighbouring countries, who could work in the offices or do businesses and earn money. There was neither a Marriage Act or Citizenship Laws forbidding a Bhutanese marrying a foreign wife then. The laws were enacted later with retroactive effect. Had there been such laws, probably no Bhutanese would have married a foreign spouse. The Royal Government's senseless action of implementing these laws shows its irresponsibility and indifference towards its citizens' difficulties. It is a well-planned conspiracy to depopulate southern Bhutan. In any case, marriage is too personal a matter for the state to intervene.

Both the Citizenship Act and the Marriage Act are racist, biased and discriminatory against *Lhotshampa* women of southern Bhutan. Moreover, the law is also implemented in a discriminatory manner; very rigidly against the *Lhotshampas* and not at all against Ngalung/ Drukpas, who for example have a Chinese, English, Italian or American wives. For example, Mr. Ugen Tshering, a Drukpa married to an Italian wife in the early eighties has today been promoted as

Foreign Secretary. Similarly, the then Chief Justice of the High Court was promoted even though he had an English wife. Today, of course, aside from bringing about a denial of benefits, marriage to non-Bhutanese wife has resulted in the very denial of citizenship rights to the *Lhotshampa* husbands. Both the Citizenship Law, 1985 and the Marriage Acts have stripped several thousand *Lhotshampas* of their nationality. As a consequences of not granting citizenship to the foreign wives of *Lhotshampa* husbands, more than 60,000 children were deprived of their rightful claim to Bhutanese citizenship. This is more than 20 per cent of the total children population of Bhutan. Refugee children constitute about 10 per cent of the country's total population of around 767,000 of Bhutan.

More than 10,000 *Lhotshampa* wives are deprived of their right to nationality. The government must repeal the discriminatory Citizenship Act, 1985 and the Marriage Act. It must enact new citizenship and marriage laws conforming to the international standards, and protect the right to nationality of all its citizens

Nationality Issues in Bhutan

Discriminatory and Racist Citizenship and Marriage Laws

The roots of the current political crisis in Bhutan and the refugees lie in Bhutan's geopolitics and population politics. A study of various policies of the Royal Government of Bhutan (RGOB) in the last two decades reflects the Ngalung/Drukpa dominated government's motive to uproot Nepali speaking *Lhotshampa* population from Bhutan and reduce their number by all means. Be it Drukpanization or Bhutanization programmes, Citizenship and Marriage Acts or NOCs/PCCs, all are directed against *Lhotshampas* of the south. It was a long standing and intrinsic ruling elites' security perception that the domestic demand for political change (democracy) would come from the *Lhotshampas* in the south. The south is bordered by the democratic India. Moreover, the *Lhotshampas* are economically well-off and more educated than their brethren in the north and east. The northern borders with China is closed. In order to pre-empt the demand for democracy, the government devised a clever strategy to depopulate the *Lhotshampas* from southern Bhutan. Hence, the *Lhotshampas* suddenly became the geopolitical scapegoats and security threat to the absolute monarchy.

Thus, the government devised various strategies to bring about a favourable demographic balance favouring a Drukpa galung nation by reducing the number of *Lhotshampas* to around 25 per cent and to prevent the demand for democracy from southern Bhutan. The failed implementation of the forced assimilation policies reinforced this insecurity. This resulted in denationalization, deprivation and virtual confiscation of *Lhotshampa* citizenship rights through manipulation of the Citizenship Act and through changing the definition of citizenship. The current political crisis and the refugee problems owe their origin to the enactment of two racist and discriminatory laws, viz., Citizenship Act of 1985 and Marriage Act of 1977 and implementation of a number of racist and discriminatory policies. These laws and policies were designed to reduce the number of *Lhotshampa* population and their mass eviction.

Citizenship Act

Question of nationality and methods employed to determine citizenship form a backdrop of all other issues and events in southern Bhutan. Bhutan's first attempt to define its citizenship came with National Law of Bhutan, 1958. The regime enacted a new Citizenship Act, 1985.

This Act was given a retrospective implementation of thirty years, that is, from 1958. It declared 31 December, 1958 as the cut-off year for granting citizenship. The Act was forcefully implemented in 1988. The wives of Bhutanese citizens married from outside the country and children born of such parents were not granted citizenship and were deprived of their legitimate citizenship status. This Act defined three criteria for granting of citizenship: by birth, by registration, and through naturalisation. This Act is the origin of the refugee problems and the looming danger of statelessness for *Lhotshampas*. The National Law, 1958 prescribed 'fatherhood' as the criteria for granting citizenship-which is normal. But the new Act repealed the previous citizenship law and prescribed 'parenthood' as the sole criteria for grant of citizenship by birth, thus denying citizenship to anyone whose mother was married from outside the country, even if the mother was granted citizenship according to previous law. Since the Act was given a retrospective implementation of 1958, all children born of a marriage between a Bhutanese father and a non-Bhutanese mother, between 1958 to 1988 were declared non-citizens and so-called 'illegal' and 'economic migrants'. The National Assembly in 1988 confirmed 14,442 marriages between a Bhutanese citizen and a non-citizen during last twenty years. The number was too insignificant for the government to grant citizenship rights.

Article 3 of the Act codified a new basis for granting citizenship - a proof of residence in Bhutan since before December 31, 1958 was required. It says that " A person permanently domiciled in Bhutan on or before 31st December, 1958, and, whose name is registered in the census register maintained by the Ministry of Home Affairs shall be deemed to be a citizen of Bhutan by registration". The government subsequently brought all *Lhotshampas* under the purview of citizenship by registration only. They were considered citizens by registration and not by birth, even though they were born and reared in Bhutan since the 17th century much before the establishment of the current ruling Wangchuchk dynasty in 1907 and granted citizenship by previous laws.

De-Nationalization

The Act arbitrarily imposes an impossible burden upon the *Lhotshampas* of providing the documentary evidence of their presence in Bhutan on 31 December, 1958, while the other ethnic groups did not have to prove anything to retain their citizenship. The government insisted on production of documents such as land tax receipts only of 1958. Documents of earlier years including the citizenship certificates issued on the basis of previous laws were arbitrarily rejected. The proper census record maintained by Chief District Officer were arbitrarily rejected. The government was fully aware that the requirements of the new Act just did not exist then in Bhutan and that most of the *Lhotshampas* would not be able to fulfil them. The Act demands that the person concerned must prove that his name was registered in the census register, though the register was maintained by the government. The government demand is not only ridiculous but totally unjustified since, the Council of Ministers including the Ministry of Home responsible for maintaining the census register was itself created in 1968. The enumeration in the census record was started only in 1972.

Following the first census of 1981, all citizens were issued with citizenship identity cards. The foreigners were issued with alien cards and the non-national labours were issued with contract permits. By 1982 all people in Bhutan were registered. Bhutanese government initially claimed that any documentary evidence whatsoever, land ownership deeds or documents showing sale, gift, and inheritance of land, tax receipts of any kind etc., showing that the person concerned was resident in Bhutan in 1958 is taken as conclusive proof of citizenship. But later the government contended that payment of property tax in itself is hardly a proof of Bhutanese citizenship. This is especially unfair since some of the documentary proof required by the census team just did not exist in the year 1958, i.e., enumeration in the census records.

Those who could not produce the documentary evidence of their presence on 31 December, 1958 were declared illegal immigrants. How is it possible for illiterate villagers to keep documents that will be demanded by the government after 30 years. Moreover, government had already issued citizenship certificates to all *Lhotshampas* making the safe keeping of the documents unimportant. The Act was also discriminatory enforced against the *Lhotshampas* and not at all against other ethnic groups. Many Ngalungs have Italian, English, Chinese and Singaporean wives, but they do not have to prove anything. However, the law prescribes a number of discriminatory criteria against the wives of *Lhotshampas* from Nepal or India and their children. They are treated at par with aliens seeking for naturalisation. Under the naturalisation process, these wives must prove their prior residence of 15-20 years in Bhutan. A child born of such mothers needs to reach the age of fifteen when he/she may apply for naturalisation. Naturalization again, is not a matter of law but subject to government approval The Act was applied in an arbitrary manner to create mass statelessness. The dissidents accused of speaking or criticising the king's government was stripped of citizenship. Many *Lhotshampas* were deprived of their nationality for having fled Bhutan to escape suppression, because their fleeing amounts to disloyalty to the state according to the regime.

The Act enabled the government to claim that the refugees are not Bhutanese citizens. The authorities confiscated the documentary evidences, particularly the citizenship identification card and land documents issued to them by the government. It was a well planned strategy and conspiracy of the, government to depopulate and reduce the number of *Lhotshampas*. No appeal on the subject was allowed. The Act also forbids the return of citizens leaving the country. Since the government alleges that refugees have voluntarily emigrated to Nepal, their return will not be possible until this Act is repealed. Even, the European Parliament's resolution has urged Bhutan to amend this Act for the return of refugees.

Marriage Laws

After enacting a draconian Citizenship Act in 1985 to reduce the *Lhotshampa* population, the government simultaneously introduced the new Marriage Act which had an even larger content of discrimination against *Lhotshampa* women and their children. The Act declared all foreign wives of the Bhutanese citizens as non-citizens, even though most of them were granted citizenship under previous citizenship laws. In contravention of all international norms and civilised behaviour, the Royal Government denied several i thousand children (born out of marriages between *Lhotshampa* husbands and Nepali speaking wives from Nepal or India) of their right to nationality. They were evicted along with their parents. This Act was only enforced against the *Lhotshampas*.

The Marriage Act was enacted in 1980 and was forcefully implemented in 1988 to especially target the wives of *Lhotshampas*. This discriminatory law imposes a number of denial of benefits to those who married non-Bhutanese wives. The *Lhotshampas* who married non-Bhutanese wife did not have the right to vote in (became ineligible for election to) the National Assembly (Parliament) elections, they were to be denied promotion in civil services, denied training and fellowships and medical treatment abroad, they were also denied business and agricultural grants and loans given by the government and could not avail of government supplied fertilisers, seeds and farm machineries on subsidies. They could not get jobs in the Foreign Service and Armed Forces. This posed enormous problems for the *Lhotshampas*.

There are many reasons as to why the *Lhotshampa* chose foreign wives of their own ethnic groups from Nepal and India. Some reasons are enumerated as follows: Bhutan stepped out of its isolation in the midsixties. The government did not encourage cultural socialization of various ethnic groups. Some ethnic groups were not allowed to own properties in the Ngalung dominated areas. Even in-country migration and in-country travel were restricted for some ethnic groups. The transport and communications were also not developed. This led to the cultural isolation of various ethnic groups. Thus, each ethnic group developed their own intra-ethnic group matrimonial alliances.

Lhotshampas had a wide ethnic area in Darjeeling, Sikkim and Nepal to choose their spouse from. As a result many *Lhotshampas* got their spouses from their own ethnic groups from these places.

The most important factor that prevented the encouragement of inter-ethnic group matrimonial alliances is culture. The *Lhotshampas* are by and large Hindus. Culturally and traditionally, they are entirely different from ruling Ngalungs. Their language is a dialect of or is derived from Sanskrit, the oldest language. They prefer to live in the hot climate of the southern foot hills. The Ngalungs are nurtured in Drukpa Kargyupa Buddhist culture. They speak Tibetan stock Dzonkha language which is entirely different from Nepali. They wear robe like dresses and prefer to live in cool climate of the north.

While strict cultural values of the *Lhotshampas* triggered the search for wives from outside Bhutan, limited domestic society and geography also facilitated such marriages. The lack of communication and infrastructure within Bhutan were also factors which made *Lhotshampas* get their wives from neighbouring Indian states and Nepal as it was easier to travel to neighbouring countries than to visit other districts of Bhutan. Because of the lack of roads, Bhutanese are still required to travel through India to reach from east to west in the south and south to north. Darjeeling district had excelled as a centre of education during the British rule in India. It is still regarded as the best place for education in the entire region of Bhutan, Nepal and Northeast India.

Jesuit fathers and Christian missionaries established the best schools in Darjeeling. Due to the absence of good schools and colleges throughout the sixties, seventies and the eighties in Bhutan, the government used to send young Bhutanese for studies to Darjeeling on Indian government scholarships. Most *Lhotshampa* students married with their schoolmates of their own ethnic community from Darjeeling, Sikkim and Nepal.. Bhutan does not have enough colleges to cater to the need of students. Its only college is affiliated with Delhi University. Bhutanese students had to go to Darjeeling as it is less expensive to study in neighbouring Darjeeling than in Delhi or Calcutta.

As a consequence of increasing developmental activities after 1960 more opportunities were being created for educated people in the government services and in the private sector. Bhutan had a very low female literacy rate. The available manpower was not sufficient to meet the demand. As a result, educated *Lhotshampa* took educated and conscious wives of their own ethnicity from neighbouring countries, who could work in the offices or do businesses and earn money.

In 1988, the government reported of 11,442 marriages between Bhutanese and non-Bhutanese during the preceding 20 years. There was neither a Marriage Act or Citizenship Laws forbidding a Bhutanese marrying a foreign wife then. The laws were enacted later with retroactive effect. Had there been such laws, probably no Bhutanese would have married a foreign spouse. The Royal Government's senseless action of implementing these laws shows its irresponsibility and indifference towards its citizens' difficulties. It is a well-planned conspiracy to depopulate southern Bhutan. In any case, marriage is too personal a matter for the state to intervene.

Both the Citizenship Act and the Marriage Act are racist, biased and discriminatory against *Lhotshampa* of southern Bhutan. Moreover, the law is also implemented in a discriminatory manner; very rigidly against the *Lhotshampas* and not at all against Drukpas, who for example have a Chinese, English, Italian or American wives. For example, Mr. Ugen Tshering, a Drukpa married to an Italian wife in the early eighties has today been promoted as Foreign Secretary. Similarly, the then Chief Justice of the High Court was promoted even though he had an English wife. Today, of course, aside from bringing about a denial of benefits, marriage to non-Bhutanese wife has resulted in the very denial of citizenship rights to the *Lhotshampa* husbands.

Both the Citizenship Law, 1985 and the Marriage Acts have stripped several thousand *Lhotshampas* of their nationality. As a consequences of not granting citizenship to the foreign wives of *Lhotshampa* husbands, more than 60,000 children were deprived of their rightful claim to Bhutanese citizenship. This is more than 20 per cent of the total children population of Bhutan. Refugee children constitute about 10 per cent of the country's total population of around 700,000 of Bhutan.

More than 10,000 *Lhotshampa* wives are deprived of their right to nationality. The government must repeal the discriminatory Citizenship Act, 1985 and the Marriage Act. It must enact new citizenship and marriage laws conforming to the international standards, and protect the right to nationality of all its citizens. "The 1985 Citizenship Act of Bhutan contains a number of vague provisions, and appears to have been applied in an arbitrary manner. It also contains provisions which could be used to exclude from citizenship many people who are not members of the dominant ethnic group, as well as those who oppose Government policy by peaceful means" according to Amnesty International's report, "Bhutan : Forcible Exile", August, 1994.

Status of Children in Bhutan

Status of Bhutanese Chilren : A child is the true reflection of the socio-economic realities of a society and the nation. Children are the true representative of a country's future. BWCO recognises the child as an inherent and integral component of society deserving the best the society has to offer. It believes that every child has an inherent right to survival, protection, security, development, love, care, education, health care, justice, peace and freedom. It believes that the grassroots social movement is required for the effective realisation of the rights of the child. Child development and welfare are definitely not a charity. The child must be the basis of any national development programme. Hence the child development and welfare policy must emphasise the participation of entire communities, society and the national government itself.

Bhutan ratified the Convention on the Rights of the Child on May 23, 1990, but submitted its initial report to the Committee on the Rights of the Children only on 20 April 1999, after five reminders and seven years of its due date on 01 September 1992. The report is full of distortion and fallacies. Bhutanese children are denied their rights under Articles 2, 3, 4, 5, 6, 7, 8, 12, 13, 14, 15, 28, 30, 32 of the Convention. Bhutan continues its policy of discrimination against *Lhotshampa* children, thus violating Article 2, the cardinal General Principles of the Convention.

Bhutan is a nation of younger population. According to a 1989 government report, 65 per cent of her population is below 30 years of age, around 40 per cent of Bhutan's population was below 15 years of age. According to the same report, the child population under 19 years (01-19 years) was 50 per cent of population. A child is legally defined as anyone not attaining the ages of 16 years in the case of girls and 18 in the case of boys according to Bhutan's Initial report submitted to the Committee on the Rights of the Child in September, 1990.

While, most child workers between 10-14 ages are found in Asia, Bhutan accounts for the highest per centage (55%) of the child labour in the age-group between 10 to 14 according to an ILO report, 1999, higher than Nepal, Bangladesh and India. It has made a mockery of such an important Convention. Although the Royal

Government of Bhutan claims to have introduced universal primary education in the country, the per centage of enrolment at the primary level is only about 20 per cent and 80 per cent of children remain without education. They are compelled to work in the agricultural farms and tend cattle. They also work as household and construction workers. Child labour exploitation is a consequence of the feudal social system, poverty, deprivation, illiteracy and lack of awareness among the parents.

Education beyond the primary level is strictly regulated in accordance with the manpower requirements of the various government departments. Nation-wide Common Examinations are held at class (standard) six and eight levels. Almost 60 per cent of students drop out at class six and more than 50 per cent at class eight. These examinations are nothing but a process of elimination and implemented to ensure that the country need not suffer agricultural labourers. The government thinks that if all receive higher education, there will be none to attend to the agricultural farms. Only a few manage to go up to class ten, where they are again screened. By the time they enter Junior college and college, only a handful remain in the education system.

No one really knows what happens to those thousands of children who drop out at class six. Rich families can always take their children to India for education even if they have failed in the Common Examinations. But poor children, once they have failed in the Common Examinations, are denied further education. There is only one Bachelors degree college in Bhutan as the higher education is deliberately restricted. The government fears that the educated unemployed youth might create political opposition to the government.

Police Clearance or no Objection Certificates

In 1990, the government introduced a draconian rule requiring all *Lhotshampa* citizens to produce a No Objection Certificates (NOCs) or Police Clearance Certificates (PCC) or Security Clearance Certificates (SCC) from the police stating that none of their kith and kin has been involved in the peaceful pro-human rights and pro-democratic movement of September-October, 1990. Every *Lhotshampa* was required to produce PCCs for getting admission of their children into schools. However, other ethnic groups were not mandated to produce the PCCs.

Through the introduction of a draconian rule requiring the

issue of the Police Clearance Certificate by the police, the Government has effectively blocked the Southern Bhutanese children of their right to education. This certificate is required at the time of admission to schools in the country. This certificate is denied to any person whose family members was suspected to be the sympathisers of the human rights movement. No civilised society can bear the accusations of a six year child denied the right to education, a penalty the child is made to pay for the convictions, right or wrong, of older relatives, who have sympathised with human rights movement. The Government has closed all schools in southern Bhutan. A few schools are opened, where only the children of security forces and government officials are allowed.

The government declared all sympathisers of pro-human rights movement and who opposed its racist and discriminatory policies ant-national and not eligible for PCCs. Other family members of those taking part in the peaceful protest rallies, who had not participated in them were also declared anti-national and evicted. PCCs were never issued to the *Lhotshampa*. Consequently, these children have landed in the refugee camps in Nepal.

Child Soldiers

The Royal Bhutan Army conscripts the underage minor children into the security forces. There are instance of 14 years old children forcefully recruited into the army, but making them to write their age as 20 years and not the real age under threat. Militia forces have been raised at various times in the past, including during internal disturbances in the early 1990s. Up to 30 per cent of militia recruits in the early 1990s were school and village children; after three months training they were reportedly deployed in auxiliary support to the army. The presence of Indian militant fighters ULFA and Bodo in Bhutan, engaged in the conflicts in neighbouring Indian states has posed a growing security problem in Bhutan. A system of village defence committees is used for local patrolling in the border region. Children under 18 are regularly used for such duties. Children who failed their school examinations are compelled to join the armed forces. Families having more than three sons are also required to send at least one for military service In the government armed forces, which has a total strength of 11,000, 5 per cent or around 550, were children below 18 years. Child soldiers below the age of 18 formed approximately 10 per cent, or around 200, of the Militias, the government paramilitary. Reports stated that one detachment of 200 soldiers contained 3 soldiers under 15 years, and that another 400 contained 15 who were under 16 years. In one group of 300 militia recruits there were 25 to 30 "very young boys". (Source: Radda Barnen, Childwar database, citing UN, Graca Machel, Case Study on Bhutan, 1994-1995).

Refugee Children

Several thousand Bhutanese children were forcefully evicted by the Government along with their parents. Nearly 45,000 Bhutanese children under the age of 18 are now compelled to live the life of refugees in Nepal and India. The refugee children comprises around 14 per cent of the total child population of Bhutan. They are deprived of their basic right to nationality and rendered stateless.

According to Bhutanese law they forfeited their right to return to their country. Since, 1991, seventeen thousand children were born in the Bhutanese refugee camps in Nepal. A nine-member delegation of the European Union Parliament visited Nepal. They also visited the Bhutanese refugee camps in Jhapa, Nepal on April 22, 2000. Mr. Gerard Collins, leader of the delegation and the chairman of the European Parliament Delegation for Relations with South Asian Countries and SAARC on his visit to Bhutanese refugee camp in Timai, Jhapa, Nepal on April 22, 2000 expressed concern about the uncertain fate and predicament of these refugee children born in the refugee camps. He said. "What will happen to the 17,000 children born in the camps, it is a matter for concern even for us."

Bhutanese refugee children are the victims of human rights abuses by the Government of Bhutan. In the good old days in Bhutan, most of these children were students. Today they are destitute, who have no present and no future. Although the international aid agencies do their best to take care of their needs. However, the most important issue today is, how long these students remain destitute and what help and assistance can the international community offer to resolve their problems so that they can go back to their motherland and live a normal life?.

Children's Educational Programme

There are more than 30,000 Bhutanese refugees living outside of the refugee camps in Nepal and India, without any relief and assistance. Many late comer refugees were denied a place in the refugee camps. They do not have any regular sources of income. So, many poor and needy Bhutanese refugee children living outside of the camps are finding it difficult to attend the schools due to very bad financial conditions of their parents. Their parents are not in a position to send them to schools due to their poor financial conditions.

In view of the above, Bhutan Women and Children Organisation (BWCO) started a children's educational programme in 1998, to help a few poor needy refugee children to receive education. Currently, ten refugee children are studying in the schools in Kathmandu.

These children get socialisation in their own culture, tradition and community. Socialisation in their own community will help them build their vision for their society. In the long run the children as growing individuals must learn to respect and appreciate other religions, cultures and people of different ethnic background along with their own. This might sound paradoxical to the racial hatreds and religious and social discrimination these children vividly encountered while in Bhutan. But it is necessary as a need for the development of cultured and civilised people and society. This prepares the refugee children to live more harmoniously with their fellow brethren when they return home.

Missions and Objectives of BWCO

Mission

BWCO is dedicated to the establishment of human rights and democracy in Bhutan and promoting the principles of human rights, democratic values, women' rights, gender justice, social justice, child rights, rule of law among Bhutanese people and creating a culture of peace through education, training, publication and dissemination. By implementing principles of non-discrimination, human rights, women' rights, child rights, civil, political, social, economic, cultural rights and fostering international public law instruments, BWCO aims to reformulate the existing gender-discriminatory system in public policies and social system and cultivate social justice in the development of a sustainable peaceful Bhutanese society .

Vision

A gender-equitable peaceful democratic society in Bhutan which is just, equitable and where women and men from all background are empowered and are able to contribute equally in the mainstream development process and able to exercise their rights, define and articulate their interests and needs in public policy.

Goals

- To work for the establishment of human rights and democracy in Bhutan through peaceful and non-violent means.
- To promote and propagate the principles, ideals and values of democracy; principles, and provisions of non-discrimination, equality, social justice and rule of law according to international standards among Bhutanese people.
- To work for the empowerment and advancement of Bhutanese women through better opportunities of education, gainful and equal employment, economic, political and legal empowerment, gender equality and an equitable share in decision making and for their full participation in all spheres of society.
- To combat against all forms of discrimination, injustices, exploitation, and oppression against women and work for their elimination.
- To promote and propagate the principles and provisions of International Human Rights Instruments, Beijing Platform for Action, CEDAW, CRC, non-discrimination, equality, social justice, rule of law in Bhutan.
- To work for legislative reforms and influence the legislative reforms and official policies on promotion and protection of human rights, interests of children and women, gender equality, women's empowerment and gender-equitable development.
- To work for the protection and promotion of the rights of Bhutanese children and work for elimination of all forms of exploitation and discrimination against children.
- To work for the early repatriation of Bhutanese refugees with dignity and honour.

Aims and Objectives

The aims and objectives of BWCO are:

1. To work for the establishment of human rights and democracy in Bhutan through peaceful and nonviolent means.
2. To work for the protection and promotion of women's human

rights as enshrined in various International Human Rights Instruments including the Convention on the Elimination of All Forms of Discrimination Against Women, the Platform for Action and the Beijing Declaration, 1995 in Bhutan and to work for elimination of all forms of exploitation, discrimination, violence against women and trafficking.

3. To organising training, seminar and workshop for raising awareness and consciousness of Bhutanese women about the principles of non-discrimination, human rights, civil, political, social, economic, cultural and legal rights, rule of law, gender equality, gender justice and social justice as contained in various International Human Rights Instruments, including the Convention on the Elimination of All Forms of Discrimination Against Women, Declaration on the Elimination of Violence against Women and Platform for Action, Beijing Declaration among the Bhutanese people at grassroots level for achie-ving gender equality, gender justice and social justice.
4. To educate Bhutanese women about phenomenon of cruelty, violence, sexual exploitation, trafficking and discrimination against them and mobilize them to combat against all forms of discrimination, exploitation and violence against them (PA).
5. To raise women's consciousness about the social, cultural, economic, religious and legal injustices, gender issues and discrimination against them and develop their consciousness, self-confidence and esteem through training, discussions, workshops, publications, awareness raising and leadership development programmes.
6. To develop Bhutanese women's consciousness, capabilities and leadership roles for women's empowerment and advancement through better opportunities of better education, gainful employment, economic empowerment and a share in decision making in all spheres and work for their full participation in society. Work for removing the obstacles to women's full participation in decision making at all levels of family, social, economic, political and national life in compliance with the Platform of Action, Beijing Declaration.
7. To intensify the grassroots movement for effective promotion, propagation, and dissemination of the principles and provisions of International Human Rights Instruments

including Convention on the Elimination of All Forms of Discrimination Against Women (CEDAW) and Beijing Declaration and Platform for Action among the Bhutanese people at grassroots level for achieving gender equality, gender justice and social justice.

8. To advocate and monitor gender representation and balance in national programmes, policies and processes. To contribute to the institutionalisation of gender perspectives in major national development programmes.
9. To campaign and advocate for the enactment of national legislation on elimination of all forms of discrimination and exploitation against women based on the Convention on the Elimination of All Forms of Discrimination Against Women (CEDAW) and Platform for Action, Beijing Declaration. To promote observance of practical application of the provisions of International Human Rights Instruments.
10. To promote women's right to health and create awareness about AIDS among the Bhutanese refugee community as a part of prevention education. To initiate safe motherhood and child health programmes for Bhutanese refugees in the refugee camps.

Children: Objectives

11. To work for the promotion and protection of the rights of Bhutanese children and work for elimination of all forms of exploitation and discrimination against children.
12. To raise awareness of Bhutanese people about the principles and provisions of the Convention on the Rights of the Child and other International Instruments on Child Rights through various demonstrative activities, publication, seminars, training and talk programmes. To intensify the grassroots movement for effective promotion, propagation, and dissemination of the principles and provisions of the Convention on the Rights of the Child among the Bhutanese people at grassroots level.
13. To organise seminars, workshops, training and public meetings with the objectives of educating and training Bhutanese people in the defence of child rights.
14. To develop critical thinking on the rights of child through training, campaign, advocacy, education and publication and to advocate and campaign for the implementation of the

provisions of convention on the Rights of Child and its incorporation into the national law of Bhutan and promote observance of practical application of all international instruments on children.

15. To work for elimination of exploitation and oppression of Bhutanese children, child labour and all forms of discrimination and deprivation against them.
16. To combat child labour, trafficking and sexual exploitation and abuses of children and initiate local, regional and international alliances for the promotion and protection of the Rights of the Child in Bhutan.
17. To intensify the grassroots movement for effective realization of the rights of the child through promotion, propagation, and dissemination of the principles and provisions of the Convention on the Rights of Child among the Bhutanese people at grassroots level.
18. Initiate programmes for rehabilitation of children at risk and under difficult circumstances. Develop and establish educational fund for helping the under privileged, deprived and poor Bhutanese children who have no access to formal education.
19. To take initiatives to establish child health care programmes for Bhutanese. To provide preventive medical and counselling services against communicable diseases to them, promote and maintain their good health, prevent and remedy their poor health. Provide child health care education including nutrition to the parents and children.
20. To serve as a centre for dissemination of information, documentation and publication concerning the status of Bhutanese women and children.

US State Department Country Reports on Human Rights Practices -2001

Bhutan

Bhutan is ruled by a hereditary monarch, King Jigme Singye Wangchuk, who governs with the support of a National Assembly and a Council of Ministers. There is no written constitution to protect fundamental political and human rights. Since ascending the throne in 1972, the King has continued the efforts toward social and political modernization begun by his father. In the last few years, Bhutan has improved rapidly services in education, health care, sanitation, and communications, with parallel but slower development of representative governance and decision making. In recent years, Bhutan has adopted some measures to increase the power of the National Assembly. The judiciary is not independent of the King.

The Royal Bhutan Police (RBP), assisted by the Royal Bhutan Army (including those assigned to the Royal Body Guard), and a national militia maintain internal security. Some members of these forces committed human rights abuses. The economy is based on agriculture and forestry, which provide the main livelihood for 90 per cent of the population and account for approximately half of the gross domestic product (GDP). The gross national product (GNP) per capita is estimated to be $600. Agriculture largely consists of subsistence farming and animal husbandry. Citrus fruit, cardamom, and other spices are the leading agricultural exports. Cement and electricity are the other important exports. Strong trade and monetary ties link the economy closely to that of India. Hydroelectric power production potential and tourism are key resources, although the Government limits tourism because of inadequate infrastructure and environmental and cultural concerns. Tourist arrivals also are limited by a requirement that tourists purchase a high minimum daily rate holiday package before visiting the country.

The Government's human rights record remained poor, and problems remain in several areas. Citizens do not have the right to change their government. The King exercises strong, active, and direct power over the Government. The Government discourages political parties, and none operate legally. Arbitrary arrest and detention remain problems, and reports continue of torture and abuse of detainees. Impunity for those who commit abuses also is a problem. Judges serve at the King's pleasure, and the Government limits significantly the right to a fair trial. In April 2000, the Government established the Department of Legal Affairs as a result of a review of the Basic Law. Programmes to build a body of written law and to train lawyers are progressing. The Government limits significantly citizens' right to privacy. The Government restricts freedom of speech, press, assembly, and association. Citizens face significant limitations on freedom of religion. Approximately two-thirds of the government-declared population of 600,000 persons is composed of' Buddhists with cultural traditions akin to those of

Tibet. The Buddhist majority consists of two principal ethnic and linguistic groups: The Ngalongs of the western part of the country and the Sharchops of the eastern part of the country. The remaining third of the population, ethnic Nepalese, most of whom are Hindus, live in the country's southern districts. Government efforts to institute policies designed to preserve the cultural dominance of the Ngalong ethnic group, to change citizenship requirements, and to control illegal immigration resulted in political protests, ethnic conflict, and repression of ethnic Nepalese in southern districts during the late 1980's and early 1990's. Tens of thousands of ethnic Nepalese left the country in 1991-92, many of whom were expelled forcibly. According to the U.N. High Commissioner for Refugees (UNHCR), as of mid-June 2000, 98,269 ethnic Nepalese remained in 7 refugee camps in eastern Nepal; upwards of 15,000 reside outside of the camps in the Indian states of Assam and West Bengal. The Government maintains that some of those in the camps never were citizens, and therefore have no right to return. In 1998 the Government began resettling Buddhist Bhutanese from other regions of the country on land in southern districts vacated by the ethnic Nepalese living in refugee camps in Nepal, which is likely to complicate any future return of the ethnic Nepalese. The Government continues its negotiation with the Government of Nepal on procedures for the screening and repatriation of ethnic Nepalese in the refugee camps. A ministerial-level bilateral meeting in November failed to resolve disputes concerning the categorization of refugees in terms of eligibility for their eventual repatriation. The Government restricts worker rights. The Government claims that it has prosecuted government personnel for unspecified abuses committed in the early 1990's; however, there is little indication that the Government has investigated adequately or punished any security force officials involved in torture, rape, and other abuses committed against ethnic Nepalese residents.

Respect for Human Rights

Section I Respect for the Integrity of the Person, Including Freedom From:

(a) *Arbitrary and Unlawful Deprivation of Life.* There were no reports of arbitrary or unlawful deprivations of life committed by the Government or its agents. Domestic human rights groups allege that the Government has taken no action to punish a government official for the 1998 killing of Buddhist monk

Gomchen Karma. The Government stated that the shooting was accidental, that the official responsible has been suspended from duty and charged in connection with the incident, and that his case was being heard as of September 2000.

(b) *Disappearance.* There were no reports of politically motivated disappearances.

(c) *Torture and Other Cruel, Inhuman, or Degrading Treatment or Punishment.* The law prohibits torture and abuse; however, human rights advocates state that in practice the security forces ignore these provisions. No one was prosecuted in connection with violating prohibitions against torture during the year. In 1999 and 2000 there were reports that security forces stopped ethnic Nepalese refugees attempting to return to the country, beat them or tortured them, and sent them back across the border. Refugee groups state that this has discouraged others from trying to return to the country. Refugee groups credibly claim that persons detained as suspected dissidents in the early 1990's were tortured and/or raped by security forces. During those years, the Government's ethnic policies and the crackdown on ethnic Nepalese political agitation created a climate of impunity in which the Government tacitly condoned the physical abuse of ethnic Nepalese. The Government denies that these abuses occurred but also claims that it has investigated and prosecuted three government officials for unspecified abuses of authority during that period. Details of these cases have not been made public.

Prison conditions reportedly are adequate, if austere. Visits by the International Committee of the Red Cross (ICRC) and the opening of a new prison in Thimphu (in 1994) contributed to improving conditions of detention. However, human rights groups active outside the country maintain that prison conditions outside of the capital city of Thimpu remain oppressive.

The Government and the ICRC signed a new Memorandum of Understanding in September 1998, extending the ICRC prison visits programme for another 5 years. The ICRC conducted two prison visits during the year, as it has done for each of the past 7 years, and was allowed unhindered access.

(d) *Arbitrary Arrest, Detention, or Exile* : Arbitrary arrest and detention remain problems. Under the law, police may not arrest a person without a warrant and must bring an arrested person before a court within 24 hours, exclusive of travel time from place of arrest. However, legal protections are incomplete, due to the lack of a fully developed criminal procedure code and to deficiencies in police training and practice.

Incommunicado detention, particularly of Nepalese refugees returning without authorization, is still known to occur. Incommunicado detention of suspected militants was a serious problem in the early 1990's, but the initiation of ICRC prison visits and the, establishment of an ICRC mail service between detainees and family members has helped to allay this problem. Of those detained in connection with political dissidence and violence in southern areas in 1991-92, 29 continue to serve sentences after conviction by the High Court.

On May 6, Damber Pulami, a refugee living in a camp in Nepal, was arrested in the country. Pulami reportedly was a member of the Youth Organization of Bhutan (the youth wing of the banned Bhutan People's Party) and had gone to the country to check on the internal resettlement of non-Nepalese to the south. Amnesty International (AI) has not received a response to queries about the charges against him, his whereabouts, and his physical condition, although according to one human rights group Pulami is in Chemgang Jail in Thimpu. According to AI, Tul Man Tamang, a 30-year old construction worker was arrested in June on suspicion of organizing political activities. He reportedly was taken to a police station at Chimakothi in Chhukha district where he allegedly was tortured, held incommunicado in a dark cell, and forced to sign a statement saying he was leaving the country voluntarily before being forcibly exiled to India. Ugyen Tenzing, a member of the Druk-Yul Peoples' Democratic Party, reportedly was arrested in Samtse district in June. N.L. Katwal, a central committee member of the Bhutan Gorkha National Liberation Front, was one of more than 55 persons arrested during a demonstration in Phuntsholing in April 2000. In December 2000 he was sentenced to 13 years and 6 months in prison. He was serving his sentence in Chamgang Jail at year's end.

Rongthong Kunley Dorji, former leader of the Druk National Congress (DNC) and United Front for Democracy in Bhutan (UFD), was arrested in India in April 1997, following the issuance of an extradition request by Bhutanese authorities. Human rights groups contend that the charges brought against Dorji by the Bhutanese government are motivated politically and constitute an attempt by the Government to suppress his prodemocracy activities. In June 1998, an Indian court released Dorji on bail but placed restrictions on his movements. Dorj i's extradition case still is pending in the Indian courts and is proceeding slowly. According to a refugee-based human rights group, only one prosecution witness, a Joint Secretary in India's Ministry of External Affairs, has been cross-examined in the last 40 months. The next witness, another Indian government official, is scheduled to testify in February 2002.

In the past, according to AI, many persons have been detained on suspicion of being members or supporters of the DNC. Only one such arrest was reported in 2000 and one during the year, but human rights groups allege that arrest and abuse of refugees returning to the country without authorization continue to occur but go unreported by the Government. There were no peaceful protest marches from India to Bhutan during the year, perhaps due to fear of arrests and deportation, as occurred in previous years after such marches. Persons holding peaceful marches from India to Bhutan charge that in 1999 the Bhutanese police assaulted them, injuring several demonstrators, and then arrested and deported all of the marchers to Nepal (see Section 5). By one estimate, approximately 100 marchers were arrested and deported in 1999. The Government acknowledged that 58 persons whom it described as terrorists were serving sentences at the end of 1998 for crimes including rape, murder, and robbery.

Although the Government does not use exile formally as punishment, many accused political dissidents freed under Government amnesties state that they were released on the condition that they depart the country. Many of them subsequently registered at refugee canips in Nepal. The Government denies this.

(e) *Denial of Fair Public Trial.* There is no written constitution, and the judiciary is not independent of the King. The judicial system consists of district courts and a High Court in Thimphu. Judges are appointed by the King on the recommendation of the Chief Justice and may be removed by the King. Village headmen adjudicate minor offenses and administrative matters.

An Office of Legal Affairs (OLA) was established in March

2000. The responsibilities of the OLA are to conduct state prosecutions, draft and review legislation, and render legal counsel. By September a department head and all staff were in place. The OLA is composed of a Legal Services Division (which eventually is to become the Ministry of Law and Justice) with domestic, international and human rights sections, and a Prosecution Division (which eventually is to become the Attorney General's office), with a criminal section and a civil section.

Criminal cases and a variety of civil matters are adjudicated under a legal code established in the 17th century and revised in 1958 and 1965. State appointed prosecutors file charges and prosecute cases for offenses against the State. In other cases, the relevant organizations and departments of government file charges and conduct the prosecution. Defendants are supposed to be presented with written charges in languages that they understand and given time to prepare their own defense. However, according to some political dissidents this practice is not always followed. In cases where defendants cannot write their own defense, courts assign judicial officers to assist defendants. There were reports that defendants receive legal representation at trial, and that they may choose from a list of 150 government-licensed and employed advocates to assist with their defense; however, it is not known how many defendants actually receive such assistance. A legal education programme gradually is building a body of persons who have received formal training abroad in the law. For example, the Government sends many lawyers to India and other countries for legal training; 54 persons have completed legal studies abroad, and 43 more are enrolled. Village headmen, who have the power to arbitrate disputes, constitute the bottom rung of the judicial system. Magistrates, each with responsibility for a block of villages, can review their decisions. Magistrates' decisions can be appealed to district judges, of which there is one for each of the country's 20 districts. The High Court in Thimphu is the country's supreme court.

Defendants have the right to appeal to the High Court and may make a final appeal to the King, who traditionally delegates the decision to the Royal Advisory Council. Trials are supposed to be conducted in open hearings, but there are allegations that this is not always the case in practice.

Questions of family law, such as marriage, divorce, and

adoption, traditionally are resolved according to a citizen's religion: Buddhist tradition for the majority of the population and Hindu tradition for the ethnic Nepalese. Nonetheless the Government states that there is one formal law that governs these matters.

Some or all of the approximately 75 prisoners serving sentences for offenses related to political dissidence or violence, primarily by ethnic Nepalese during 1991-92, may be political prisoners (see Section 1.e.). On December 17, 1999, the King pardoned 200 prisoners to mark National Day; all reportedly were released. Among them were 40 persons convicted of "antinational" offenses, including Tek Nath Rizal, a prominent ethnic Nepalese dissident, and internationally recognized political prisoner. He was convicted in 1992 of "antinational" crimes, including writing and distributing political pamphlets and attending political meetings. In 2000 Rizal was granted permission to leave the country to receive medical treatment in India. He has since returned to the country. According to AI, property confiscated from Rizal during his arrest has not been restored to him.

Arbitrary Interference with Privacy, Family, Home, or Correspondence

There are no laws providing for these rights. According to human rights groups, police regularly conduct house-to-house searches for suspected dissidents without explanation or legal justification. The Government requires all citizens, including minorities, to wear the traditional dress of the Buddhist majority when visiting Buddhist religious buildings, monasteries, or government offices; in schools, and when attending official functions and public ceremonies.

Section 2 Respect for Civil Liberties, Including:

(a) ***Freedom of Speech and Press*** : The Government restricts freedom of speech, and to a lesser extent freedom of the press. The country's only regular publication is *Kuensel*, a weekly newspaper with a circulation of 15,000. It also reports stories on a daily basis through its on-line edition. *Kuensel* was formerly government-run, and human rights groups in the past stated that government ministries reviewed editorial material and suppressed or changed content. According to the Government, *Kuensel* is independent and is funded entirely through advertising and subscription revenue. Its board

consists of a mix of senior civil servants and private individuals. *Kuensel*, which is published simultaneously in the English, Dzongkha, and Nepali languages, supports the Government but does occasionally report criticism of the King and of government policies in the National Assembly. The Government maintains that there are no restrictions on individuals starting new publications, but that the market is too small to support any. Nepalese, Indian, and other foreign newspapers and magazines are available, but readership is in the hundreds and primarily limited to government officials.

After a 10-year ban on private television reception, in 1999 the Government introduced local television broadcasting with the inauguration of the Bhutan Broadcasting Service. The service broadcasts locally produced and foreign Programmes. In late 1999 the Government began licensing cable operators. There are more than 27 cable providers in the country with more than 10,000 subscribers. A large variety of programming is available, including CNN, and BBC. The Government does not censor cable content. The Government radio station broadcasts each day in the four major languages (Dzongkha, Nepali, English, and Sharchop). The Government inaugurated the country's first Internet service provider, Druknet, in June 1999; it had 1,820 subscribers as of late 2000. There are internet cafes in Thimpu, Phuentsholing and Bumthang. The Government does not censor any content on Druknet except for pornography, which is blocked. There are no reported restrictions on academic freedom.

(b) ***Freedom of Peaceful Assembly and Association*** : The Government restricts freedom of assembly and association. Citizens may engage in peaceful assembly and association only for purposes approved by the Government. Although the Government allows civic and business organizations, there are no legally recognized political parties. The Government regards parties organized by ethnic Nepalese exiles – the Bhutan People's Party (BPP), the Bhutan National Democratic Party (BNDP), and the Druk National Congress-- as "terrorist and antinational" organizations and has declared them illegal. These parties, which seek the repatriation of refugees and democratic reform, do not conduct activities inside the country.

(c) ***Freedom of Religion*** : The Government restricts freedom of religion. The Drukpa branch of the Kagyupa School of Mahayana Buddhism is the state religion. Approximately two-thirds of the population practice either Drukpa Kagyupa or Ningmapa Buddhism.

The Drukpa branch is practiced predominantly in the western and central parts of the country, which are inhabited mainly by ethnic Ngalongs (descendants of Tibetan immigrants who predominate in government and the civil service, and whose cultural norms have been declared to be the standard for all citizens). The Ningmapa school is practiced predominantly in the eastern part of the country, although there are adherents, including the royal family, in other areas. Most of those living in the east are ethnic Sharchops--the descendants of those thought to be the country's original inhabitants. The Government subsidizes monasteries and shrines of the Drukpa sect and provides aid to approximately one-third of the Kingdom's 12,000 monks. The Government also provides financial assistance for the construction of Drukpa Kagyupa and Ningmapa Buddhist temples and shrines. In the early 1990's, the Government provided funds for the construction of new Hindu temples and centers of Sanskrit and Hindu learning and for the renovation of existing temples and places of Hindu learning. The Drukpa branch of Buddhism enjoys statutory representation in the National Assembly (Drukpa monks occupy 10 seats in the 150-member National Assembly) and in the Royal Advisory Council (Drukpa monks hold 2 of the I I seats on the Council); the Drukpa branch is an influential voice on public policy. Citizens of other faiths, mostly Hindus, enjoy freedom of worship but may not proselytize. Followers of religions other than Buddhism and Hinduism generally are free to worship in private homes but may not erect religious buildings or congregate in public. Under the law, conversions are illegal.

Some of the country's few Christians, mostly ethnic Nepalese living in the south, state that they are subject to harassment and discrimination by the Government; local authorities, and non-Christian citizens. The King has declared major Hindu festivals to be national holidays, and the royal family participates in them. Foreign missionaries are not permitted to proselytize, but international Christian relief organizations and Jesuit priests are active in education and humanitarian activities. The Government restricts the import into the country of printed religious matter; only

Buddhist religious texts can be imported. According to dissidents living outside of the country, Buddhist religious teaching, of both the Drukpa Kagyupa and Ningniapa sects is permitted in the schools, but teaching of other religious faiths is not. Applicants for government services sometimes are asked their religion before services are rendered. All government civil servants, regardless of religion, are required to take an oath of allegiance to the King, the country, and the people. The oath does not have religious content, but a Buddhist lama administers it.

(d) ***Freedom of Movement Within the Country, Foreign Travel, Emigration, and Repatriation .*** Citizens traveling in border regions are required to show their citizenship identity cards at immigration check points, which in some cases are located at a considerable distance from what is infect an open border with India. By treaty citizens may reside and work in India.

The country is not a signatory to the 1951 U.N. Convention Relating to the Status of Refugees or its 1967 Protocol (See Section 5). The Government states that it recognizes the right to asylum in accordance with international refugee law; however, the Government has not formulated a policy regarding refugees, asylees, first asylum, or the return of refugees to countries in which they fear persecution.

According to one credible human rights source, until recently the Government systematically arrested and imprisoned Tibetan refugees crossing the border with Tibet. This policy was followed under a tacit agreement with China. So invariable was this policy that Tibetan leaders advised refugees not to use routes of escape through Bhutan, and refugees have not done so for several years. Since Tibetans effectively are the only refugee population seeking first asylum in the country, the issue of first asylum did not arise during the year.

Section 3 Respect for Political Rights: The Right of Citizens to Change their Government

Citizens do not have the right to change their government. The country is a monarchy with sovereign power vested in the King. In 1998 the King devolved his day-to-day executive powers to the Council of Ministers, who are elected by the National Assembly from among themselves, but reserved control of "matters of national sovereignty and national security " for himself. He also introduced term limits for his Council of Ministers and proposed measures to increase the role of the National Assembly in the formation of his Government.

The National Assembly elected a new Council of Ministers and Government in July 1998 to a 5-year term. In July the National Assembly elected six Royal Advisory Councilors. There are elected or partially elected assemblies at the local, district, and national levels, and the Government claims to encourage decentralization and citizen participation. These elections are conducted in much the same way as National Assembly elections. Since 1969 the National Assembly has had the power to remove ministers whom the King appoints, but it never has done so. Political authority ultimately resides in the King, and decisionmaking involves only a small number of officials. Officials subject to questioning by the National Assembly routinely make major decisions, but the National Assembly is not known to have overturned any decisions reached by the King and government officials. Political parties do not exist legally, and the Government discourages their formation as divisive. The Government has banned parties established abroad by ethnic Nepalese (see Section 2.b).

The National Assembly has 150 members. Of these, 105 are elected indirectly by heads of household, 10 are selected by a part of the Buddhist clerg , and the remaining 35 are appointed by the King to represent the Government. The National Assembly, which meets irregularly, has little independent authority. However, there are efforts underway to have the National Assembly meet on a more regular basis, and in recent years the King and the Council of Ministers have been more responsive to the National Assembly's concerns. The procedures for the nomination and election of National Assembly members state that in order to be eligible for nomination as a candidate, a person must be a citizen of Bhutan; be at least 25 years of age; not be married to a foreign national, not have been terminated or compulsorily retired for misconduct from government service; not have committed any act of treason against the King, the populace, and country; have no criminal record or any criminal case pending against him; have respect for the nation's laws, and be able to read and write in Dzongkha (the language, in several dialects, spoken by Bhutanese Buddhists).

Each National Assembly constituency consists of a number of villages. Each village is permitted to nominate one candidate but must do so by consensus. There is no provision for self-nomination, and the law states that no person may campaign for the candidacy or canvass through other means. If more than one village within a constituency puts forward a candidate, an election is conducted by the district development committee, and the candidate obtaining a simple majority of votes cast is declared the winner. Individuals do not have the right to vote, every family in a village is entitled to one Vote in elections. The law does not make clear how a candidate is selected if none achieves a simple majority. However, it does state that in case of a tie among the candidates in the election, selection shall be made through the drawing of lots. The candidate whose name is drawn shall be deemed to be elected.

Human rights activists claim that the only time individual citizens have any involvement in choosing a National Assembly representative is when they are asked for consensus approval of a village candidate by the village headman. The name put to villagers for consensus approval by the headman is suggested to him by district officials, who in turn take their direction from the central Government. Consensus approval takes place at a public gathering. Human rights activists state that there is no secret ballot. The National Assembly enacts laws, approves senior government appointments, and advises the King on matters of national importance. Voting is by secret ballot, with a simple majority needed to pass a measure. The King may not formally veto legislation, but may return bills for further consideration. The Assembly occasionally rejects the King's recommendations or delays implementing them, but in general, the King has enough influence to persuade the Assembly to approve legislation that he considers essential or to withdraw proposals he opposes. The Assembly may question government officials and force them to resign by a two-third vote of no confidence; however, the National Assembly never has compelled any government official to resign. The Royal Civil Service Commission is responsible for disciplining subministerial level government officials and has removed several following their convictions for crimes, including embezzlement.

In 1998 the King issued a decree setting out several measures intended to increase the role of the National Assembly in the formation and dissolution of his Government. The decree, later adopted by the 76th session of the National Assembly, provided that all cabinet ministers are to be elected by the National Assembly and that the roles and responsibilities of the cabinet ministries are to be spelled out. Each cabinet minister is to be elected by simple majority in a secret ballot in the National Assembly from among candidates nominated by the King. The King is to select nominees for cabinet office from among senior government officials holding the rank of secretary or above. The King is to determine the portfolios of his ministers, whose terms are limited to 5 years, after which they must pass a vote of confidence in the National Assembly in order to remain in office. Finally the decree provided that the National Assembly, by a two-thirds vote of no confidence, can require the King to abdicate and to be replaced by the next person in the line of succession. After adopting the decree, the National Assembly elected a new council of ministers consistent with it. Human rights groups maintain that since only the King may nominate candidates for cabinet office, their election by the National Assembly is not a sionificant democratic reform. The King removed himself as Chairman of the Council of Ministers in 1998. Based on an election held in the National Assembly in 1998, Cabinet Ministers who received the most votes rotate the position on a yearly basis. The Chairman of the Council of Ministers serves as Prime Minster and Head of Government. In August Trade and Industry Minister Khundu Wangchuk became Chairman.

The per centage of women in government or politics does not correspond to their numbers in the population. The persistence of traditional gender roles apparently accounts for a low proportion of women in government, although women have made visible gains. A total of 15 women hold seats in the National Assembly, 23 per cent of civil service employees are women, and women hold more than 30 per cent of positions at the Ministry of Foreign Affairs.

There are 105 elected people's representatives in the National Assembly. All major ethnic groups are represented in the National Assembly, including 14 ethnic Nepalese.

Section 4 Governmental Attitude Regarding International and Non-governmental Investigation of Alleged Violations of Human Rights. There are no legal human rights non-governmental organizations (NGO's) in the country. The Government regards human rights groups established by ethnic Nepalese exiles—the Human Rights Organization of Bhutan, the People's Forum for Human Rights in Bhutan, and the Association of Human Rights Activists-Bhutan—as political organizations and does not permit them to operate in the country. AI was permitted to visit in 1998, and later released a report.

ICRC representatives continue twice yearly prison visits, and the Government has allowed them unhindered access to detention facilities, including those in southern districts inhabited by ethnic Nepalese. The chairman and members of the U.N. Human Rights Commission Working Group on Arbitrary Detention have made two visits to the country.

Section 5 Discrimination Based on Race, Sex, Religion, Disability, Language, or Social Status

Ongoing government efforts to cultivate a national identity rooted in the language, religion, and culture of the Ngalong ethnic group restrict cultural expression by other ethnic groups. In the late 1980's and early 1990's, the Government instituted policies designed to preserve the Cultural dominance of the Ngalong ethnic group. It also committed many abuses against the ethnic Nepalese which led to the departure of tens of thousands of them. Many ethnic Nepalese were expelled forcibly, and almost 100,000 of them remain in refugee camps in Nepal. At the time, the Government claimed that it was concerned about the rapid population growth of and political a-itation by the ethnic Nepalese. The Government claims that ethnic and gender discrimination in employment is not a problem. It claims that ethnic Nepalese fill 22 per cent of government jobs, which is slightly less than their proportion of the total population. Bhutanese human rights groups active outside the country claim that ethnic Nepalese actually make up approximately 35 per cent of the country's population and that the Government underreports their number. Women are accorded respect in the traditions of most ethnic groups, although some exile groups claim that gender discrimination is a problem.

Women

There is no evidence that rape or spousal abuse are extensive problems. For example, in 1999 there were 10 reported rapes nationwide. In the south, in the early 1990s, there were widespread reports of the rape of large numbers of ethnic Nepalese women, including by go vernment forces. The Government denied these reports.

In 1996 the National Assembly adopted a revised Rape Act. The law contains a clear definition of criminal sexual assault and specifies penalties. In cases of rape involving minors, sentences range from 5 to 17 years. In extreme cases, a rapist may be imprisoned for life. There are few known instances of sexual harassment.

Women constitute 48 per cent of the population and participate freely in the social and economic life of the country. Approximately 43 per cent of enrollment in school is female. Inheritance law provides for equal inheritance among all sons and daughters, but traditional inheritance practices, which vary among ethnic groups, may be observed if the heirs choose to forego legal challenges. Dowry is not customary, even among ethnic Nepalese Hindus. Among some groups, inheritance practices favoring daughters reportedly account for the large numbers of women who own shops and businesses and for an accompanying tendency of women to drop out of higher education to go into business. However, female school enrollment has been growing in response to government policies. Women increasingly are found among senior officials and private sector entrepreneurs, especially in the tourism industry. Women in unskilled jobs generally are paid slightly less than men.

Polygamy is allowed, provided the first wife gives her permission. Marriages may be arranged by the marriage partners themselves as well as by their parents. Divorce is common. Existing legislation requires that all marriages must be registered; it also favors women in matters of alimony.

Children

The Government has demonstrated its commitment to child welfare by its rapid expansion of primary schools, healthcare facilities, and immunization Programmes. Mortality rates for both infants and children under 5 years dropped significantly since 1989. The Government provides free and compulsory primary school education, and primary school enrollment has increased 9 per cent per year since 199 1, with enrollment of girls increasing at an even higher rate. Government policies aimed at increasing enrollment of girls increased the proportion of girls in primary schools from 39 per cent in 1990 to 45 per cent during the year. In 1999 the participation rate for children in primary schools was estimated at 72 per cent, with the rate of completion of 7 years of schooling at 60 per cent for girls and at 59 per cent for boys. There is no law barring ethnic Nepalese children from attending school. However, most of the 75 primary schools in southern areas heavily populated by ethnic Nepalese that were closed in 1990 remain closed. The closure of the schools acts as an effective barrier to the ability of the ethnic Nepalese in southern areas to obtain a primary education. Exile groups claim that Nepalese students scoring highly on national exams are not always given the same advantages as other students (such as the chance to study abroad at government expense), particularly if they are related to prominent dissidents or refugees. There is no societal pattern of abuse against children. Children enjoy a privileged position in society and benefit from international development Programmes focused on maternal and child welfare. A study by the United Nations Children's Fund (UNICEF) found that boys and girls receive equal treatment regarding nutrition and health care and that there is little difference in child mortality rates between the sexes.

Persons with Disabilities

There is no evidence of official discrimination toward persons with disabilities, but the Government has not passed legislation mandating accessibility for persons with disabilities. Societal discrimination against persons with disabilities remains a problem.

National/Racial/Ethnic Minorities

Ethnic Nepalese have lived in the southern part of the country for centuries, and the early phases of economic development at the turn of the century brought a large influx of additional ethnic Nepalese. Early efforts at national integration focused on assimilation, including financial incentives for intermarriage, education for some students in regions other than their own, and an increase in development funds for the south. However, in the late 1980's, concern over the increase in the population of and political agitation among ethnic Nepalese prompted aggressive government efforts to assert a national culture, to tighten control over southern regions, to control illegal immigration, to expel ethnic Nepalese, and to promote national integration.

Beginning in 1989, more discriminatory measures were introduced, aimed at shaping a new national identity known as Drukpa. Dr Ukpa is based on the customs of the non-ethnic Nepalese Ngalong ethnic group predominant in the western part of the country. Measures included a requirement that national dress be worn for official occasions and as a school uniform, the teaching of Dzongkha is a second language in all schools, and an end to instruction in Nepali as a second language. During the mid- and late 1980's, citizenship became a highly contentious matter. Requirements for citizenship first were formalized in the Citizenship Law of 1958, which granted citizenship to all adults who owned land and had lived in the country for at least 10 years. However, in 1985 a new citizenship law significantly tightened requirements for citizenship and resulted in the denaturalization of many), ethnic Nepalese. The 1985 law required that both parents be citizens in order to confer citizenship on a child, and that persons seeking to prove citizenship through their own or their parents' residency in 1958 be able to prove residency in the country at that time. In many cases, persons were unable to produce the documentation necessary, such as land tax receipts from 1958, to show residency. The law permits residents who lost citizenship under the 1985 law to apply for naturalization if they can prove residence during the 15 years prior to that time. The Government declared all residents who could not meet the new citizenship requirements to be illegal immigrants. Beginning in 1988, the Government expelled large numbers of ethnic Nepalese through enforcement of the new citizenship laws.

The 1985 Citizenship Act also provides for the revocation of the citizenship of any naturalized citizen who "has shown by act or speech to be disloyal in any manner whatsoever to the King, country, and people of Bhutan." The Home Ministry later declared in a circular that any nationals leaving the country to assist "antinationals," and the families of such persons, would forfeit their citizenship. Human rights groups allege that these provisions were used widely to revoke the citizenship of ethnic Nepalese who subsequently were expelled or otherwise departed from the country. In response to the perceived repression, ethnic Nepalese protested, sometimes violently. The protests were led by the Bhutan Peoples' Party (BPP), which advocated full citizenship rights for ethnic Nepalese and for democratic reforms. Characterizing the BPP as a "terrorist" movement backed by Indian sympathizers, the authorities cracked down on its activities and ordered the closure of local Nepalese schools, clinics, and development Programmes after several were raided or bombed by dissidents. There were credible reports that many ethnic Nepalese activists were beaten and tortured while in custody, and that security forces committed acts of rape. There also were credible reports that militants, including BPP members, attacked and killed census officers and other officials, and engaged in bombings.

Local officials took advantage of the climate of repression to coerce ethnic Nepalese to sell their land below its fair value and to emigrate. Beginning in 1991, ethnic Nepalese began to leave southern areas of the country in large numbers and take refuge in Nepal.

Many ethnic Nepalese also were forced to sign "voluntary migration forms" wherein they agreed to leave the country, after local officials threatened to fine or imprison them for failing to comply. According to UNHCR, there were 98,269 ethnic Nepalese refugees in seven refugee camps in eastern Nepal as of June 2000. An additional 15,000 refugees, according to UNHCR estimates, are living outside the camps in Nepal and India.

Ethnic Nepalese political groups in exile complain that the revision of the country's citizenship laws in 1985 denaturalized tens of thousands of former residents of Bhutan. They also complain that the new laws have been applied selectively and make unfair demands for documentation on a largely illiterate group in a country that only recently has adopted basic administrative procedures. They claim that many ethnic Nepalese whose families have been in the country for generations were expelled because they were unable to document their claims to residence. The Government denies this and asserts that a three-member village committee, typically ethnic Nepalese in southern districts, certifies in writing that 4 resident is a Bhutanese citizen in cases where documents cannot be produced.

The Government maintains that many of those who departed the country in the early 1990's were Nepalese or Indian citizens who came to the country after the enactment of the 1958 Citizenship law but were not detected until a census in 1988. The Government also claims that many persons registered in the camps as refugees never may have resided in the country. Finally the Government contends that some ethnic Nepalese left the country voluntarily, thus renouncing their Bhutanese citizenship. Human rights organizations credibly dispute this claim. A royal decree in 1991 made forcible expulsion of a citizen a criminal offense. Nevertheless only three officials ever were punished for abusing their authority during this period (see Section I.c.). According to the UNHCR, the overwhelming majority of refugees who entered the camps since screening began in June 1993 have documentary proof of Bhutanese nationality. Random checks and surveys of camp residents—including both pre-and post-June 1993 arrivals—bear this out.

Since 1994 there has been a series of negotiations between

Nepal and Bhutan to resolve the Bhutanese refugee problem. In late December 2000, the two countries agreed upon a system to verify the nationality of Bhutanese refugees in Nepal in preparation for their return to the country. Refugee verifications began in March. By December all the residents of the first camp had been interviewed, and the Bhutanese verification team went back to Thimpu pending the start of verification at the next camp. Refugee groups are concerned that at the present rate, verification will take several years. Bilateral negotiations on repatriation issues in November failed to arrive at an agreement, and the matter was deferred to a proposed future session of ministerial-level talks. In 1996, 1998, and 1999, refugees held a series of "peace marches" from Nepal to Bhutan to assert their right to return to Bhutan. The marchers charged that the Bhutanese police assaulted them during each march, injuring several demonstrators, and then arrested and deported all of the marchers. A resolution adopted by the National Assembly in 1997 prohibits the still-resident family members of ethnic Nepalese refugees from holding jobs with the Government or in the armed forces. Under the resolution, those holding such jobs were to be retired involuntarily. The Government made clear that for the purposes of this resolution, a family member would be defined as a parent, a child, a sibling, or a member of the same household. The Government states that 429 civil servants, many of them ethnic Nepalese, were retired compulsorily in accordance with the resolution, and that the program was abrogated in November 1997. The Government states that those forced to retire were accorded retirement benefits in proportion to their years of government service.

The Government also began a program in 1998 of resettling Buddhist Bhutanese from other regions of the country on land in the southern part of the country vacated by the ethnic Nepalese living in refugee camps in Nepal. Human rights groups maintain that this action prejudices any eventual outcome of negotiations over the return of the refugees to the country. The Government maintains that this is not its first resettlement program and that Bhutanese citizens who are ethnic Nepalese from the south sometimes are resettled on more fertile land in other parts of the country. The failure of the Government to permit the return of ethnic Nepalese refugees has tended to reinforce societal prejudices against this group, as has the Government's policy on the forced retirement of refugee family members in government service and the resettlement of Buddhists on land vacated by expelled ethnic Nepalese in the south.

Section 6 Worker Rights

(a) *The Right of Association* Trade unions are not permitted, and there are no labour unions. Workers do not have the right to strike, and the Government is not a member of the International Labour Organization. The Government maintains that, with very little industrialization, there is little labour to be organized.

(b) *The Right to Organize and Bargain Collectively.* There is no collective bargaining in industry. Industry accounts for approximately 25 per cent of the GDP, but employs only a minute fraction of the total work force. The Government affects wages in the manufacturing sector through its control over wages in state owned industries. There are no export processing zones.

(c) *Prohibition of Forced or Compulsory Labour.* 'The Government prohibits forced or compulsory labour, and there were no reports that such practices occurred. There is no evidence to suggest that domestic workers are subjected to coerced or bonded labour. The law does not specifically prohibit forced and bonded labour by children, but there were no reports that such practices occur.

(d) *Status of Child Labour Practices and Minimum Age for Employment.* The law sets the minimum age for employment at 18 years for citizens and 20 years for noncitizens. A UNICEF study suggested that children as young as 11 years sometimes are employed with roadbuilding teams, which usually are made up of non-Bhutanese guest workers. Children often do agricultural work and chores on family farms. The law specifically does not prohibit forced and bonded labour by children, but such practices are not known to occur (see Section 6.c.). The country has not ratified ILO Convention 182 on the Worst Forms of Child Labour; however, as a state party to the U.N. Convention on the Rights of the Child, the Government supports the provisions contained therein. The country lacks a large pool of ready labour; for major projects, such as road works, the Government brings in hired labourers from India.

(e) *Acceptable Conditions of Work.* A circular that went into effect in 1994 established wage rates, rules and regulations for labour recruiting agencies, and the regulations for payment of workmen's compensation. Wage rates are revised periodically, and range upward from a minimum of roughly $2.50 (100 ngultrums) per day plus various allowances paid in cash or kind. This minimum wage provides a decent standard of living for a worker and family. The workday is defined as 8 hours with a 1hour lunch break. Work in excess of this must be paid at one and one-half times normal rates. Workers paid on a monthly basis are entitled to I day's paid leave for 6 days of work and 15 days of leave annually. The largest salaried work force is the government service, which has an administered wage structure last revised in 1988 but supplemented by special allowances and increases. The last such increase was in 1999. According to the latest Census of Manufacturing Industries, only 38 industrial establishments employ more than 50 workers. Smaller industrial units include 39 plants of medium size, 345 small units, 832 cottage industry units, and 2,154 "mini" units. The Government favours family-owned farms. Land laws prohibit a farmer from selling his or her last 5 acres and require the sale of holdings in excess of 25 acres. This, along with the country's rugged geography, results in a predominantly self-employed agricultural workforce. Workers are entitled to free medical care within the country. Cases that cannot be dealt with in the country are flown to other countries (usually India) for treatment. Workers are eligible for compensation for partial or total disability, and in the event of death their families are entitled to compensation. Existing labour regulations do not grant workers the right to remove themselves from work situations that endanger health and safety without jeopardizing their continued employment.

(f) *Trafficking in Persons.* The law does not specifically prohibit trafficking in persons; however, there were no reports that persons were trafficked to, from, or within the country.

Amnesty International Country Report December 2000

Amid increased international attention, there was a breakthrough in negotiations between Bhutan and Nepal on the right of almost 100,000 Nepali speaking people in refugee camps in eastern Nepal to return to Bhutan. Torture by police was reported.

Leaders of political parties in exile were reportedly arrested on their return.

Background

Finance Minister Yeshi Zimba took office as Chairman to the Council of Ministers in August. A new system of "security clearance certificates", issued by the Royal Bhutan Police, replaced "no objection certificates" and "police clearance certificates". However, there were continuing concerns that members of the Nepali-speaking community would continue to face discrimination when applying for such certificates in order to be able to obtain work, promotion or business licences or to travel abroad, on the basis that they had contacts with "antinationals" in refugee camps in Nepal. As part of strengthening the country's legal framework, new charge-sheets were introduced on which police must enter the sections of the law under which a person is to be charged.

Nepali-speaking Refugees

Several high-level delegations visited the country to discuss with the authorities the plight of people living in refugee camps in Nepal since the early 1990s. Among them were US State Department officials who visited in January and December.

After her visit in April, the UN High Commissioner for Refugees reported that Bhutan was ready to proceed with joint verification of people living in the camps to determine their eligibility for inclusion in a future voluntary repatriation programme. However, in May the ninth round of ministerial talks between Bhutan and Nepal failed to reach agreement. Bhutan's position was that individuals over the age of 18 should be verified individually while Nepal wanted the unit of verification to be the head of the family. A compromise formula, put forward by the High Commissioner was initially rejected by Bhutan. In late December, Nepal and Bhutan finally reached an agreement on the mechanisms and unit of verification. A joint verification team - consisting of five officials from each government - was mandated to first validate the family units and then proceed to verify heads of families and individual units.

In September the European Parliament passed a resolution calling on "the Governments of Bhutan and Nepal, in cooperation with all parties involved, to reach an agreement which will allow the early and voluntary repatriation of the refugees to their country of origin".

Torture

Torture by police was reported. Tul Man Tamang, a 30-year-old construction worker, was arrested on 27 June on suspicion of organizing political activities. He was taken to the police station at Chimakothi in. Chhukha district where he was allegedly kicked and beaten with a cane, leather belt and rifle butt on his back, legs and buttocks. He was reportedly held incommunicado in a dark cell for three days before being taken to the police station at Phuntsholing on the border with India. He was forced to sign a statement saying he was leaving the country of his own free will and was forcibly exiled to India.

Arrests of Politicians

Several leaders of political parties in exile who returned to Bhutan were arrested. Some remained held at the end of the year. N.L. Katwal, a central committee member of the Bhutan Gorkha National Liberation Front, was reportedly among more than 50 people arrested during a demonstration in Phuntsholing in April. Ugyen Tenzing, a member of the Druk-Yul Peoples Democratic Party, was reportedly arrested in Samtse district in June and taken to Thimphu police headquarters.

5

Women's Participation in Government

The process of all-round development of Bhutan in terms of both the beneficiaries and the contributors - is women. Women population, which comprises almost half of the total population in Bhutan, has been so far neglected, discriminated and exploited. They have been deprived of most of the opportunities including access to business and industry, gainful employment, skill development training, education, health etc. They do not have access to education, gainful employment, economic resources, political process and decision-making institutions. Their representation at the policy and decision making bodies is negligible. In total, the status of women is very low in Bhutan. The social attitudes, traditional practices and outlook against women have contributed to the exploitation of women.

This has made Bhutanese women lacking in confidence in handling the issues generally affecting themselves even in their day-to-day life. The situation in Bhutan is such that majority of women are not even aware of their basic rights. The practice of discrimination, gender-inequality and exploitation of women are not sudden emergence in the Asian societies. These are the legacy of the past feudal societies.

Bhutan is still a feudal and autocratic society. Therefore, the presence of discrimination, gender inequality and exploitation of women in one or other form is the main characteristics of feudal society of Bhutan. Bhutanese patriarchal system reflects male supremacy making women subservient to men. Government has made no efforts to protect and promote women's rights even though it has ratified the International Convention on the

Elimination of All Forms of Discrimination Against Women. Participation by women in national life is almost nil. Women have least access to higher post in the government. They have never been appointed as Ministers, Judges, Chief District Officers, Ambassadors or to other senior important posts.

Women comprising around 49 % of the population have least access to gainful employment. They do not have economic autonomy. More than 95 % women are illiterate and are engaged in traditional agricultural farming.

The government has done nothing to improve their lot. Less than 0.5% women are employed in the civil service (bureaucracy). They are mostly employed in lower level jobs like, telephone operators, typists, clerks etc. Less than 0.5% women are engaged in business. Around 0.2% are engaged in other occupation and 3.5% of women have no identifiable occupation. The plight of rural women is worse. They are most neglected lot.

Sexual exploitation, illiteracy, superstition, disease, child mortality and ignorance are rampant in the rural villages. The real condition of women do not come to the light of the foreigners. Bhutan does not have newspaper, its only weekly bulletin is owned by the government. The external media is not allowed to Bhutan. Whereas, the government churns out glossy picture of the economic indicators in the international forums. They are only meant for the consumption of international community without reality.

Bhutanese refugee women and children constitute around 49% and 40% of the total refugee population in exile. Hundreds of women were raped during the army crackdown after peaceful protests in 1990. While male members were jailed for joining the peaceful rallies, women folk were abused, tortured and terrorised to flee the country. A number of reports prepared by the International human rights organisations, like, Amnesty International, IMADAR, Japan depicted cases of torture, dishonour and rape of Bhutanese women by the security forces.

Marriage Act

In 1980, the government of Bhutan simultaneously introduced the new Marriage Act which had an even larger content of discrimination against *Lhotshampa* women and their children. The Act declared all foreign wives of the Bhutanese citizens as non-citizens, even though most of them were granted citizenship under previous citizenship laws.

In contravention of all international norms and civilised behaviour, the Government denied several thousand children (born out of marriages between *Lhotshampa* husbands and Nepali speaking wives from Nepal or India) of their right to nationality. They were evicted along with their parents. This Act was only enforced against the *Lhotshampas.*

The Marriage Act was enacted in 1980 and was forcefully implemented in 1983 to especially target the wives of *Lhotshampas.* This discriminatory law imposes a number of denial of benefits to those who married non-Bhutanese wives. The *Lhotshampas* who married non-Bhutanese wife did not have the right to vote in (became ineligible for election to) the National Assembly (Parliament) elections, they were denied promotion in civil services, denied training and fellowships and medical treatment abroad, they were also denied business and agricultural grants and loans given by the government and could not avail of government supplied fertilisers, seeds and farm machineries on subsidies. They could not get jobs in the Foreign Service and Armed Forces.

This posed enormous problems for the *Lhotshampas*. There are many reasons as to why the *Lhotshampa* chose foreign wives of their own ethnic groups from Nepal and India. Some reasons are enumerated as follows:

Bhutan stepped out of its isolation in the mid-sixties. The government did not encourage cultural socialization of various ethnic groups. Some ethnic groups were not allowed to own properties in the ruling Ngalung dominated areas. Even in-country migration was restricted. In-country travel was also restricted for some ethnic groups The transport and communications were also not developed. This led to the cultural isolation of various ethnic groups. Thus, each ethnic group developed their own intra-ethnic group matrimonial alliances. *Lhotshampas* had a wide ethnic area in Darjeeling, Sikkim and Nepal to choose their spouse from. As a result many *Lhotshampas* got their spouses from their own ethnic groups from these places. The most important factor that prevented the encouragement of inter-ethnic group matrimonial alliances is culture.

The Lhotshampas are by and large Hindus. Culturally and

traditionally, the Lhotshampas are entirely different from ruling Ngalung ethnic group. Their language is a dialect of or is derived from Sanskrit, the oldest language. They prefer to live in the hot climate of the southern foot hills. The Ngalungs are nurtured in Drukpa Kargyupa Buddhist culture. They speak Tibetan stock Dzonkha language which is entirely different from Nepali. They wear robe like dresses and prefer to live in cool climate of the north. While strict cultural values of the Lhotshampas triggered the search for wives from outside Bhutan, limited domestic society and geography also facilitated such marriages.

The lack of communication and infrastructure within Bhutan were also factors which made *Lhotshampas* get their wives from neighbouring Indian states and Nepal as it is easier to travel to neighbouring countries than to visit other districts of Bhutan. Because of the lack of roads, Bhutanese are required to travel through India to reach from east to west in the south and south to north. Darjeeling district had excelled as a centre of education during the British rule in India. It is still regarded as the best place for education in the entire region of Bhutan, Nepal and Northeast India. Jesuit fathers and Christian missionaries established the best schools in Darjeeling.

Due to the absence of good schools and colleges throughout the sixties, seventies and the eighties in Bhutan, the government used to send young Bhutanese for studies to Darjeeling on Indian government scholarships. Most *Lhotshampa* students married with their schoolmates of their own ethnic community from Darjeeling, Sikkim and Nepal.. Bhutan does not have enough colleges to cater to the need of students. Its only college is affiliated with Delhi University.

Therefore, Bhutanese students have no alternatives but to go to Darjeeling as it is less expensive to study in neighbouring Darjeeling than in Delhi or Calcutta. As a consequence of increasing developmental activities after 1960 more opportunities were being created for educated people in the government services and in the private sector. Bhutan has a very low literacy rate. The available manpower was not sufficient to meet the demand. As a result, educated *Lhotshampa* took educated and conscious wives of their own ethnicity from neighbouring countries, who could work in the offices or do businesses and earn money.

There was neither a Marriage Act or Citizenship Laws

forbidding a Bhutanese marrying a foreign wife then. The laws were enacted later with retroactive effect. Had there been such laws, probably no Bhutanese would have married a foreign spouse. The Royal Government's senseless action of implementing these laws shows its irresponsibility and indifference towards its citizens' difficulties. It is a well-planned conspiracy to depopulate southern Bhutan. In any case, marriage is too personal a matter for the state to intervene.

Both the Citizenship Act and the Marriage Act are racist, biased and discriminatory against *Lhotshampa* women of southern Bhutan. Moreover, the law is also implemented in a discriminatory manner; very rigidly against the *Lhotshampa*s and not at all against Ngalung/Drukpas, who for example have a Chinese, English, Italian or American wives. For example, Mr. Ugen Tshering, a Drukpa married to an Italian wife in the early eighties has today been promoted as Foreign Secretary.

Similarly, the then Chief Justice of the High Court was promoted even though he had an English wife. Today, of course, aside from bringing about a denial of benefits, marriage to non-Bhutanese wife has resulted in the very denial of citizenship rights to the Lhotshampa husbands. Both the Citizenship Law, 1985 and the Marriage Acts have stripped several thousand Lhotshampas of their nationality.

As a consequences of not granting citizenship to the foreign wives of Lhotshampa husbands, more than 60,000 children were deprived of their rightful claim to Bhutanese citizenship. This is more than 20 percent of the total children population of Bhutan. Refugee children constitute about 10 percent of the country's total population of around 767,000 of Bhutan. More than 10,000 Lhotshampa wives are deprived of their right to nationality. The government must repeal the discriminatory Citizenship Act, 1985 and the Marriage Act. It must enact new citizenship and marriage laws conforming to the international standards, and protect the right to nationality of all its citizens

Discriminatory issues in Bhutan

The roots of the current political crisis in Bhutan and the refugees lie in Bhutan's geopolitics and population politics. A study of various policies of the Royal Government of Bhutan (RGOB) in the last two decades reflects the Ngalung/Drukpa dominated government's motive to uproot Nepali speaking Lhotshampa population from Bhutan and reduce their number by all means. Be it Drukpanization or Bhutanization programmes, Citizenship and Marriage Acts or NOCs/PCCs, all are directed against Lhotshampas of the south. It was a long standing and intrinsic ruling elites' security perception that the domestic demand for political change (democracy) would come from the Lhotshampas in the south. The south is bordered by the democratic India.

Moreover, the Lhotshampas are economically well-off and more educated than their brethren in the north and east. The northern borders with China is closed. In order to pre-empt the demand for democracy, the government devised a clever strategy to depopulate the Lhotshampas from southern Bhutan. Hence, the Lhotshampas suddenly became the geopolitical scapegoats and security threat to the absolute monarchy. Thus, the government devised various strategies to bring about a favourable demographic balance favouring a Drukpa/Ngalung nation by reducing the number of Lhotshampas to around 25% and to prevent the demand for democracy from southern Bhutan.

The failed implementation of the forced assimilation policies reinforced this insecurity. This resulted in denationalization, deprivation and virtual confiscation. of Lhotshampa citizenship rights through manipulation of the Citizenship Act and through changing the definition of citizenship. The current political crisis and the refugee problems owe their origin to the enactment of two racist and discriminatory laws, viz., Citizenship Act of 1985 and Marriage Act of 1977 and implementation of a number of racist and discriminatory policies. These laws and policies were designed to reduce the number of Lhotshampa population and their mass eviction.

Citizenship Act

Bhutan's first attempt to define its citizenship came with National Law of Bhutan, 1958. The regime enacted a new Citizenship Act, 1985. This Act was given a retrospective implementation of thirty years, that is, from 1958. It declared 31 December, 1958 as the cut-off year for granting citizenship. The Act was forcefully implemented in 1988. The wives of Bhutanese citizens married from outside the country and children born of such parents were not granted citizenship and were deprived of their legitimate citizenship status. This Act defined three criteria for granting of citizenship: by birth, by registration, and through naturalisation. This Act is the origin of the refugee problems and the looming danger of statelessness for Lhotshampas.

The National Law, 1958 prescribed 'fatherhood' as the criteria for granting citizenship-which is normal. But the new Act repealed the previous citizenship law and prescribed 'parenthood' as the sole criteria for grant of citizenship by birth, thus denying citizenship to anyone whose mother was married from outside the country, even if the mother was granted citizenship according to previous law.

Since the Act was given a retrospective implementation of 1958, all children born of a marriage between a Bhutanese father and a non-Bhutanese mother, between 1958 to 1988 were declared non-citizens and so-called 'illegal' and 'economic migrants'. The National Assembly in1988 confirmed 14,442 marriages between a Bhutanese citizen and a non-citizen during last twenty years. The number was too insignificant for the government to grant citizenship rights.

Article 3 of the Act codified a new basis for granting citizenship - a proof of residence in Bhutan since before December 31, 1958 was required. It says that " A person permanently domiciled in Bhutan on or before 31st December, 1958, and, whose name is registered in the census register maintained by the Ministry of Home Affairs shall be deemed to be a citizen of Bhutan by registration".

The government subsequently brought all Lhotshampas under the purview of citizenship by registration only. They were considered citizens by registration and not by birth, even though they were born and reared in Bhutan since the 17th century much before the establishment of the current ruling Wangchuchk dynasty in 1907 and granted citizenship by previous laws.

The Act arbitrarily imposes an impossible burden upon the Lhotshampas of providing the documentary evidence of their presence in Bhutan on 31 December, 1958, while the other ethnic groups did not have to prove anything to retain their citizenship. The government insisted on production of documents such as land tax receipts only of 1958. Documents of earlier years including the citizenship certificates issued on the basis of previous laws were arbitrarily rejected. The proper census record maintained by Chief District Officer were arbitrarily rejected.

The government was fully aware that the requirements of

the new Act just did not exist then in Bhutan and that most of the Lhotshampas would not be able to fulfil them. The Act demands that the person concerned must prove that his name was registered in the census register, though the register was maintained by the government. The government demand is not only ridiculous but totally unjustified since, the Council of Ministers including the Ministry of Home responsible for maintaining the census register was itself created in 1968. The enumeration in the census record was started only in 1972.

Following the first census of 1981, all citizens were issued with citizenship identity cards. The Foreigners were issued with alien cards and the non-national labours were issued with contract permits. By 1982 all people in Bhutan were registered.

Bhutanese government initially claimed that any documentary evidence whatsoever, land ownership deeds or documents showing sale, gift, and inheritance of land, tax receipts of any kind etc., showing that the person concerned was resident in Bhutan in 1958 is taken as conclusive proof of citizenship.

But later the government contended that payment of property tax in itself is hardly a proof of Bhutanese citizenship. This is especially unfair since some of the documentary proof required by the census team just did not exist in the year 1958, i.e., enumeration in the census records. Those who could not produce the documentary evidence of their presence on 31 December, 1958 were declared illegal immigrants. How is it possible for illiterate villagers to keep documents that will be demanded by the government after 30 years.

Moreover, government had already issued citizenship certificates to all Lhotshampas making the safe keeping of the documents unimportant. The Act was also discriminatorily enforced against the Lhotshampas and not at all against other ethnic groups. Many Ngalungs have Italian, English, Chinese and Singaporean wives, but they do not have to prove anything. However, the law prescribes a number of discriminatory criteria against the wives of Lhotshampas from Nepal or India and their children.

They are treated at par with aliens seeking for naturalisation. Under the naturalisation process, these wives must prove their prior residence of 15-20 years in Bhutan. A child born of such mothers needs to reach the age of fifteen when he/she may apply for naturalisation. The Act was applied in an arbitrary manner to create mass statelessness. The dissidents accused of speaking or criticising the king's government was stripped of citizenship.

Many Lhotshampas were deprived of their nationality for having fled Bhutan to escape suppression, because their fleeing amounts to disloyalty to the state according to the regime.

The Act enabled the government to claim that the refugees are not Bhutanese citizens. The authorities confiscated the documentary evidences, particularly the citizenship identification card and land documents issued to them by the government. It was a well planned strategy and conspiracy of the government to depopulate and reduce the number of Lhotshampas. No appeal on the subject was allowed. The Act also forbids the return of citizens leaving the country. Since the government alleges that refugees have voluntarily emigrated to Nepal, their return will not be possible until this Act is repealed. Even, the European Parliament's resolution has urged Bhutan to amend this Act for the return of refugees. After enacting a draconian Citizenship Act in 1985 to reduce the Lhotshampa population, the government simultaneously introduced the new Marriage Act which had an even larger content of discrimination against Lhotshampa women and their children. The Act declared all foreign wives of the Bhutanese citizens as non-citizens, even though most of them were granted citizenship under previous citizenship laws.

In contravention of all international norms and civilised behaviour, the Royal Government denied several thousand children (born out of marriages between Lhotshampa husbands and Nepali speaking wives from Nepal or India) of their right to nationality. They were evicted along with their parents. This Act was only enforced against the Lhotshampas.

Gender Issues

Bhutanese women comprise 48 percent of the population and play a major role in the development of the country. They do not suffer from gender discrimination, as they have equal status with men and enjoy the same level of freedom under the law. Indeed, property inheritance laws are particularly favourable to women, and most households are headed by women. Women's participation in decision making at community meetings is as high as 70 percent.

The percentage is lower at district and block levels, but

participation is being actively promoted at those levels and is increasing. Representation in the National Assembly and employment in government service have a high percentage of men but these imbalances were mostly due to low girl's school enrolment in the past, when education facilities were often located far from their place of domicile.

These imbalances have been slowly improved through the vast expansion of school facilities all over the country particularly in the 1990s. However, some gender imbalance exists in the secondary school enrolment rates. In terms of vocational and tertiary education, there is still marked imbalance. Despite the absence of gender discrimination in Bhutan, and the approximate and improving balance found in many areas of social life, there are a number of issues that impact severely on women.

Education for Women

The Bhutan government provides free education to the people in Bhutan. The primary school enrolment ratio had reached 72 percent (over 100,000 children) by 1999-up from 12 percent in 1980 and from 25 percent as recently as 1990-which suggests that a 95 percent ratio may be reached in 2002 and universal primary enrolment soon after that. Girls now comprise some 45 percent of primary schoolchildren, or over 60 percent of the gross enrolment ratio, and they tend to have lower dropout rates than primary school boys. Aside from such quantitative improvements, both the quality and the internal efficiency of primary education have improved.

A curriculum known as the New Approach to Primary Education, introduced in the mid-1980s and extended to all primary schools in 1993, seeks to provide a curriculum based on Bhutanese values and circumstances and to develop skills that are useful to those who leave school at the end of their primary education. The survival rate in primary school increased from 35 percent in 1987 to 64 percent in 1998.

As a result of these improvements, the adult literacy rate rose from 17 percent in 1977 to 23 percent in 1980, 38 percent in 1990, and 54 percent in 1998. However, the adult rate is only 28 percent for women, and is particularly low - even 10 percent - in some of the more remote rural areas. The situation is being addressed through nonformal education programs. Secondary education has also expanded rapidly, although a shortage of trained, competent teachers at these higher levels remains a major constraint to faster growth.

Even so, the Government has built new secondary schools, recruited expatriate teachers (mainly from India) and, importantly, expanded boarding facilities (now covering 23,366 students) as an inducement to rural students generally and to girls in particular. The gender balance is about 53:47 in favour of boys in junior high schools, 57:43 in high schools, and 52:48 in private schools. At tertiary and vocational levels, males dominate. Notwithstanding the major improvements in basic education facilities, the country faces an acute shortage of skilled and semiskilled workers.

The problems thus far have been that the technical and vocational training system has not been demand-driven, the quality of training provided has not been up to the required standard, the institutions offering training have been weak, and job seekers with even basic educational qualifications have been reluctant to accept training for many vocational occupations or trades. The problems are being addressed as a matter of urgency by the Government, with the assistance of ADB and other aid agencies. But inadequate technical skills will continue to be a major barrier to reduced dependence on expatriate labour, to industrial growth, and to the local, productive absorption of an expanding population.

Major environmental concerns relate to (i) the high rates of population growth resulting in increasing pressure on the natural resource base, especially on land resources (with negative impacts in terms of land degradation and soil erosion as all arable lands are currently utilized and new marginal lands are being brought under cultivation); (ii) additional risks of land degradation and diminished regeneration capacity of pastures and forests, due to higher demand for livestock products and possible increases in overgrazing; (iii) higher deforestation risks, due to population growth and related demands in terms of fuelwood, materials, and nonwood forest products; (iv) increased risks of soil erosion due to rapid and improper road network development; (v) high rural-urban migration flows and increasing pressure on the already poor urban infrastructures and adjacent land resources, especially in terms of inadequate solid waste management and sanitation systems; (vi) possible negative effects on the environment and cultural integrity that could result from rapid and unplanned tourism development; and (vii) additional possible negative impacts due to industrialization, water resources development (including hydropower), and the indiscriminate growth of mining activities.

Recognizing the need to achieve sustainable development, the Government established the National Environmental Committee in 1989 with a broad mandate in environmental planning and management: overall responsibility for the introduction of regulations, standards, and administrative procedures to control pollution, preserve natural resources, and achieve sustainable development.

Accordingly, in the past decade, the Government undertook a number of activities, including the preparation of the National Environment Strategy (NES) and the implementation of a program for institutionalizing and strengthening the environmental assessment process in the country. Various line agencies have started to revise rules and regulations in their areas of responsibility to incorporate the different environmental requirements, including environmental impact assessment (EIA) procedures.

Another piece of environmental legislation, the Forest and Nature Conservation Act, was approved in 1995. More recently, the Government embarked on a comprehensive exercise to further upgrade its environmental management capacities by establishing additional environmental institutions and administrative mechanisms to prepare for the introduction of the required regulatory and strategy/policy implementation framework. Major efforts are now focusing on:

(i) the rapid formulation of the National Environmental Action Plan to implement the recommendations of the NES;
(ii) effective implementation of the recently adopted Environmental Impact Assessment Act;
(iii) adoption of a comprehensive (umbrella) environmental act (the National Environment Protection Act); and
(iv) the gradual but firm introduction of policy measures and institutional programs to improve the enforcement of environmental regulations, environmental monitoring, interagency coordination, and the overall mainstreaming of environmental concerns into the economic planning

and investment decisionmaking process, also through the adoption of market-based instruments.

While economic development in Bhutan will continue to be based mainly on hydropower, wood, agriculture, minerals, and services, major development constraints relate to (i) potential competition for alternative land and water uses; (ii) topographical factors increasing the cost of power, transport, and communications; and (iii) limited access to and supply of raw materials located in remote areas. In consideration of such key environmental constraints, there is a strong need to incorporate and integrate environmental management criteria in the overall development planning, decision-making, and industrial policy formulation process.

6

National Policy

Women in Bhutan have been mostly involved in activities related to housekeeping, agriculture, animal husbandry and cottage industries but they also play as vital a role as men in the rural and urban economy. Women own a slightly smaller area than men, 2.4 acres per household compared to 3.0 acres. As for other farm assets, women own almost the same number of cattle, draught cattle, milch cows and pack animals. Since they generally inherit land, and they have been making substantial contributions to meeting their families basic needs for food, clothing, housing and health care. The socio-economic position of women in Bhutan is strong in terms of women's influence on intra-household decisions and their ownership of assets. Women in Bhutan score high compared to most developing countries.

Bhutan Development Finance Corporation (BDFC)

The only programme worth noting is the Rural Credit Programme launched by the Bhutan Development Finance Corporation (BDFC) in 1982, which provides rural credit facilities. During the first 12 years of continuous operation in the rural financial scene, BDFC provided loans to several thousand clients and as of 31 December 1993 its total loan disbursement under the programme stood at Nu. 96.03 million.

Women obtained loans mostly for weaving, purchase of seasonal agricultural inputs and livestock, vegetable cultivation, tailoring and knitting. The BDFC's Rural Credit Programme provides credit services to both sexes through its network of 20 District Branch Offices located in each and every district headquarter. A close examination of the fully computerised Management Information System (MIS) of BDFC reveals that women constitute only 32 per cent of the total number of active clients of BDFC. The past due amounts (27 per cent) and portfolio areas (16.6 per cent) of female clients were also smaller than that of male clients. These observations indicate that Bhutanese women are better repayers of loans than men and thus it is also possible that they could be more creditworthy than male clients on the average.

The single biggest problem confronting BDFC now remains to be that of low recovery rates. Low recovery rates not only result in suspension of accrued interest income, but it also makes it necessary for the corporation to put aside substantial amounts for provisions for the past due loans as per the Prudential Guidelines of the Royal Monetary Authority.

To check further growth of the bad debt base, freezing of new loan disbursement is currently imposed in Gewogs or Blocks that do not achieve the minimum average on-time recovery rate of the particular Dzongkhag as of 31 December of the preceding year or a cut off-rate of 40 per cent, whichever is higher. By this arrangement blocks, which have lower recovery rates than the district average recovery rate of the previous year end of the minimum cut-off rate of 40 per cent become ineligible for fresh loans, till the Block recovery rate is improved to this minimum level.

As when this is achieved, the block becomes eligible for a new loan. This freezing arrangement is expected to not only enhance the recovery rates and increase the sustainability of the rural credit operations, but it is also intended to instill financial and credit discipline among clients and public representatives. The rural credit programmes have made a significant difference in improving the incomes and quality of life of rural communities, especially women, directly or indirectly.

Extension of credit facilities have not only enabled women to be more receptive to new technologies, but improved practices of farming, utilisation of new seeds, seedlings or-plants, and application of fertilisers and plant protection chemicals, have also made it possible for them to actually obtain and use the various new extension packages developed. The credit facilities also indirectly helped the rural clients by enhancing the success of extension programmes, which are geared to boost the production, productivity and income levels of the people.

Women's credit programmes

The Rural Credit Programme (RCP) of BDFC are funded by resources received from various donors such as UNCDF, IFAD, ADB and HELVETAS besides the revolving fund loan provided by the Royal Monetary Authority. In spite of several teething problems faced initially, the RCP has now gained a good momentum and is operating satisfactorily after proper streamlining and strengthening of the manage-ment system of the BDFC. The increased credit demand is attributed to two major factors:

- Increased loan recovery rates which have enhanced the eligibility of more Gewogs or Blocks and its clients in all the districts;
- Enhanced loan ceilings from Nu. 20,000 to Nu. 50,000 during the later half of 1992. While the actual credit demand would spiral in the years to come with serious efforts made to improve clients services, client- institution relationships, lending coverage and volume, recovery rates and overall accountability, and the availability of additional resources for further on-lending would become a constraint as the flow of donor funds are getting phased out and there is little or no possibility of obtaining fresh funds from new sources.

The BDFC is required to mobilise the necessary financial resources from other possible sources. Of all the alternatives which are available, the savings mobilisation scheme tends to offer the most potential for supplementing a certain portion of fund deficit for on-lending. There are several advantages to the introduction of the savings and mobilisation scheme.

The BDFC is already providing credit services nation-wide through its branch offices in all the 20 Dzongkhags with a minimum of two staff members in each Dzongkhag and incurring certain overhead costs irrespective of the volume of workload and profitability of the branches.

Introduction of a savings mobilisation scheme could increase the cost effectiveness of the entire operations, making it a really viable undertaking. With the existing network of branch offices in all the Dzongkhag headquarters, the BDFC has a good and wide coverage of the countryside and clients are also well aware of its operations and functions. The Bank of Bhutan which is the only bank in the country does not provide banking services in all the Dzongkhags. This justifies that a second financial insti-tution like the BDFC should provide a savings mobilisation scheme nationwide. The services provided by the Bank of Bhutan are very poor and inadequate and the situation would not improve unless the BDFC or any second financial institution competes for the business.

Like in most countries, where both credit and savings services are usually provided by the same financial institution, it would be convenient for the clients as well as the BDFC if it provides both credit and savings services. Access to credit facilities is in fact a precondition to mobilisation of savings, especially among the rural people as they should be provided first with some cash in hand to understand and think to save a portion of it. Therefore, increasing the access of women to formal credit facilities could have very positive bearing on the quantum of savings that may be mobilised.

Provision of larger amounts of loans to women, both in terms of increased number of clients and loan sizes, would enhance the productivity and income of women, which in turn could further facilitate new investments for generation of additional incomes.

The additional income thus generated and earned could provide them the opportunity and the means to save. Having a certain amount of savings, in turn, could further increase their creditworthiness, which generally increases their chances for obtaining bigger loans for larger investment that are expected to result in higher profits and cash flows that would end in more savings to be mobilised.

Women's Access to Financial Institutions

The financial institutions have been extending liberal credit facilities and services nationwide, especially the rural credit programme by the Bhutan Development Finance Corporation (BDFC). However, there are certain impedi-ments which restrict the access of women to credit facilities offered by the financial institutions.

Out of 9,652 active clients of the nationwide BDFC implemented Rural Credit Programme, there were only 3,044 female clients (32 per cent) as against 6,608 male clients (68 per cent). One that pertains to the woman client's own individual limitations, and the other to conditions enforced by the financial institutions involved in the delivery of the credit system.

The first category of constraints that restrict access of women to credit relate to factors such as landownership, decision-making authority, control of resources, low literacy, remoteness of, villages, lack of markets, and limited investment opportunities. Women's ownership of land and other properties and the registration record of these, enables them to be either eligible or not eligible for participation in the credit programme implemented by the financial institutions and the local district administration. Individuals who have a land or house registered in their name could become eligible for a loan and this automatically excludes the participation of landless women in the credit programme. Moreover, local public representatives become increasingly reluctant to endorse the loan application requests of landless persons who are usually considered not creditworthy.

Women enjoying adequate authority in making their family's household decisions or having control over its resources, tend to have better access to and participation in credit programmes than women of families where they are denied such freedom. The low literacy level of women is a significant factor restricting their access to credit facilities. Most rural women being illiterate are not aware of the utility, benefits, and the related procedures for obtaining a loan. Some get scared applying for one, fearing that they may not be able to repay it later.

In cases where loans were availed, putting them to productive uses have been a common problem of several female clients, who in the mean time utilised the loan for other domestic consumption purposes. It has been observed that women participating in the credit programmes successfully are usually the ones who are better exposed to or aware of the real benefits and utility of the credit facilities.

Credit services are utilised by women mainly for financing of activities such as production of cash crops, vegetables, handicrafts, weaving, knitting, etc., but for most of these local products there are no established markets. Residents of the locality produce similar commodities or items and not many outsiders come to purchase the surplus production.

The lack of markets not only reduces the demand for credit, but it also restricts further participation of women in credit programmes as they fail to clear their earlier loans because of their inability to sell and encash their production. The demand and the extent of enhancing the access to credit are to a large degree dependent on the micro-enterprise and economic investment opportunities of a specific locality.

In most of Bhutanese rural communities and villages there are not many opportunities for making profitable investments, thereby limiting the credit absorptive capacity of individual women clients. This is a serious problem which needs to be investigated through the collective efforts of the national government, local district administrations, sector, agencies and the financial institutions.

Major constraints that restrict women's access to credit due to limitations of financial institutions include the complicated and lengthy procedures, rigid formalities and requirements, restrictive procedures and arrangements, high cost of obtaining credit, inflexible repayment conditions, inadequate credit promotions and improvements in the credit delivery system.

The existing system and related formalities are still found to be complicated, lengthy, and not conducive enough to attract maximum participation of women and the rural people. Further streamlining and modification of the prevailing credit delivery system is warranted to enhance the access of women to formal credit facilities.

The basic identification requirements of applicants such as land or house registration numbers, census records, properties owned, endorsement of agricultural and animal husbandry supervisors, and the local public representatives like village head man often posed certain hindrances for women to have access to credit facilities.

Although these basic formalities are a necessity, a certain portion of these formalities can and should be made more flexible to improve the access of the poorest of the poor which consist mainly of women. Relaxation of these rigid formalities in processing of loans by financial institution could greatly enhance the accessibility of women to credit facilities.

Procedures of lending institutions such as having to make disbursements in cash, by cheque, to the client in person, in the presence of a witness, which are actually meant to avoid fraud and ensure proper receipt of credit by the clients for the intended purpose, often restrict easy access to the credit service that it provides.

The actual cost of obtaining credit, including the opportunity cost of filling-up the application forms, getting endorsements of local public representatives and sectoral heads or persons in-charge, travelling from the village to district head-quarters, waiting for the loans to be processed and sanctioned, receiving the loan, getting it encashed from the bank, and returning home to the village often adds up to a substantial amount. This, at times, makes it quite unattractive to think of getting loans, specially smaller amounts of seasonal nature, although the interest rates charged by the financial institutions for the actual loan is just 14 per cent.

In most cases, more than the impediments to access of women to credit, it is the lack of credit promotions that actually limits participation of clients in the existing credit facilities. Increasing the awareness of credit services and the benefits that may be derived from credit among the rural commu-nities could greatly improve the participation of women in the credit programme.

The new strategy for improvement of the Rural Credit delivery system that the BDFC is already promoting and intends to pursue mainly consists of the following seven key aspects:

- Realisation of all past due loan outstanding with the appointment of loan recovery Commission Agents in consultation with the District Administrations.
- Formation and implementation of Gewog Loan Committees (GLCs) to further decentralise the credit delivery system at the grass roots level.
- Establishment of self-help groups for delivery of credit to the rural communities based on the group's collective assurances for repayments.
- Introduction of savings mobilisation scheme along with the credit programme for meeting full financial services needs of the clients.
- Expansion of credit coverage by incorporating additional scheme for purchase of land, loans for trading by village based small businessmen and loans for marketing of agricultural produces.

- Carrying out of location specific, activity specific, purpose specific, and demand and supply specific micro- economic or enterprise investment opportunity studies jointly with the district administrations and the sectoral agencies.
- Establishment of appropriate linkages of the credit programme with the extension packages.

Women employment and poverty alleviation programmes should ultimately lead to the formation of mass organisations of poor women, at the regional, national and international levels. Only then can the poor women of the world hope to bring about the fulfilment of their practical and strategic needs. They can form strategic alliances with other organisations of the poor—such as trade unions and farmers and tenant farmers groups—and thus involve men in the change process as well.

Most important, these federations must remain wholly autonomous and maintain a supra-political stance to prevent the co-optation and dilution of the empowerment process by pervasive patriarchal forces. They should run as candidates of existing parties, not as representatives of autonomous women's federations.

Human Rights Practices in Bhutan

Bhutan is under the rule of King Jigme Singye Wangchuk, who governs with the support of a National Assembly and a Council of Ministers. There is no written constitution to protect fundamental political and human rights.

Since ascending the throne in 1972, the King has continued the efforts toward social and political modernization begun by his father. In the last few years, Bhutan has improved rapidly services in education, health care, sanitation, and communications, with parallel but slower development of representative governance and decisionmaking.

Bhutan has adopted some measures to increase the power of the National Assembly. The judiciary is not independent of the King. The Royal Bhutan Police (RBP), assisted by the Royal Bhutan Army (including those assigned to the Royal Body Guard), and a national militia maintain internal security. Some members of these forces committed human rights abuses.

Agriculture and foresty are the economic asset for the country. The gross national product (GNP) per capita is estimated to be $600. Agriculture largely consists of subsistence farming and animal husbandry. Citrus fruit, cardamom, and other spices are the leading agricultural exports.

Cement and electricity are the other important exports. Strong trade and monetary ties link the economy closely to that of India. Hydroelectric power production potential and tourism are key resources, although the Government limits tourism because of inadequate infrastructure and environmental and cultural concerns.

Tourist arrivals also are limited by a requirement that tourists purchase a high minimum daily rate holiday package before visiting the country. The Government's human rights record remained poor, and problems remain in several areas. Citizens do not have the right to change their government. The King exercises strong, active, and direct power over the Government. The Government discourages political parties, and none operate legally. Arbitrary arrest and detention remain problems, and reports continue of torture and abuse of detainees. Impunity for those who commit abuses also is a problem. Judges serve at the King's pleasure, and the Government limits significantly the right to a fair trial.

In April 2000, the Government established the Department of Legal Affairs as a result of a review of the Basic Law. Programs to build a body of written law and to train lawyers are progressing. The Government limits significantly citizens' right to privacy. The Government restricts freedom of speech, press, assembly, and association. Citizens face significant limitations on freedom of religion. Approximately two-thirds of the government-declared population of 600,000 persons is composed of Buddhists with cultural traditions akin to those of Tibet.

The Buddhist majority consists of two principal ethnic and linguistic groups: The Ngalongs of the western part of the country and the Sharchops of the eastern part of the country. The remaining third of the population, ethnic Nepalese, most of whom are Hindus, live in the country's southern districts. Government efforts to institute policies designed to preserve the cultural dominance of the Ngalong ethnic group, to change citizenship requirements, and to control illegal immigration resulted in political protests, ethnic conflict, and repression of ethnic Nepalese in southern districts during the late 1980's and early 1990's. Tens of thousands of ethnic Nepalese left the country in 1991-92, many of whom were expelled forcibly.

According to the U.N. High Commissioner for Refugees (UNHCR), as of mid-June 2000, 98,269 ethnic Nepalese remained in

7 refugee camps in eastern Nepal; upwards of 15,000 reside outside of the camps in the Indian states of Assam and West Bengal. The Government maintains that some of those in the camps never were citizens, and therefore have no right to return. In 1998 the Government began resettling Buddhist Bhutanese from other regions of the country on land in southern districts vacated by the ethnic Nepalese living in refugee camps in Nepal, which is likely to complicate any future return of the ethnic Nepalese. The Government continues its negotiation with the Government of Nepal on procedures for the screening and repatriation of ethnic Nepalese in the refugee camps. A ministerial-level bilateral meeting in November failed to resolve disputes concerning the categorization of refugees in terms of eligibility for their eventual repatriation.

The Government restricts worker rights. The Government claims that it has prosecuted government personnel for unspecified abuses committed in the early 1990's; however, there is little indication that the Government has investigated adequately or punished any security force officials involved in torture, rape, and other abuses committed against ethnic Nepalese residents. Domestic human rights groups allege that the Government has taken no action to punish a government official for the 1998 killing of Buddhist monk Gomchen Karma. The Government stated that the shooting was accidental, that the official responsible has been suspended from duty and charged in connection with the incident, and that his case was being heard as of September 2000.

The law prohibits torture and abuse; however, human rights advocates state that in practice the security forces ignore these provisions. No one was prosecuted in connection with violating prohibitions against torture during the year. In 1999 and 2000 there were reports that security forces stopped ethnic Nepalese refugees attempting to return to the country, beat them or tortured them, and sent them back across the border. Refugee groups state that this has discouraged others from trying to return to the country. Refugee groups credibly claim that persons detained as suspected dissidents in the early 1990's were tortured and/or raped by security forces.

During those years, the Government's ethnic policies and the crackdown on ethnic Nepalese political agitation created a climate of impunity in which the Government tacitly condoned the physical abuse of ethnic Nepalese. The Government denies that these abuses occurred but also claims that it has investigated and prosecuted three government officials for unspecified abuses of authority during that period. Prison conditions reportedly are adequate, if austere. Visits by the International Committee of the Red Cross (ICRC) and the opening of a new prison in Thimphu (in 1994) contributed to improving conditions of detention.

However, human rights groups active outside the country maintain that prison conditions outside of the capitol city of Thimpu remain oppressive. The Government and the ICRC signed a new Memorandum of Understanding in September 1998, extending the ICRC prison visits program for another 5 years. The ICRC conducted two prison visits during the year, as it has done for each of the past 7 years, and was allowed unhindered access.

Under the law, police may not arrest a person without a warrant and must bring an arrested person before a court within 24 hours, exclusive of travel time from place of arrest. However, legal protections are incomplete, due to the lack of a fully developed criminal procedure code and to deficiencies in police training and practice. Incommunicado detention, particularly of Nepalese refugees returning without authorization, is still known to occur.

Incommunicado detention of suspected militants was a serious problem in the early 1990's, but the initiation of ICRC prison visits and the establishment of an ICRC mail service between detainees and family members has helped to allay this problem. Of those detained in connection with political dissidence and violence in southern areas in 1991-92, 29 continue to serve sentences after conviction by the High Court.

On May 6, Damber Pulami, a refugee living in a camp in Nepal, was arrested in the country. Pulami reportedly was a member of the Youth Organization of Bhutan and had gone to the country to check on the internal resettlement of non-Nepalese to the south.

Amnesty International (AI) has not received a response to queries about the charges against him, his whereabouts, and his physical condition, although according to one human rights group Pulami is in Chemgang Jail in Thimpu. According to AI, Tul Man Tamang, a 30-year-old construction worker was arrested in June on suspicion of organizing political activities. He reportedly was taken to a police station at Chimakothi in Chhukha district where he allegedly was tortured, held incommunicado in a dark cell, and forced to sign a statement saying he was leaving the country voluntarily before being forcibly exiled to India. Ugyen Tenzing, a member of the Druk-Yul Peoples' Democratic Party, reportedly was arrested in Samtse district in June. N.L. Katwal, a central committee member of the Bhutan Gorkha National Liberation Front, was one of more than 55 persons arrested during a demonstration in Phuntsholing in April 2000. In December 2000 he was sentenced to 13 years and 6 months in prison. He was serving his sentence in Chamgang Jail at year's end.

Rongthong Kunley Dorji, former leader of the Druk National Congress (DNC) and United Front for Democracy in Bhutan (UFD), was arrested in India in April 1997, following the issuance of an extradition request by Bhutanese authorities. Human rights groups contend that the charges brought against Dorji by the Bhutenese government are motivated politically and constitute an attempt by the Government to suppress his prodemocracy activities.

In June 1998, an Indian court released Dorji on bail but placed restrictions on his movements. Dorji's extradition case still is pending in the Indian courts and is proceeding slowly. According to a refugee-based human rights group, only one prosecution witness, a Joint Secretary in India's Ministry of External Affairs, has been cross-examined in the last 40 months. The next witness, another Indian government official, is scheduled to testify in February 2002. In the past, according to AI, many persons have been detained on suspicion of being members or supporters of the DNC. Only one such arrest was reported in 2000 and one during the year, but human rights groups allege that arrest and abuse of refugees returning to the country without authorization continue to occur but go unreported by the Government.

There were no peaceful protest marches from India to Bhutan during the year, perhaps due to fear of arrests and deportation, as occurred in previous years after such marches. Persons holding peaceful marches from India to Bhutan charge that in 1999 the Bhutanese police assaulted them, injuring several demonstrators, and then arrested and deported all of the marchers to Nepal. By one estimate, approximately 100 marchers were arrested and deported in 1999. The Government acknowledged that 58 persons whom it described as terrorists were serving sentences at the end of 1998 for crimes including rape, murder, and robbery. Although the Government does not use exile formally as punishment, many accused political dissidents freed under Government amnesties state that they were released on the condition that they depart the country.

The judicial system consists of district courts and a High Court in Thimphu. Judges are appointed by the King on the recommendation of the Chief Justice and may be removed by the King. Village headmen adjudicate minor offences and administrative matters. An Office of Legal Affairs (OLA) was established in March 2000. The responsibilities of the OLA are to conduct state prosecutions, draft and review legislation, and render legal counsel. By September a department head and all staff were in place.

The OLA is composed of a Legal Services Division (which eventually is to become the Ministry of Law and Justice) with domestic, international, and human rights sections; and a Prosecution Division (which eventually is to become the Attorney General's office), with a criminal section and a civil section. Criminal cases and a variety of civil matters are adjudicated under a legal code established in the 17th century and revised in 1958 and 1965. State-appointed prosecutors file charges and prosecute cases for offences against the State. In other cases, the relevant organizations and departments of government file charges and conduct the prosecution.

Defendants are supposed to be presented with written charges in languages that they understand and given time to prepare their own defense. However, according to some political dissidents this practice is not always followed. In cases where defendants cannot write their own defense, courts assign judicial officers to assist defendants. There were reports that defendants receive legal representation at trial, and that they may choose from a list of 150 government-licensed and employed advocates to assist with their defense; however, it is not known how many defendants actually receive such assistance.

A legal education program gradually is building a body of persons who have received formal training abroad in the law. For example, the Government sends many lawyers to India and other countries for legal training; 54 persons have completed legal studies abroad, and 43 more are enrolled. Village headmen, who have the power to arbitrate disputes, constitute the bottom rung of the judicial system. Magistrates, each with responsibility for a block of villages, can review their decisions. Magistrates' decisions can be appealed to district judges, of which there is one for each of the country's 20 districts. The High Court in Thimphu is the country's supreme court.

There are no laws providing for these rights. According to

human rights groups, police regularly conduct house-to-house searches for suspected dissidents without explanation or legal justification. The Government requires all citizens, including minorities, to wear the traditional dress of the Buddhist majority when visiting Buddhist religious buildings, monasteries, or government offices; in schools, and when attending official functions and public ceremonies.

The Government restricts freedom of speech, and to a lesser extent freedom of the press. The country's only regular publication is Kuensel, a weekly newspaper with a circulation of 15,000. It also reports stories on a daily basis through its on-line edition. Kuensel was formerly government-run, and human rights groups in the past stated that government ministries reviewed editorial material and suppressed or changed content.

According to the Government, Kuensel is independent and is funded entirely through advertising and subscription revenue. Its board consists of a mix of senior civil servants and private individuals. Kuensel, which is published simultaneously in the English, Dzongkha, and Nepali languages, supports the Government but does occasionally report criticism of the King and of government policies in the National Assembly. The Government maintains that there are no restrictions on individuals starting new publications, but that the market is too small to support any. Nepalese, Indian, and other foreign newspapers and magazines are available, but readership is in the hundreds and primarily limited to government officials.

After a 10-year ban on private television reception, in 1999 the Government introduced local television broadcasting with the inauguration of the Bhutan Broadcasting Service. The service broadcasts locally produced and foreign programs. In late 1999 the Government began licensing cable operators. There are more than 27 cable providers in the country with more than 10,000 subscribers. A large variety of programming is available, including CNN, and BBC. The Government does not censor cable content. The Government radio station broadcasts each day in the four major languages (Dzongkha, Nepali, English, and Sharchop). The Government inaugurated the country's first Internet service provider, Druknet, in June 1999: it had 1,820 subscribers as of late 2000. There are internet cafes in Thimpu, Phuentsholing and Bumthang. The Government does not censor any content on Druknet except for pornography, which is blocked.

The Government restricts freedom of assembly and association. Citizens may engage in peaceful assembly and association only for purposes approved by the Government. Although the Government allows civic and business organizations, there are no legally recognized political parties. The Government regards parties organized by ethnic Nepalese exiles—the Bhutan People's Party (BPP), the Bhutan National Democratic Party (BNDP), and the Druk National Congress—as "terrorist and antinational" organizations and has declared them illegal. These parties, which seek the repatriation of refugees and democratic reform, do not conduct activities inside the country.

The Government restricts freedom of religion. The Drukpa branch of the Kagyupa School of Mahayana Buddhism is the state religion. Approximately two-thirds of the population practice either Drukpa Kagyupa or Ningmapa Buddhism. The Drukpa branch is practiced predominantly in the western and central parts of the country, which are inhabited mainly by ethnic Ngalongs (descendants of Tibetan immigrants who predominate in government and the civil service, and whose cultural norms have been declared to be the standard for all citizens). The Ningmapa school is practiced predominantly in the eastern part of the country, although there are adherents, including the royal family, in other areas.

Citizens travelling in border regions are required to show their citizenship identity cards at immigration check points, which in some cases are located at a considerable distance from what is in effect an open border with India. By treaty citizens may reside and work in India. The country is not a signatory to the 1951 U.N. Convention Relating to the Status of Refugees or its 1967 Protocol. The Government states that it recognizes the right to asylum in accordance with international refugee law; however, the Government has not formulated a policy regarding refugees, asylees, first asylum, or the return of refugees to countries in which they fear persecution.

According to one credible human rights source, until recently the Government systematically arrested and imprisoned Tibetan refugees crossing the border with Tibet. This policy was followed under a tacit agreement with China. So invariable was this policy that Tibetan leaders advised refugees not to use routes of escape through Bhutan, and refugees have not done so for several years. Since Tibetans effectively are the only refugee population seeking first asylum in the country, the issue of first asylum did not arise during the year.

In 1998 the King devolved his day-to-day executive powers to the Council of Ministers, who are elected by the National Assembly from among themselves, but reserved control of "matters of national sovereignty and national security" for himself. He also introduced term limits for his Council of Ministers and proposed measures to increase the role of the National Assembly in the formation of his Government.

The National Assembly elected a new Council of Ministers and Government in July 1998 to a 5-year term. In July the National Assembly elected six Royal Advisory Councilors. There are elected or partially elected assemblies at the local, district, and national levels, and the Government claims to encourage decentralization and citizen participation. These elections are conducted in much the same way as National Assembly elections. Since 1969 the National Assembly has had the power to remove ministers whom the King appoints, but it never has done so. Political authority ultimately resides in the King, and decisionmaking involves only a small number of officials. Officials subject to questioning by the National Assembly routinely make major decisions, but the National Assembly is not known to have overturned any decisions reached by the King and government officials.

The National Assembly has 150 members. Of these, 105 are elected indirectly by heads of household, 10 are selected by a part of the Buddhist clergy, and the remaining 35 are appointed by the King to represent the Government. The National Assembly, which meets irregularly, has little independent authority.

The procedures for the nomination and election of National Assembly members state that in order to be eligible for nomination as a candidate, a person must be a citizen of Bhutan; be at least 25 years of age; not be married to a foreign national; not have been terminated or compulsorily retired for misconduct from government service; not have committed any act of treason against the King, the populace, and country; have no criminal record or any criminal case pending against him; have respect for the nation's laws; and be able to read and write in Dzongkha. Each National Assembly constituency consists of a number of villages. Each village is permitted to nominate one candidate but must do so by consensus. There is no provision for self-nomination, and the law states that no person may campaign for the candidacy or canvass through other means. If more than one village within a constituency puts forward a candidate, an election is conducted by the district development committee, and the candidate obtaining a simple majority of votes cast is declared the winner.

Election

Individuals do not have the right to vote; every family in a village is entitled to one vote in elections. The law does not make clear how a candidate is selected if none achieves a simple majority. However, it does state that in case of a tie among the candidates in the election, selection shall be made through the drawing of lots. The candidate whose name is drawn shall be deemed to be elected. Human rights activists claim that the only time individual citizens have any involvement in choosing a National Assembly representative is when they are asked for consensus approval of a village candidate by the village headman. The name put to villagers for consensus approval by the headman is suggested to him by district officials, who in turn take their direction from the central Government. Consensus approval takes place at a public gathering. Human rights activists state that there is no secret ballot.

The National Assembly enacts laws, approves senior government appointments, and advises the King on matters of national importance. Voting is by secret ballot, with a simple majority needed to pass a measure. The King may not formally veto legislation, but may return bills for further consideration. The Assembly occasionally rejects the King's recommendations or delays implementing them, but in general, the King has enough influence to persuade the Assembly to approve legislation that he considers essential or to withdraw proposals he opposes,

The Assembly may question government officials and force them to resign by a two-thirds vote of no confidence; however, the National Assembly never has compelled any government official to resign. The Royal Civil Service Commission is responsible for disciplining subministerial level government officials and has removed several following their convictions for crimes, including embezzlement. In 1998 the King issued a decree setting out several measures intended to increase the role of the National Assembly in the formation and dissolution of his Government. The decree, later adopted by the 76th session of the National Assembly, provided that all cabinet ministers are to be elected by the National Assembly and that the roles and responsibilities of the cabinet ministries are to be spelled out. Each cabinet minister is to be elected by simple majority in a secret ballot in the National Assembly from among candidates nominated by the King.

The King is to select nominees for cabinet office from among senior government officials holding the rank of secretary or above. The King is to determine the portfolios of his ministers, whose terms are limited to 5 years, after which they must pass a vote of confidence in the National Assembly in order to remain in office. Finally the decree provided that the National Assembly, by a two-thirds vote of no confidence, can require the King to abdicate and to be replaced by the next person in the line of succession. After adopting the decree, the National Assembly elected a new council of ministers consistent with it.

Human rights groups maintain that since only the King may nominate candidates for cabinet office, their election by the National Assembly is not a significant democratic reform. The King removed himself as Chairman of the Council of Ministers in 1998. Based on an election held in the National Assembly in 1998, Cabinet Ministers who received the most votes rotate the position on a yearly basis. The Chairman of the Council of Ministers serves as Prime Minster and Head of Government. In August Trade and Industry Minister Khundu Wangchuk became Chairman.

The percentage of women in government or politics does not correspond to their numbers in the population. The persistence of traditional gender roles apparently accounts for a low proportion of women in government, although women have made visible gains. A total of 15 women hold seats in the National Assembly, 23 percent of civil service employees are women, and women hold more than 30 percent of positions at the Ministry of Foreign Affairs.

There are no legal human rights nongovernmental organizations (NGO's) in the country. The Government regards human rights groups established by ethnic Nepalese exiles—the Human Rights Organization of Bhutan, the People's Forum for Human Rights in Bhutan, and the Association of Human Rights Activists-Bhutan—as political organizations and does not permit them to operate in the country. ICRC representatives continue twice yearly prison visits, and the Government has allowed them unhindered access to detention facilities, including those in southern districts inhabited by ethnic Nepalese. The chairman and members of the U.N. Human Rights Commission Working Group on Arbitrary Detention have made two visits to the country.

In the late 1980's and early 1990's, the Government instituted policies designed to preserve the cultural dominance of the Ngalong ethnic group. It also committed many abuses against the ethnic Nepalese, which led to the departure of tens of thousands of them. Many ethnic Nepalese were expelled forcibly, and almost 100,000 of them remain in refugee camps in Nepal. At the time, the Government claimed that it was concerned about the rapid population growth of and political agitation by the ethnic Nepalese.

The Government claims that ethnic and gender discrimination in employment is not a problem. It claims that ethnic Nepalese fill 22 percent of government jobs, which is slightly less than their proportion of the total population. Bhutanese human rights groups active outside the country claim that ethnic Nepalese actually make up approximately 35 percent of the country's population and that the Government under reports their number. Women are accorded respect in the traditions of most ethnic groups, although some exile groups claim that gender discrimination is a problem.

There is no evidence that rape or spousal abuse are extensive problems. For example, in 1999 there were 10 reported rapes nationwide. In the south, in the early 1990s, there were widespread reports of the rape of large numbers of ethnic Nepalese women, including by government forces. The Government denied these reports. In 1996 the National Assembly adopted a revised Rape Act.

The law contains a clear definition of criminal sexual assault and specifies penalties. In cases of rape involving minors, sentences range from 5 to 17 years. In extreme cases, a rapist may be imprisoned for life. There are few known instances of sexual harassment. Women constitute 48 percent of the population and participate freely in the social and economic life of the country. Approximately 43 percent of enrolment in school is female. Inheritance law provides for equal inheritance among all sons and daughters, but traditional inheritance practices, which vary among ethnic groups, may be observed if the heirs choose to forego legal challenges.

Dowry is not customary, even among ethnic Nepalese Hindus. Among some groups, inheritance practices favouring daughters reportedly account for the large numbers of women who own shops and businesses and for an accompanying tendency of women to drop out of higher education to go into business. However, female school enrolment has been growing in response to government policies. Women increasingly are found among senior officials and private sector entrepreneurs, especially in the tourism industry. Women in unskilled jobs generally are paid slightly less than men. Polygamy is allowed, provided the first wife gives her permission. Marriages may be arranged by the marriage partners themselves as well as by their parents. Divorce is common. Existing legislation requires that all marriages must be registered; it also favours women in matters of alimony.

The Government has demonstrated its commitment to child welfare by its rapid expansion of primary schools, healthcare facilities, and immunization programs. Mortality rates for both infants and children under 5 years dropped significantly since 1989. The Government provides free and compulsory primary school education, and primary school enrolment has increased 9 percent per year since 1991, with enrolment of girls increasing at an even higher rate.

Government policies aimed at increasing enrolment of girls increased the proportion of girls in primary schools from 39 percent in 1990 to 45 percent during the year. In 1999 the participation rate for children in primary schools was estimated at 72 percent, with the rate of completion of 7 years of schooling at 60 percent for girls and at 59 percent for boys. There is no law barring ethnic Nepalese children from attending school. However, most of the 75 primary schools in southern areas heavily populated by ethnic Nepalese that were closed in 1990 remain closed. The closure of the schools acts as an effective barrier to the ability of the ethnic Nepalese in southern areas to obtain a primary education. Exile groups claim that Nepalese students scoring highly on national exams are not always given the same advantages as other students, particularly if they are related to prominent dissidents or refugees. There is no societal pattern of abuse against children. Children enjoy a privileged position in society and benefit from international development programs focused on maternal and child welfare. A study by the United Nations Children's Fund (UNICEF) found that boys and girls receive equal treatment regarding nutrition and health care and that there is little difference in child mortality rates between the sexes.

Ethnic Nepalese have lived in the southern part of the country for centuries, and the early phases of economic development at the turn of the century brought a large influx of additional ethnic Nepalese. Early efforts at national integration focused on assimilation, including financial incentives for intermarriage, education for some students in regions other than their own, and an increase in development funds for the south.

However, in the late 1980's, concern over the increase in the population of and political agitation among ethnic Nepalese prompted aggressive government efforts to assert a national culture, to tighten control over southern regions, to control illegal immigration, to expel ethnic Nepalese, and to promote national integration. Beginning in 1989, more discriminatory measures were introduced, aimed at shaping a new national identity known as Drukpa. During the mid- and late 1980's, citizenship became a highly contentious matter. Requirements for citizenship first were formalized in the Citizenship Law of 1958, which granted citizenship to all adults who owned land and had lived in the country for at least 10 years. However, in 1985 a new citizenship law significantly tightened requirements for citizenship and resulted in the denaturalization of many ethnic Nepalese. The 1985 law required that both parents be citizens in order to confer citizenship on a child, and that persons seeking to prove citizenship through their own or their parents' residency in 1958 be able to prove residency in the country at that time.

In many cases, persons were unable to produce the documentation necessary, such as land tax receipts from 1958, to show residency. The law permits residents who lost citizenship under the 1985 law to apply for naturalization if they can prove residence during the 15 years prior to that time. The Government declared all residents who could not meet the new citizenship requirements to be illegal immigrants. Beginning in 1988, the Government expelled large numbers of ethnic Nepalese through enforcement of the new citizenship laws. The 1985 Citizenship Act also provides for the revocation of the citizenship of any naturalized citizen who "has shown by act or speech to be disloyal in any manner whatsoever to the King, country, and people of Bhutan."

The Home Ministry later declared in a circular that any nationals leaving the country to assist "antinationals," and the families of such persons, would forfeit their citizenship. Human rights groups allege that these provisions were used widely to revoke the citizenship of ethnic Nepalese who subsequently were expelled or otherwise departed from the country. In response to the perceived repression, ethnic Nepalese protested, sometimes violently. The protests were led by the Bhutan Peoples' Party (BPP), which advocated full citizenship rights for ethnic Nepalese and for democratic reforms.

Characterizing the BPP as a "terrorist" movement backed by Indian sympathizers, the authorities cracked down on its activities and ordered the closure of local Nepalese schools, clinics, and development programs after several were raided or bombed by dissidents. There were credible reports that many ethnic Nepalese activists were beaten and tortured while in custody, and that security forces committed acts of rape. There also were credible reports that militants, including BPP members, attacked and killed census officers and other officials, and engaged in bombings. Local officials took advantage of the climate of repression to coerce ethnic Nepalese to sell their land below its fair value and to emigrate.

Beginning in 1991, ethnic Nepalese began to leave southern areas of the country in large numbers and take refuge in Nepal. Many ethnic Nepalese also were forced to sign "voluntary migration forms" wherein they agreed to leave the country, after local officials threatened to fine or imprison them for failing to comply. According to UNHCR, there were 98,269 ethnic Nepalese refugees in seven refugee camps in eastern Nepal as of June 2000. An additional 15,000 refugees, according to UNHCR estimates, are living outside the camps in Nepal and India. Ethnic Nepalese political groups in exile complain that the revision of the country's citizenship laws in 1985 denaturalized tens of thousands of former residents of Bhutan.

They also complain that the new laws have been applied selectively and make unfair demands for documentation on a largely illiterate group in a country that only recently has adopted basic administrative procedures. They claim that many ethnic Nepalese whose families have been in the country for generations were expelled because they were unable to document their claims to residence. The Government denies this and asserts that a three-member village committee, typically ethnic Nepalese in southern districts, certifies in writing that a resident is a Bhutanese citizen in cases where documents cannot be produced.

The Government maintains that many of those who departed the country in the early 1990's were Nepalese or Indian citizens who came to the country after the enactment of the 1958 Citizenship law but were not detected until a census in 1988. The Government also claims that many persons registered in the camps as refugees never may have resided in the country. Finally the Government contends that some ethnic Nepalese left the country voluntarily, thus renouncing their Bhutanese citizenship.

Human rights organizations credibly dispute this claim. A royal decree in 1991 made forcible expulsion of a citizen a criminal offence. Nevertheless only three officials ever were punished for abusing their authority during this period. According to the UNHCR, the overwhelming majority of refugees who entered the camps since screening began in June 1993 have documentary proof of Bhutanese nationality. Since 1994 there has been a series of negotiations between Nepal and Bhutan to resolve the Bhutanese refugee problem.

In late December 2000, the two countries agreed upon a system to verify the nationality of Bhutanese refugees in Nepal in preparation for their return to the country. Refugee verifications began in March. By December all the residents of the first camp had been interviewed, and the Bhutanese verification team went back to Thimpu pending the start of verification at the next camp. Refugee groups are concerned that at the present rate, verification will take several years.

Bilateral negotiations on repatriation issues in November failed to arrive at an agreement, and the matter was deferred to a proposed future session of ministerial-level talks. In 1996, 1998, and 1999, refugees held a series of "peace marches" from Nepal to Bhutan to assert their right to return to Bhutan. The marchers charged that the Bhutanese police assaulted them during each march, injuring several demonstrators, and then arrested and deported all of the marchers.

A resolution adopted by the National Assembly in 1997 prohibits the still-resident family members of ethnic Nepalese refugees from holding jobs with the Government or in the armed forces. Under the resolution, those holding such jobs were to be retired involuntarily. The Government made clear that for the purposes of this resolution, a family member would be defined as a parent, a child, a sibling, or a member of the same household. The Government states that 429 civil servants, many of them ethnic Nepalese, were retired compulsorily in accordance with the resolution, and that the program was abrogated in November 1997.

The Government also began a program in 1998 of resettling Buddhist Bhutanese from other regions of the country on land in the southern part of the country vacated by the ethnic Nepalese living in refugee camps in Nepal. Human rights groups maintain that this action prejudices any eventual outcome of negotiations over the return of the refugees to the country. The Government maintains that this is not its first resettlement program and that Bhutanese citizens who are ethnic Nepalese from the south sometimes are resettled on more fertile land in other parts of the country. The failure of the Government to permit the return of ethnic Nepalese refugees has tended to reinforce societal prejudices against this group, as has the Government's policy on the forced retirement of refugee family members in government service and the resettlement of Buddhists on land vacated by expelled ethnic Nepalese in the south.

Trade unions are not permitted, and there are no labour unions. Workers do not have the right to strike, and the Government is not a member of the International Labour Organization. The Government maintains that, with very little industrialization, there is little labour to be organized. There is no collective bargaining in industry. Industry accounts for approximately 25 percent of the GDP, but employs only a minute fraction of the total work force. The Government affects wages in the manufacturing sector through its control over wages in state-owned industries.

The Government prohibits forced or compulsory labour, and there were no reports that such practices occurred. There is no evidence to suggest that domestic workers are subjected to coerced or bonded labour. The law does not specifically prohibit forced and bonded labour by children, but there were no reports that such practices occur. The law sets the minimum age for employment at 18 years for citizens and 20 years for noncitizens. A UNICEF study suggested that children as young as 11 years sometimes are employed with roadbuilding teams, which usually are made up of non-Bhutanese guest workers.

Children often do agricultural work and chores on family farms. The law specifically does not prohibit forced and bonded labour by children, but such practices are not known to occur. The country has not ratified ILO Convention 182 on the Worst Forms of Child Labour; however, as a state party to the U.N. Convention on the Rights of the Child, the Government supports the provisions contained therein. The country lacks a large pool of ready labour; for major projects, such as road works, the Government brings in hired labourers from India.

7

Woman in Politics

In 1985, the government enacted a new Citizenship Act. In 1988 the government began taking a census in southern Bhutan based on the 1985 Act. The census was one of inclusion and not exclusion – each person was expected to prove he/she was domiciled in Bhutan in 1958 to qualify as a Bhutanese by registration according to the 1985 Citizenship Act. The government started with a fresh slate; the onus was on the individual to prove his or her credentials. It was not made easy by officials who demanded tax receipts for exactly the year 1958, not even ones issued earlier would do ostensibly because that might imply the person may have left the country before 1958 and returned only after the cutoff year. The ridiculously stringent conditions above were to impact on the legal status of many more people because of two amendments to nationality laws.

The Marriage Act of 1977 had prescribed that only children born of Bhutanese fathers, not either spouse as before, would be considered Bhutanese citizens. The 1985 Citizenship Act tightened this requirement further and required both parents to be Bhutanese for citizenship by birth. Applied retrospectively and in tandem with the 1958 tax receipt stipulation, the government could declare tens of thousands of legal southern Bhutanese as non-nationals.

A person born in Bhutan in 1959 suddenly became an illegal resident during the 1988 census when either parent could not prove his/her presence in the country in 1958, the cutoff year. Thus began the woes of southern Bhutanese.

Attempts by southern Bhutanese to persuade the government to review the census implementation exercise were unsuccessful. The government deemed one such attempt, the submission of a petition by Royal Advisor Councillors Tek Nath Rizal and B.P.Bhandari in April 1988, an act of sedition. Youth in schools, colleges and villages became agitated and began to express dissent. This gave the government an excuse to become more aggressive and overtly discriminatory.

The 'One Nation, One People' policy was adopted stringently with a uniform compulsory dress code and dropping of the Nepali language from the school curriculum. A green-belt plan was unveiled that threatened to make a third of all southern Bhutanese homeless. When the people reacted by rising up in mass protests all over southern Bhutan, the government began a massive crackdown. Thousands were arrested and among them hundreds detained for years without trial.

Starting from a small group of dissidents who escaped the crackdown launched by the authorities, the refugee community grew as security forces plundered and terrorised villagers in the south following the protest demonstrations of September-October 1990. But the exodus peaked during in the first half of 1992 when the government initiated a campaign of systematic expulsion by forcing people to sign "voluntary" emigration forms before deporting them. The flood of refugees eventually stopped, but not before a hundred thousand had been forced to leave Bhutan.

All but a few hundred of the refugees from Bhutan are Lhotsampa, Bhutanese Hindus of Nepali origin who lived in the southern plains of Bhutan. Most fled to Nepal and India between late 1990 and 1992 to escape what refugee leaders called an "ethnic cleansing" campaign by the Bhutanese authorities. Bhutan, an isolated Himalayan kingdom, is ruled by Buddhist Drupkas who live mostly in the country's mountainous north. The Drupka historically excluded the Lhotsampa from the country's political and economic mainstream. The refugees complained of being denied citizenship and political rights, prevented from studying in the Nepalese language, and forced to wear traditional Drupka clothing. They also said they were subjected to widespread human rights abuses. The Bhutanese government not only denied the refugees' charges, but it also claimed that most of the refugees were either illegal immigrants to Bhutan or not from Bhutan at all.

Since 1993, there has been a stalemate between Bhutan and Nepal over the refugees' future. The two governments have held numerous talks, but with no concrete results. Although the flow of new refugees slowed to a trickle after 1992, discrimination in Bhutan did not end. In January 1998, Bhutan adopted a resolution dismissing 219 Lhotsampa government workers from their posts simply because of their ethnicity. The Bhutanese authorities have also resettled hundreds of Drupka families onto land belonging to the refugees.

In June, Bhutan's King, Jigme Singye Wangchuk, introduced several measures that limited his own power and introduced more democracy into the political process. Although some observers thought that might signal hope for the refugees, other expressed doubt.

The New Delhi-based South Asia Human Rights Documentation Centre (SAHRDC) said that the changes might not be as significant as they appeared, and that the King was probably only making them as "political concessions [to domestic political opponents] in order to preserve the monarchy." SAHRDC added that the King and the Bhutanese government still appeared intent on preventing the return of the refugees.

Beginning in late 1997, several hundred ethnic Sharchops (or Sarchops) from eastern Bhutan fled into Arunachal Pradesh in India. Although their number was small, the exodus of a second group of refugees from tiny Bhutan called attention to what SAHRDC called "another of the [South Asia] region's subterranean hot spots."

In a 1998 report on Bhutanese refugees, SAHRDC said that the exodus was the result of Bhutan's political persecution of Sharchops, Bhutan's second largest ethnic group. The government crackdown was aimed at stifling political opposition among Sharchops for the Druk National Congress (DNC), a political party seeking more democratic reform and human rights protection in Bhutan. The Bhutanese authorities arrested scores of Sharchops in 1997, including community leaders, monks, and relatives of exiled DNC leader Rongthong

Kunley Dorji. Coincidentally, the authorities in India also arrested Dorji in 1997, though they released him on bail in June 1998.

After 1972, Bhutan has rapidly improved services in education, health care, sanitation, and communications, with parallel but slower developments of the role of representatives in governance and decision making. In recent years, Bhutan has adopted some measures to transfer power from the King to the National Assembly. The judiciary is not independent of the King.

Approximately two-thirds of the government-declared population of 600,000 is composed of Buddhists with cultural traditions akin to those of Tibet. The Buddhist majority consists of two principal ethnic and linguistic groups: the Ngalongs of the western part of the country and the Sharchops of the eastern part of the country.

The remaining third of the population, ethnic Nepalese, most of whom are Hindus, live in the country's southern districts. Bhutanese dissident groups claim that the actual population is between 650,000 and 700,000 and that the Government underreports the number of ethnic Nepalese in the country.

The rapid growth of this ethnic Nepalese segment of the population led some in the Buddhist majority to fear for the survival of their culture.

Government efforts to tighten citizenship requirements and to control illegal immigration resulted in political protests and led to ethnic conflict and repression of ethnic Nepalese in southern districts during the late 1980's and early 1990's.

Tens of thousands of ethnic Nepalese left the country in 1991-92, many forcibly expelled. Approximately 97,000 ethnic Nepalese remain in refugee camps in Nepal and upwards of 15,000 reside outside of the camps in the Indian states of Assam and West Bengal. The Government maintains that some of those in the camps were never citizens, and therefore have no right to return.

In 1998 the Government began resettling Buddhist Bhutanese from other regions of the country on land in southern districts vacated by the ethnic Nepalese now living in refugee camps in Nepal.

A National Assembly resolution adopted in 1997 prohibits still-resident immediate family members of ethnic Nepalese refugees from holding jobs with the Government or the armed forces. In early 1998, the Government implemented the resolution, and had dismissed 429 civil servants by November 1998, when implementation of the resolution was discontinued.

The Royal Bhutan Police, assisted by the Royal Bhutan Army, including those assigned to the Royal Body Guard, and a national militia, maintain internal security. Some members of these forces committed human rights abuses against ethnic Nepalese. The economy is based on agriculture and forestry, which provide the main livelihood for 90 per cent of the population and account for about half of the gross domestic product.

Agriculture consists largely of subsistence farming and animal husbandry. Cardamon, citrus fruit, and spices are the leading agricultural exports. Cement and electricity are the other important exports. Strong trade and monetary ties link the economy closely to that of India.

Hydroelectric power production potential and tourism are key resources, although the Government limits foreign tourist arrivals for reasons of lack of adequate tourist infrastructure and environmental concerns. Tourist arrivals are limited by means of pricing policies.

Bhutan is a poor country. The gross national product (GNP) per capita is estimated to be $470. The Government significantly restricts the rights of the Kingdom's citizens, and problems remain in several areas. The King exercises strong, active, and direct power over the Government. Citizens do not yet have the right to change their government. The Government discourages political parties, and none operate legally. There were reports that security forces beat ethnic Nepalese refugees who entered the country to demonstrate.

Arbitrary arrest and detention remain problems. Judges serve at the King's pleasure, and the Government limits significantly the right to a fair trial. Criminal cases and a variety of civil matters are adjudicated under a legal code established in the 17th century and revised and modernised in 1958 and 1965. In late 1998, the Government formed a special committee of jurists and government officials to review the country's basic law and propose changes. Programs to build a body of written law and to train lawyers are progressing. For example, the Government sends many lawyers to India and other countries for legal training.

The Government limits significantly citizens' right to privacy. The Government restricts freedom of speech, the press, assembly, and association. The Government launched the country's first indigenous television service in June, modifying a ban on private television reception that had been in place since 1989. Citizens face significant limitations on freedom of religion.

In July 1998, the Government initiated steps to renew negotiations with the Government of Nepal on procedures for the screening and repatriation of ethnic Nepalese in the refugee camps, and the two governments held a series of meetings during the second half of that year. After a 3-year hiatus, ministerial-level bilateral talks resumed in September. The Government restricts worker rights.

The Government claims that it has prosecuted government personnel for unspecified abuses committed in the early 1990's; however, public indications are that it has done little to investigate and prosecute security force officials responsible for torture, rape, and other abuses committed against ethnic Nepalese residents.

Human rights groups allege that Gomchen Karma, a Buddhist monk arrested in October 1997 during a peaceful demonstration in the eastern part of the country, was shot and killed by a government official. The Government stated that the shooting was accidental, that the official responsible has been suspended from duty and charged in connection with the incident, and that his case was being heard as of the end of 1998.

The law prohibits torture and abuse; however, human rights advocates state that in practice security forces ignore these provisions. There were reports that numerous ethnic Nepalese refugees attempting to return to the country were captured by security forces, beaten, and sent back across the border. Persons holding peaceful marches from India to Bhutan report that during the year, the police assaulted them, injuring several demonstrators, and then arrested and deported all of the marchers to Nepal. Instances of torture of ethnic Nepalese who attempted to return to the country occurred in 1996.

Refugee newspapers published in Nepal allege that Nima Gyaltsen, a prisoner detained since 1997 without charge or trial in Zilnon Namgyeling jail in Thimphu, died after being subjected to torture during his incarceration. Amnesty International reported that 19-year-old Needup Phuntso was expelled from school in March 1998 and was tortured by members of the Royal Bhutanese police after his arrest in Thimphu in July 1998. Refugee groups credibly claim that persons detained as suspected dissidents in the early 1990's were tortured by security forces, who also committed acts of rape.

During those years, the Government's ethnic policies and the crackdown on ethnic Nepalese political agitation created a climate of impunity in which the Government tacitly condoned the physical abuse of ethnic Nepalese.

The Government denies these abuses but also claims it has investigated and prosecuted three government officials for unspecified abuses of authority during that period. Details of these cases have not been made public, and there is little indication that the Government has adequately investigated or punished any security force officials involved in the widespread abuses of 1989-92.

Human rights groups allege that a Buddhist monk arrested in October 1997, Thinley Oezor Kenpo, was tortured in custody in 1997.

According to Amnesty International, Kenpo was one of 120 persons arrested for political reasons since 1997 who by December 1998 had been sentenced to up to 15 years in prison. Prison conditions are reportedly adequate, if austere. In 1993 the International Committee of the Red Cross (ICRC) began a program of visits to prisons in the capital, Thimphu.

The Government and the ICRC signed a new Memorandum of Understanding in September 1998, extending the ICRC prison visits program for another 5 years. During the same month, an ICRC team visited 54 inmates in Chemgang central jail and 127 inmates in Thimphu district jail. The ICRC conducted two prison visits during the year, as it has done for each of the past six years. Arbitrary arrest and detention remain problems. Under the Police Act of 1979, police may not arrest a person without a warrant and must produce an arrested person before a court within 24 hours of arrest, exclusive of travel time from place of arrest. Legal protections are incomplete, however, due to the lack of a fully elaborated criminal procedure code and to deficiencies in police training and practice. Incommunicado detention is known to occur.

Incommunicado detention of suspected militants was a serious problem in 1991 and 1992, but the initiation of ICRC prison visits and the establishment of an ICRC mail service between detainees and family members has helped to allay this problem. Of those detained in connection with political dissidence and violence in southern areas in 1991-92, 1,685 were ultimately amnestied, 58 are serving sentences after conviction by the High Court, 9 were acquitted by the High Court, and 71 were released after serving prison sentences.

Four persons were arrested in February 1997 in Trashi and charged with involvement in seditious activities. They were convicted by the High Court and are currently serving prison sentences. Human rights groups allege that in July and August 1997, the Royal Bhutan Police (RBP) in and around Samdrup Jongkar town in the east arrested some 50 suspected supporters of a Bhutanese dissident group active outside the country.

The Government states that only 16 persons were arrested during this period and that they have been charged with involvement in seditious activities and are awaiting trial. Many were said to be supporters of one-time Druk National Congress (DNC) and United Front for Democracy in Bhutan (UFD) leader Rongthong Kunley Dorji, who was arrested in India in April 1997, following the issuance of an extradition request by Bhutanese authorities. Dorji faces extradition proceedings in India and possible return to Bhutan to face charges of fraud, nonpayment of loans, and incitement to violence.

The original Bhutanese extradition request included a third charge, "anti-national activities", but this was later dropped when it became clear that Indian law would preclude his extradition to face political charges.

Human rights groups contend that the charges brought against Dorji are politically motivated and constitute an attempt by the government to suppress his prodemocracy activities. In

June 1998 an Indian court granted Dorji bail, but placed restrictions on his movements. Dorji's extradition case still is pending in the Indian courts. According to an Amnesty International report released during the year, 30 persons were detained in 1998, most of them on suspicion of being members or supporters of the DNC.

Amnesty International (AI) has reported that some of those arrested are feared to be at risk of torture. Bhutanese human rights groups outside the country claim that the arrests, including those of several Buddhist monks, are aimed at imposing Ngalong norms on the eastern, Sharchop community, which has a distinct ethnic and religious identity. The Government denies that it has such a policy; many government officials, including both the former Head of Government, Foreign Minister Jigme Thinley, and the Chief Justice of the High Court Sonam Tobgye, are Sharchops. Persons holding peaceful marches from India to Bhutan charge that during the year, the police assaulted them, injuring several demonstrators, and then arrested and deported all of the marchers to Nepal. By one estimate, approximately 100 marchers were arrested and deported during the year.

The Government acknowledged that 58 persons whom it described as "terrorists" were serving sentences at the end of 1998 for crimes including rape, murder, and robbery. It stated that a total of 134 persons were arrested in connection with the October 1997 disturbances in the east; of that number, more than one-half either had been tried and acquitted or had been released after serving short sentences.

Although the Government does not formally use exile as a form of punishment, many accused political dissidents freed under Government amnesties say that they were released on the condition that they depart the country. Many of them subsequently registered at refugee camps in Nepal. The Government denies this.

The judicial system consists of district courts and a High Court in Thimphu. Judges are appointed by the King on the recommendation of the Chief Justice and may be removed by him. Village headmen adjudicate minor offences and administrative matters. Criminal cases and a variety of civil matters are adjudicated under a legal code established in the

17th century and revised in 1958 and 1965. For offences against the State, state-appointed prosecutors file charges and prosecute cases.

Defendants are supposed to be presented with written charges in languages that they understand and given time to prepare their own defence. However, this practice is not always followed, according to some political dissidents. In cases where defendants cannot write their own defence, courts assign judicial officers to assist defendants. There were reports that defendants receive legal representation at trial, and that they may choose from a list of 150 government-licensed and employed advocates to assist with their defence; however, it is not known how many defendants actually receive such assistance.

A legal education program is gradually building a body of persons who have received formal training in the law abroad. Village headmen, who have the power to arbitrate disputes, make up the bottom rung of the judicial system. Magistrates can review their decisions, each with responsibility for a block of villages. Magistrates' decisions can be appealed to district judges, of which there is one for each of the country's 20 districts. The High Court in Thimphu is the country's supreme court. Its decisions can be appealed to the King. Defendants have the right to appeal to the High Court and may make a final appeal to the King, who traditionally delegates the decision to the Royal Advisory Council. Trials are to be conducted in open hearings; however, there are allegations that this is not always the case in practice.

Questions of family law, such as marriage, divorce, and adoption, are traditionally resolved according to a citizen's religion: Buddhist tradition for the majority of the population and Hindu tradition for the ethnic Nepalese; however, the Government states that there is one formal law that governs these matters. Some or all of the approximately 75 prisoners serving sentences for offences related to political dissidence or violence, primarily by ethnic Nepalese during 1991-92, may be political prisoners. On December 17, the King pardoned 200 prisoners to mark National Day; all reportedly were released.

The Government restricts freedom of speech and of the press. The country's only regular publication is Kuensel, a government-run weekly newspaper with a circulation of 10,000. Bhutanese human rights groups state that government ministries regularly review editorial material and have the power to, and regularly do, suppress or change content.

They allege that the board of directors nominally responsible for editorial policy is appointed by and can be removed by the Government. Kuensel, which publishes simultaneous editions in the English, Dzongkha, and Nepali languages, supports the Government but does occasionally report criticism of the King and Government policies in the National Assembly. In 1989 the Government banned all private television reception and ordered that television antennas and satellite dishes be dismantled. Many homes in Paro and Thimphu nonetheless have satellite dishes and receive signals from international broadcasters. In June the Government introduced locally produced television service with the inauguration of the Bhutan Broadcasting Service.

The Government radio station broadcasts each day in the four major languages (Dzongkha, Nepali, English, and Sharchop). The Government inaugurated the country's first internet service provider, Druknet, in June. English is the medium of instruction in schools and the national language, Dzongkha, is taught as second language. The teaching of Nepali as a second language was discontinued in 1990.

The Government restricts freedom of assembly and association. Citizens may engage in peaceful assembly and association only for purposes approved by the Government. Although the Government allows civic and business organisations, there are no legally recognised political parties. The Government regards parties organised by ethnic Nepalese exiles—the Bhutan People's Party (BPP) and the Bhutan National Democratic Party (BNDP)—as well as the Druk National Congress (DNC)—as "terrorist and anti-national" organisations and has declared them illegal. These parties do not conduct activities inside the country. They seek the repatriation of refugees and democratic reform.

The Government imposes limits on freedom of religion. The Drukpa branch of the Kagyupa School of Mahayana Buddhism is the state religion. About two-thirds of the population practice either Drukpa Kagyupa or Ningmapa Buddhism.

The Drukpa branch is practiced predominantly in the western and central parts of the country, which are inhabited mainly by ethnic Ngalongs (descendants of Tibetan immigrants who predominate in government and the civil service, and whose cultural norms have been declared to be the standard for all citizens). The Ningmapa school is practiced predominantly in the eastern part of the country, although there are adherents in other areas, including the royal family. Most of those living in the east are ethnic Sharchops—the descendants of those thought to be the country's original inhabitants. The Government subsidizes monasteries and shrines of the Drukpa sect and provides aid to about one-third of the Kingdom's 12,000 monks. The Government also provides financial assistance for the construction of Drukpa Kagyupa and Ningmapa Buddhist temples and shrines.

In the early 1990's, the Government provided funds for the construction of new Hindu temples and centres of Sanskrit and Hindu learning and for the renovation of existing temples and places of Hindu learning. The Drukpa branch enjoys statutory representation in the National Assembly and in the Royal Advisory Council and is an influential voice on public policy. Citizens of other faiths, mostly Hindus, enjoy freedom of worship but may not proselytise. Under the law, conversions are illegal.

The King has declared major Hindu festivals to be national holidays, and the royal family participates in them. Foreign missionaries are not permitted to proselytise, but international Christian relief organisations and Jesuit priests are active in education and humanitarian activities. According to dissidents living outside of the country, the Government restricts the import into the country of printed religious matter; only Buddhist religious texts are allowed to enter.

Citizens travelling in border regions are required to show their citizenship identity cards at immigration check points, which in some cases are located at a considerable distance from what is in effect an open border with India. By treaty, citizens may reside and work in India.

Bhutan is not a signatory to the 1951 U.N. Convention Relating to the Status of Refugees or its 1967 Protocol. The Government states that it recognises the right to asylum in accordance with international refugee law; however, it has no official policy regarding refugees, asylum, first asylum, or the return of refugees to countries in which they fear persecution. Citizens do not yet have the right to change their government. Bhutan is a monarchy with sovereign power vested in the King.

In June 1998, the King introduced term limits for his Council of Ministers and proposed measures to increase the role of the National Assembly in the formation of his Government. The National Assembly elected a new Council of Ministers and Government in July 1998 to a 5-year term. There are elected or partially elected assemblies at the local, district, and national levels, and the Government claims to encourage decentralisation and citizen participation.

8

The Assessment

Concluding Observations of the Committee on the Rights of the Child

At its 715th and 716th meetings (CRC/C/SR. 715 and 716), held on 5 June 2001, the Committee on the Rights of the Child considered the initial report of Bhutan (CRC/C/3/Add.60), which was received on 20 April 1999, and adopted at the 721st meeting, held on 8 June 2001, the following concluding observations.

The Committee notes that the initial State party report was prepared according to the Committee's guidelines for reporting. It notes the timely submission of the informative written answers. The Committee further notes with appreciation the presence of a high-level and cross-sectoral delegation, which contributed to a frank and open dialogue.

Positive Aspects

The Committee notes that the consideration of the initial report of Bhutan marked the first occasion that the State party had appeared before a human rights treaty body.

The Committee welcomes the progress made at the Joint Verification Talks and the commencement of the verification process of the refugees in Nepal. It further welcomes the undertaking made by the head of the State party's delegation to convey to the Government the Committee's concerns on the need to accelerate the process.

The Committee welcomes the incorporation in the State party's development plans of the goals contained in the World Declaration and Plan of Action of the 1990 World Summit for Children.

The Committee welcomes the establishment of the Department of Legal Affairs, which is an important step in consolidating the rule of law in the State party.

The Committee welcomes the establishment of the Youth Development Fund and the Health Trust Fund.

The Committee appreciates the cooperation of the State party with United Nations agencies and other international organizations, such as in the formulation and signing of a Master Plan of Operations in cooperation with UNICEF.

The Committee welcomes the child-focused and holistic approach taken by the State party in formulating policies and programmes relating to aspects of the Convention.

Factors and difficulties impeding the implementation of the Convention

The Committee acknowledges that difficult topography (i.e. difficult mountainous terrain); the relatively recent socio-economic development, the pressures posed by high population growth on the provision of social services and the shortage of human and economic resources are factors impeding the implementation of some provisions of the Convention.

The Committee notes the challenges posed by the State party's aspirations to maintain its unique culture and identity amidst increasing development and openness, as well as within the regional context.

Principal subjects of concern and recommendations General measures of implementation

Legislation

While noting various legislative measures already taken or proposed with respect to child rights (e.g. amendments to the 1980 Marriage Act, the 1993 Rape Act, the draft Juvenile Justice Act, draft Civil and Criminal Codes, and the draft Immoral Trafficking Act), the Committee is concerned that they do not reflect a comprehensive rights-based approach to the implementation of the Convention.

The Committee recommends that the State party:

(a) Ensure the speedy promulgation of legislation relating to child rights;

(b) Undertake a comprehensive review of existing legislation, from a rights-based approach, to ensure its conformity with the principles and provisions of the Convention; and

(c) Consider adopting a comprehensive children's code which would incorporate the principles and provisions of the Convention.

Coordination

The Committee welcomes the information that the Government is planning to review the implementation structure for the Convention, particularly the strengthening of the role of the CRC Task Force. However, it is concerned that the CRC Task Force is not yet operational.

The Committee recommends that the State party:

(a) Pursue the preparation and development of a comprehensive national plan of action for the implementation of the Convention, through an open, consultative and participatory process;

(b) Ensure that the CRC Task Force is responsible for intersectoral coordination and cooperation (at and between national and local levels of government), dissemination and training of the Convention, coordination of NGO activities in the implementation of the Convention, as well as coordination in the preparation of the State party's reports; and

(c) Ensure that the CRC Task Force is adequately resourced (e.g. financially and professionally).

Cooperation with civil society

Noting good governmental cooperation in the development and welfare sectors with national associations, bilateral aid agencies, international organizations and NGOs, the Committee is nevertheless concerned that insufficient efforts have been made to involve civil society, particularly in the area of civil rights and freedoms, in the implementation of the Convention.

The Committee recommends that the State party:

(a) Consider a systematic approach to involving civil society, especially children's associations, throughout all stages of the implementation of the Convention, including with respect to civil rights and freedoms; and

(b) Ensure that legislation regulating NGOs conforms to

international standards on freedom of association, as a step in facilitating and strengthening their participation.

Data collection

The Committee is concerned that disaggregated data on persons under 18 years relating to the rights contained in the Convention are not systematically collected and used effectively to assess progress and design policies to implement the Convention.

The Committee recommends that the State party:

(a) Establish a mechanism to systematically collect and analyse disaggregated data on all persons under 18 years for all areas covered by the Convention, including members of the most vulnerable groups (i.e. children of different ethnicity, living in remote areas, with disabilities, of economically disadvantaged households, etc.); and

(b) Seek technical assistance from, among others, UNICEF.

Monitoring structures

The Committee is concerned at the lack of an independent mechanism with a mandate to regularly monitor and evaluate progress in the implementation of the Convention and empowered to receive and address complaints.

The Committee recommends that the State party:

(a) Consider the establishment of an independent national human rights institution, in accordance with the Paris Principles relating to the status of national institutions (General Assembly resolution 48/134), to monitor and evaluate progress in the implementation of the Convention at the national and at the local levels. This institution should be accessible to children and empowered to receive and investigate complaints of violations of child rights in a child-sensitive manner and to address them effectively; and

(b) Seek technical assistance from, among others, the OHCHR, UNICEF and the European Network of Ombudspersons for Children.

Budgetary allocation

While noting significant investment and increased budgetary allocation in the social sector, the Committee is still concerned that insufficient attention has been paid to article 4 of the Convention regarding the implementation to the "maximum extent of ... available resources" of the economic, social and cultural rights of children.

The Comittee recommends that the State party:

(a) Systematically assess the impact of budgetary allocations on the implementation of child rights;

(b) Ensure that multi-sectoral programmes are adequately funded;

(c) Ensure the distribution - to the maximum extent - of available resources at the national and local level, and, where needed, within the framework of international cooperation; and

(d) Consider its obligations under the Convention in all aspects of its negotiations with international financial institutions and other donors, to ensure that the economic, social and cultural rights of children, particularly children belonging to the most vulnerable groups, are well observed.

Training/dissemination of the Convention

Noting some efforts by the State party (e.g. radio programmes), the Committee is concerned that awareness of the Convention amongst professionals working with and for children and the general public, including children themselves, remains low. The Committee is concerned that the State party is not undertaking adequate dissemination and awareness raising activities in a systematic and targeted manner.

The Committee recommends that the State party:

(a) Develop an ongoing programme for the dissemination of information on the Convention and its implementation among children and parents, civil society and all sectors and levels of government, including initiatives to reach those vulnerable groups who are illiterate or without formal education;

(b) Develop systematic and ongoing human rights training programmes for all professional groups working for and with children (e.g. judges, lawyers, law enforcement officials, civil servants, local government officials, personnel working in institutions and places of detention for children, teachers, health personnel); and

(c) Seek assistance from, among others, OHCHR and UNICEF.

Definition of the child

The Committee notes that the 1996 amendment to the Marriage Act of 1980 raised the age of marriage of girls to 18. It further notes information from the delegation that courts generally interpret the law to include persons under 18 as children for all purposes.

The Committee recommends that the State party review its legislation with a view to ensuring that the definition of the child and minimum age requirements conform to the principles and provisions of the Convention, are gender neutral, are explicit and are enforced by law.

General principles

The right to non-discrimination

The Committee is concerned at the disparities in the enjoyment of rights experienced by children belonging to the most vulnerable groups (e.g. children living in remote areas, belonging to other ethnic groups, with disabilities from economically disadvantaged households, etc.).

The Committee recommends that the State party:

(a) Make greater efforts to ensure that all children within its jurisdiction enjoy all the rights set out in the Convention without discrimination, in accordance with article 2; and

(b) Prioritize and target social services for children belonging to the most vulnerable groups.

The Committee is concerned about the impact on children of reports of discrimination against individuals belonging to the Lhotshampas. In particular, it is concerned about reports: that these children face de facto discrimination in access to education and other services and on the basis of status, activities, or opinions of their parents, or relatives.

The Committee recommends that the State party:

(a) Take effective measures, including enacting or rescinding legislation where necessary, to prevent and eliminate discrimination, in accordance with article 2 of the Convention, in all fields of civil, economic, political, social and cultural life;

(b) Establish accessible, prompt and effective mechanisms to monitor, receive and address complaints of discrimination (e.g. prompt appeal in circumstances of denial of school enrolment); and

(c) Take all appropriate measures, such as comprehensive public education campaigns, to prevent and combat negative societal attitudes towards different ethnic groups.

Respect for the views of the child

The Committee notes the State party's efforts to respect the views of children in schools (e.g. the 1997 school code of conduct). Nevertheless, it is concerned that traditional attitudes towards children in society at large may limit the exercise of this right, especially within the family.

The Committee recommends that the State party:

(a) Continue to promote and facilitate, within the family, the school, the courts and administrative bodies, respect for the views of children and their participation in all matters affecting them, in accordance with article 12 of the Convention;

(b) Develop skills-training programmes in community settings for teachers, social workers and local officials at the village-block level to assist children to express their informed views and opinions and to have them taken into consideration; and

(c) Seek assistance from, among others, UNICEF.

Civil rights and freedoms

Birth registration

Noting the difficulties imposed by terrain and settlement patterns, the Committee is concerned that the failure of timely birth registration can have negative consequences on the full enjoyment by children of their fundamental rights and freedoms.

The Committee recommends that the State party:

(a) Make greater efforts to ensure the timely registration of all births, and issue birth certificates;

(b) Carry out awareness-raising about registration in rural areas; and

(c) Consider the establishment of mobile registration offices and registration units in schools.

Nationality

The Committee is concerned that under citizenship laws, a child of a Bhutanese mother and a non-national father must face a burdensome naturalization process, whereas this is not required if the father is Bhutanese.

The Committee recommends that the State party ensure the right of a child to a nationality without discrimination on the basis of the gender of the parent(s), in accordance with articles 2 and 7 of the Convention.

Family environment and alternative care

Family reunification

The Committee is concerned that as a result of events following the census in the late 1980s, there may be children in southern Bhutan who are separated from their parents, or whose parents are residing abroad as refugees.

The Committee recommends that the State party ensure that family reunification is dealt with in a positive, humane and expeditious manner, in accordance with article 10 of the Convention.

Violence/abuse/neglect/maltreatment

Noting the respect for children in Bhutan, the Committee is concerned that there is insufficient information and awareness of the ill-treatment of children in schools and within the family.

The Committee recommends that the State party:

(a) Conduct a study to assess the nature and extent of ill-treatment of children, and design policies and programmes to address it;

(b) Take legislative measures to prohibit all forms of physical and mental violence, including corporal punishment and sexual abuse of children in the family, schools, and in institutions;

(c) Carry out public education campaigns about the negative consequences of ill-treatment of children and promote positive, non-violent forms of discipline as an alternative to corporal punishment;

(d) Establish effective procedures and mechanisms to receive, monitor and investigate complaints, including intervention where necessary;

(e) Prosecute instances of ill-treatment, ensuring that the abused child is not victimized in legal proceedings;
(f) Train teachers, law enforcement officials, care workers, judges and health professionals in the identification, reporting and management of ill-treatment cases; and
(g) Seek assistance from, among others, UNICEF and WHO.

Basic health and welfare

Right to health and healthcare

The Committee notes significant achievements in the health sector: improvements in health indicators; increased investment; the inclusion of health education in the school curricula; and the establishment of basic health units, outreach clinics and health volunteer programmes. However, it is concerned about problems of access to services and the shortage of trained health workers.

The Committee recommends that the State party:
(a) Make greater efforts to ensure access to health services; and
(b) Continue to allocate the required resources to address the shortage of trained health workers.

Noting the State party's efforts to address adolescent health, such as the publication of pamphlets on reproductive and mental health, and drug abuse, the Committee is concerned at the effectiveness of these efforts.

The Committee recommends that the State party:
(a) Ensure that adolescents have access to and are provided with education on reproductive health and other adolescent health issues, as well as with child-sensitive and confidential counselling services;
(b) Strengthen its efforts to provide adolescent health education within the educational system; and
(c) Seek assistance from, among others, UNICEF and WHO.

Children with disabilities

Noting some efforts by the State party concerning children with disabilities (i.e. the pilot school for inclusive education and formation of a parents support group in Thimpu, and a school for visually impaired children), the Committee is concerned that children with disabilities in general have inadequate access to specialized services and education, and there is insufficient support for families.

The Committee recommends that the State party:

(a) Conduct a survey to assess the causes and extent of disability among children;
(b) Review existing policies and practice in relation to children with disabilities, taking due regard of the Standard Rules on the Equalization of Opportunities for Persons with Disabilities (General Assembly resolution 48/96) and of the Committee's recommendations adopted at its day of general discussion on "Children with disabilities" (see CRC/C/69);
(c) Involve children with disabilities and their families in the development of surveys and policy review;
(d) Undertake greater efforts to make available the necessary resources (e.g. professional and financial, including professional and financial support to families);
(e) Undertake greater efforts to promote and expand community-based rehabilitation programmes, including parent support groups, and inclusive education of children with all forms of disability; and
(f) Seek assistance from, among others, UNICEF and WHO.

Education, leisure and cultural activities

Education

Noting significant achievements in education indicators, the Committee is concerned that primary education is not compulsory; that there is still a significant gender gap in enrolment; and that there are deficiencies in access to education and the quality of teacher training.

The Committee recommends that the State party:

(a) Ensure that primary education is free and made compulsory;
(b) Make greater efforts to close the gender gap; and
(c) Allocate the required resources to address access to education and the quality of teacher training.

Noting with appreciation that the aims of education are generally in conformity with article 29 of the Convention, the Committee is concerned that human rights education, including the Convention, is not included in the school curricula.

Taking due regard of its General Comment No. 1 on the aims of education, the Committee recommends that the State party:

(a) Include human rights education in the curricula, particularly with respect to the development and respect for human rights, tolerance, and equality of the sexes and of religious and ethnic minorities; and
(b) Seek assistance from UNICEF and UNESCO.

Special measures of protection

Refugees

While noting that the verification process of refugees in camps in Nepal has commenced, the Committee is nevertheless concerned at the slow rate of this process and the serious and negative impact this has on the rights of children residing in these camps, particularly given that repatriation will begin only once all refugees have been verified.

In accordance with the principles of the best interests of the child, the right to a nationality and to the preservation of identity (articles 3, 7 and 8 of the Convention), and with a view to reaching a just and durable solution to the situation of refugees in camps in Nepal, the Committee recommends that the State party:

(a) Make greater efforts to expedite the verification process and consider the possibility of repatriating individuals within a reasonable time following individual verification;
(b) Consider a mechanism to allow individuals to appeal against decisions;
(c) Ensure that returnees are repatriated and resettled, in safety and dignity, to their place of origin or choice;
(d) Consider acceding to the 1951 Convention relating to the Status of Refugees, its 1967 Protocol, and the conventions on statelessness; and
(e) In the best interests of the children, consider seeking assistance from UNHCR.

Armed conflict

The Committee is concerned at the low age of 15 for voluntary enlistment in the armed forces.

The Committee recommends that the State party consider raising this to 18.

The Committee expresses its concern at the negative impact on children of reported armed insurgency in the south-central and south-eastern parts of the country.

In light of article 38 and other relevant articles of the Convention, the Committee recommends that the State party:

(a) At all time, ensure respect for human rights and humanitarian law aimed at the protection and care of children affected by armed conflict; and

(b) Provide physical rehabilitation and psychological recovery measures for these children.

Child labour

The Committee is concerned at the absence of legislation on the minimum age for admission to employment, as well as insufficient information on children working, including in the informal sector, such as agriculture. It is concerned that an increasing number of children are dropping out of school and taking up work in urban areas (e.g. as waiters, as bus attendants, in vehicle workshops, or as domestic workers).

The Committee recommends that the State party:

(a) Undertake a national survey on the causes and extent of child labour;

(b) Establish a minimum age for admission to employment, in accordance with the principles and provisions of the Convention, that is in conformity with the age of completion of education, and ensure that it is enforced; employers should be required to have, and to produce on demand, proof of age of all children working on their premises.

(c) Establish a mechanism to monitor the implementation of standards which is empowered to receive and address complaints of violations;

(d) Carry out campaigns to inform and sensitize the general public, especially parents and children, of work hazards; and

(e) Consider membership in ILO.

Sexual exploitation

Noting the 1993 Rape Act and the draft Immoral Trafficking Act, the Committee is concerned at the insufficient data on and awareness of the phenomenon of sexual exploitation of children in Bhutan.

The Committee recommends that the State party:

(a) Undertake a national study on the nature and extent of sexual exploitation of children (i.e. sale of children, child prostitution and child pornography), and compile and keep up to date disaggregated data to serve as a basis for designing measures and evaluating progress in this area;

(b) Review its legislation and ensure that it criminalizes the sexual exploitation of children, is gender neutral and penalizes all offenders involved, whether local or foreign, while ensuring that the child victims are not penalized;

(c) Ensure that legal procedures are simplified so that responses are appropriate, timely, and sensitive to victims;

(d) Establish rehabilitation and social reintegration programmes for child victims;

(e) Train personnel working with child victims; and

(f) Carry out awareness-raising campaigns to sensitize and mobilize the general public on the child's right to physical and mental integrity and safety from sexual exploitation.

Administration of juvenile justice

While noting the establishment of the Youth Development and Rehabilitation Centre, the Committee is nevertheless concerned at the administration of juvenile justice. In particular, it notes the absence of information on the minimum age of criminal responsibility. The Committee is also concerned that insufficient efforts have been made to ensure the speedy adoption of the draft juvenile justice and criminal procedure legislation.

The Committee recommends that the State party:

(a) Establish a minimum age of criminal responsibility that is in accordance with the principles and provisions of the Convention;

(b) Expedite the promulgation of the draft juvenile justice and criminal procedure laws;

(c) Ensure that the system of juvenile justice fully integrates into its legislation and practice the provisions of the Convention, in particular articles 37, 40 and 39, as well as other relevant international standards in this area, such as the Beijing Rules, the Riyadh Guidelines, the United Nations Rules for the Protection of Juveniles Deprived of their Liberty, and the Vienna Guidelines for Action on Children in the Criminal Justice System;

(d) Ensure that the deprivation of liberty is used only as a measure of last resort, for the shortest possible time, is authorized by the court, and that persons under 18 are not detained with adults;

(e) Ensure that children have access to legal aid and independent and effective complaints mechanisms;

(f) Consider alternative measures to deprivation of liberty, such as probation, community service, or suspended sentences;

(g) Train professionals in the area of rehabilitation and social reintegration of children;

(h) Seek assistance from, among others, OHCHR, the Centre for International Crime Prevention, the International Network on Juvenile Justice and UNICEF, through the Coordination Panel on Technical Advice and Assistance on Juvenile Justice.

Optional Protocols

The Committee encourages the State party to ratify the Optional Protocols to the Convention on the Rights of the Child on the sale of children, child prostitution and child pornography, and on the involvement of children in armed conflict.

Dissemination of documentation

Finally, the Committee recommends that in accordance with article 44, paragraph 6, of the Convention, the initial report presented by the State party be made widely available to the public at large and that consideration be given to the publication of the report along with the written answers to the list of issues raised by the Committee, the relevant summary records of the discussion, and the concluding observations adopted by the Committee following its consideration of the report. Such a document should be widely distributed in order to generate debate and awareness of the Convention and its implementation and monitoring within the Government, the Parliament and the general public, including concerned non-governmental organizations.

Bibliography

Asian Development Bank (ADB), "Statistics of South Asian Children and Women", 1997.

Filmer, D., et al., "Gender Disparity in South Asia", *Policy Research Working Paper*, World Bank, 1998.

Gurung, J., 'Gender Dimensions in Biodiversity Management: Bhutan and Nepal', 1997.

Jeffery, Patricia and Basu, Amrita (eds.), *Resisting The Sacred And The Secular: Women Activism And Politicized Religion In South Asia;* 1999.

Moser, Caroline O.N., Gender Planning in the Third World: Meeting Practical and Strategic Gender Needs, *World Development*, Vol. 17, No.11,1989.

Risseeuw, Carla and Ganesh, Kamala, *Negotiation And Social Space: A Gendered Analysis Of Changing Kin And Security Network In South Asia And Sub-Saharan Africa*, 1998.

Rosenegger, P., 'Annual Report: Bhutan' FAO/RAP Non-Wood Forest Products of Bhutan, RAP Publication, 1996.

____________, "South Asia Unites Against Domestic Violence," *Women Living Under Muslim Laws Newsheet*, Vol. X, No. 1., 1998.

Sarwar, Beena, "South Asia Unites Against Domestic Violence," *Women Living Under Muslim Laws Newsheet*. Vol. X, No. 1., 1998.

Schuler, Margaret, (ed.) *Freedom from Violence: Women's Strategies from Around the World*. New York: UNIFEM, 1992.

Sen, Gita, et al., *Poverty, Economic Growth and Gender Equity: The Asian and Pacific Experience*, Kuala Lumpur: Asian and Pacific Development Centre, 1994.

Shaikh Ali Maqsood, et al., "Towards a New Paradigm for Poverty Eradication in South Asia", *International Social Science Journal*, No. 148, June. UNESCO, 1996.

UNDP, *Human Development Report,* Oxford University Press, New York, 1997.

World Bank, *The South Asia Regional Gender Action Plan.* Washington, D.C.,1997.

World Health Organization, *Nutrition in South-East Asia,* 2000.

Index